SHAM

SHAM TO ROCK
GROWING UP
IN FORTIES AND FIFTIES DUBLIN

A memoir by
Gabriel Duffy

Introduction by
Colin Wilson

AENGUS BOOKS

First edition.
Published May 2003 by
Aengus Books
Distributed by Country Books/Ashridge Press

ISBN 0 9544868 0 3

British Library Cataloguing in Publication Data:
a catalogue record for this book is available from the British Library.

Design, typesetting and production:
Country Books, Little Longstone,
Bakewell, Derbyshire DE45 INN

Tel/Fax: 01629 640670
e-mail: dickrichardson@country-books.co.uk

Printed and bound by: Antony Rowe Ltd, Chippenham, Wiltshire

For Susan. Megan and Sally

TOPIC CONTENT

Acknowledgements

CHAPTER FIVE

For useful subsidiary information on girls' comic papers I am particularly indebted to one marvellously comprehensive study. That is: 'You're A Brick Angela!: A New Look at Girls' Fiction from 1839 to 1975' – by Mary Cadogan and Patricia Craig. Gollancz, 1976.

CHAPTER NINE

Volumes II and III of Asa Brigg's 'The History of Broadcasting in the United Kingdom', provided several items, facts and dates.

CHAPTER TWELVE

'The Fifties' by Peter Lewis (Heinemann, 1978) refreshed my memory on certain points. I also owe him for my footnote on Teddy Boys in Chapter Eleven.

With copious thanks to Dick Richardson,
a true gentleman and consummate professional.

Gratitude also to Bob, Jon, Justin, Nick, Peter and Simon;
for sound advice, support and stimulus.

INTRODUCTION BY COLIN WILSON

I met the author of this autobiography almost forty years ago and have come to regard him as one of the more interesting and remarkable characters I came to know as a result of writing a book called The Outsider.

At 21, he was brilliant, widely-read, and (like other Celts I have known) capable of drinking so much whisky that I was convinced he would die of cirrhosis of the liver before he was thirty.

But he confounded me by writing a number of books and plays with a demonic industry that revealed that he was quite unlike so many of my early Soho acquaintances, who talked about the books they intended to write but never actually got around to writing them. He even became, at one point, a highly successful businessman.

One of the earliest books he wrote – and, in my opinion, one of the best, is the present autobiography. He began it to record his experiences of Dublin in his childhood and adolescence, and sent it to me as he wrote it.

At the time, I found it charming, funny and immensely evocative, although even then I realised that its main quality is a startling truthfulness that makes it a kind of second cousin to the Confessions of Jean Jacques Rousseau. But when I re-read it more recently, I realised that sampling it piecemeal had done it an injustice, because its chief quality is a certain continuity. I also realised that it is as good an autobiography as I have ever read. And it aroused such a host of insights and ideas that I knew that I had to write an introduction to it.

Let me start off, then, by saying that my first meeting with Gabriel in 1963 was unpropitious. I had moved to Cornwall, six years earlier, to escape from the London literary scene. The Outsider (which was invariably linked with John Osborne's Look Back in Anger because they appeared at the same time) had become a *succes fou*, but the publicity involved in 'overnight success' soon turned sour and journalists became sick of endless chatter about the 'Angry Young Men.' But although Cornwall was a refuge from the snapping and snarling, I soon discovered that it had one disadvantage – that people who had disrupted my life in London by dropping in unannounced for an evening now dropped in for days at a time. I began to feel that I would have been wiser to move to a desert island.

And so on that morning in September 1963, when I woke up to be told by my wife that there was a drunken Irishman asleep on the settee, and that he had arrived late the night before (after I had gone to bed) and announced that he was a genius, I groaned and resisted the temptation to pull the sheets over my head.

My friend Bill Hopkins, who was staying with us, had apparently engaged him in conversation and finally provided him with a sleeping bag. Two other friends, Jonathan and Sue Guinness, had apparently withdrawn as they saw all prospect of reasonable conversation vanishing.

Gabriel was obviously very young, and inclined to become tongue-tied when sober. And since I am not a particularly talkative person, unless something stirs my interest, we were hardly compatible. He might have broken the ice by asking me questions, but instead suggested at one point that we should discuss 'ideas', which had the opposite effect.

Worse was to come. That evening, Bill and I took him out for a drink, and he quickly displayed the Celtic capacity for getting drunk in about five minutes flat. He also became noisy and Rabelaisian, until the owner of the first club we took him to – a very proper Englishman – had to ask me politely to take him away.

I have always hated drunks – at least, befuddled drunks – since they have voluntarily chosen to place themselves in a state in which reasonable intercourse with their fellow human beings becomes impossible. I had seen too much of them in London, particularly around Soho, and had had two choice examples living above us in Notting Hill, a pair of Scottish painters called Calquoun and MacBride, who went to enormous lengths to avoid allowing themselves to become sober. So as far as I was concerned, our drunken Irish guest was simply a nuisance. My curiosity was not even stirred by his conviction that he was a genius. In a sober Englishman this would have interested me, but I had met too many drunken Celts who announced they were a genius after their fourth large whisky, and who relapsed into incoherent depression when sober. I thought that Gabriel was simply another enthusiastic Celt who thought he was an 'Outsider' – like a thousand or so other people who had told me so since the book came out – but who lacked the self-discipline to do anything about it.

So although I cannot recall anything of that visit except the club owner asking me to take him away because shouts of 'Fuck' disturbed the other members, I have no doubt I saw him leave with relief, and hoped I had seen the last of him.

In fact Gabriel kept in touch, and in due course sent me the beginning of a novel he was writing - apparently on my advice, since I had told him that short stories were difficult to place. And although I can recall nothing about it, I can remember being suddenly impressed. He tells towards the end of the present book how a Dublin contemporary asked to see the novel he was writing, then said: 'I've always thought you were an irritating clown. I cannot believe you have written this. It is highly literate.' I experienced the same recognition on seeing the pages of his novel.

It made me aware that he was a real writer, who expressed himself easily and well. He had that capacity of articulate Irishmen to write as fluently as he talked.

Some time after that, I was astonished to learn that he had become a successful business consultant, and ran his own firm. The only thing that worried me was that the extracts he now sent me from the latest work in progress were so pregnant with ideas they could hardly walk upright, and were certainly unpublishable. This may have been my own fault, since I had introduced him by that time to the work of Edmund Husserl, whom I still feel to be the most important philosopher since Plato. My enthusiasm had impressed Gabriel, and, to do him justice, I think he understood why I thought Husserl so important.

Now the problem is that Husserl himself is virtually unreadable. His writing is as dry and abstract as a page of algebra. I had approached him by reading about him through more accessible writers, like Sartre, Merleau-Ponty, Paul Ricoeur and Maurice Natanson.

Besides, what is important in Husserl is very easy to explain, viz, the concept of 'intentionality': that in order to grasp something, you have to fire your attention at it like an arrow. And we do this so automatically that we do not realise we are doing it. Yet if you ask why a young poet, like Keats or Rimbaud or Rupert Brooke, feels almost sick with excitement on a spring morning, it is because the 'archer' who lives in the unconscious mind is drawing his bow-string back twice as far as usual. The Outsider had been about these romantics who had glimpsed this blaze of meaning, then sunk into depression because they suspected that it was all illusion. Husserl had answered the basic question I had asked in The Outsider, whether the meaning was real, and had answered it positively, not with the defeated negativity of Sartre, Beckett, Golding and the rest.

But Gabriel took my advice to study Husserl literally, and

plunged head first into works like Ideas and Formal and Transcendental Logic. He obviously read them more determinedly than I ever did. And the effect on his fiction was counter-productive., destroying that lightness of touch that had made it so readable. Fortunately, he soon recognised this, and the next chunk of typescript he sent me was the beginning of a thriller that revealed an amazing ability to grasp the essentials of the idiom of Le Carré and Frederick Forsyth. It was so smooth, competent and gripping that I had no doubt that Gabriel's days as an unpublished writer were about to end. I was unconcerned that this was not an attempt to write the great modern novel. At the age of 16, I had learned an important lesson from Balzac, who had taught himself to write by churning out appalling Gothic novels under various pseudonyms, and from Graham Greene, who wrote some excellent thrillers before he became obsessed by sin and adultery. (I find The Power and the Glory quite unreadable, but can still return with pleasure to A Gun for Hire or The Confidential Agent.)

At about this time, Gabriel's business collapsed – due, I gather, to devoting too much of his attention to writing, and not recognising soon enough the signs that he was having his pocket picked. I never learned the details, but I can imagine them. By now he was married with two daughters. What impressed me was that instead of allowing all this to make him suicidal, he saw it as an opportunity, and plunged back into writing.

And at that point I reread the autobiography, and realised that this is not only the most obviously publishable book he has written, but is also the key to his curious and complex character. I have never been able to understand why someone so obviously intelligent, literate and capable of hard work has made so many false starts. In theory, his combination of talent and determination should have achieved a breakthrough when he was in his 20s or 30s. He stopped drinking a long time ago, and although he has occasionally fallen off the wagon, alcohol has ceased to be a major problem. And where writing is concerned, he is almost as much a workaholic as I am myself.

Then he provided me with the key.

For some reason, Gabriel had omitted to send me chapters 6 and 7, or perhaps I had simply mislaid them. I asked him if I could have a copy, and they arrived a few days later. I immediately began to read Chapter 7, 'Spare the Rod', and was horrified by it. He describes his mother's frustration at having to live in the ground floor flat of a two storey house instead of in a house of her own, and her anger at his father – a policeman – for leaving her alone in the evening to drink and gamble in a pub. This was all familiar stuff to me, for my own family situation had been much the same, except that we lived in a rented council house. My own father came home from the shoe factory, had his tea, then shaved and went to the working men's club across the road, where he played cards, dominoes or darts, and occasionally spent the rent. My mother compensated by reading 'true romances' and sentimental novels. What was so different about Gabriel's childhood was that his mother took out her unhappiness and frustration on him, beating him with a cane without even recognising that it had developed into what sexologists call 'minor sadism.' And since he had nothing to compare it with, he regarded it as normal, and accepted that he was to blame for provoking the beatings.

What was worse was that the kindly Protestant neighbour who lived upstairs soothed Gabriel's mother by giving her sherry, and started her on the path to alcoholism.

When I try to analyse what shocked me so much about all this, I realise that it was not simply the beating inflicted on an only child. It was the dreadful, long-term frustration of the mother, living what Thoreau calls a life of quiet desperation.

It seemed that Gabriel's mother and father had met when he was a young policeman – *garda* – posted to a village in

Roscommon. She ran her own small shop. He was also a boxer, who trained the local lads, as well as an excellent dancer. She was a good dancer too, so when they met at the village hop, it was natural that they should be drawn together. Life must have seemed full of promise when the athletic young policeman courted the local beauty and won her. He was posted to Dublin, and there they married. Gabriel arrived in 1942. And from then on, married life became one long, dreary disappointment, until they both became more or less alcoholic, and were accustomed to the idea that – as Yeats said – life is a long preparation for something that never happens.

As I tried to understand why I found all this so upsetting, I realised that it arises from a deep-seated conviction that life ought to bring some fulfilment. For I, like Gabriel, had started off with an unpromising working class background, and had left school at 16 because my parents did not have the money to even suggest that I should go on to further education and university. Like Gabriel, I was bright and promising at school, and spent most of my spare time curled up with a book. But I had one piece of luck that was the basis of everything that followed. When I was 10, my mother gave me a chemistry set for my birthday, and after reading the instruction book from end to end a dozen times, I dishonestly helped myself to a coverless volume of Holmyard's Inorganic Chemistry that I found lying around on the top of a locker at school. This too I devoured, then found more books on chemistry in the local library, some of them huge tomes three inches thick. An aunt gave me some magazines called Armchair Science, and an uncle presented me with The Marvels and Mysteries of Science, in which a photograph of the great nebula in Andromeda drew me on to volumes on astronomy, then to books like The Mysterious Universe by Sir James Jeans, and Eddington's Nature of the Physical World. By the time I was 12 I knew I wanted to be a scientist, and had secretly resolved to become Einstein's successor.

What happened when I left school at 16 left these day-dreams in ruins. I did not have enough credits to apply for a job in ICI, which required matriculation mathematics. My old school offered me a job as a laboratory assistant if I could get the necessary credit, and lent me the books to study. But in the meantime, I worked in a wool factory, and found myself plunged into the same despair that Dickens felt in the blacking factory and Wells in the drapery emporium. When I was young I had been led to feel that life always rewarded talent; now I felt that I might spend my whole life on a kind of treadmill. I was not even elated when I passed my maths exam with the necessary credit, for in the few months in the wool factory, I had started to read poetry as some kind of emotional relief – I had discovered it through Palgrave's Golden Treasury when I was about 14 – and had lost all my interest in science.

The next year was depressing, as I took a job as a civil servant – when my school threw me out – and hated it as much as the wool factory. The RAF, where I did my National Service as a clerk, was no better, and even the natural optimism of youth could not disguise from me that the rest of my life might be just as boring and frustrating.

Since this is not supposed to be my own autobiography, I will simply add that, after a shotgun wedding and a brief and unsuccessful marriage, I gambled everything on becoming a writer, became a kind of 'beatnik' long before that term existed, and was eventually inspired to write a novel about 'outsiders' from which The Outsider was an offshoot. I began it on Christmas Day, 1954, when I was 23, and a publisher had accepted it a few months later. It appeared a month before my twenty fifth birthday, was reviewed on the same day as Osborne's Look Back in Anger, and brought me the kind of recognition I had dreamed about, but in such lavish quantities that it soon ceased to be a pleasure. And so I fled to Cornwall with my girlfriend Joy, and not long thereafter received a letter from Gabriel Duffy explaining that he was an Outsider…

So by the time he came to visit me in Cornwall, the fear I had experienced at 16, that life would prove to be 'a long preparation for something that never happens' – was behind me. Admittedly, my books were violently attacked and often ignored, but I was published in several countries, and could make a living by writing. And those long years of working without encouragement (and the years from 16 to 24 had seemed endless) had prepared me to weather the lack of critical interest in my work.

Now it can be seen why I was so strangely upset by the story of Gabriel's mother. It brought back suddenly the depression I had experienced from the age of 16, the feeling that there is no law of nature that says that effort always leads to success, and that life is bound to bring some kind of fulfilment. I found myself so deeply saddened by her story that I found it hard to be indignant about the beatings.

But I am quite certain that Gabriel is correct when he attributes some of his later problems to his mother. He quotes the psychiatrist Abraham Maslow who remarked that his own mother was 'the type that's called schizophrenogenic… she's the one who makes crazy people, crazy children', and who made Maslow wonder later why he never went insane. A mother who beats her son may not qualify as schizophrenogenic, but she is certainly not going to build up the kind of self-confidence that a young writer needs to believe in his own work. Gabriel admits that one of his own main reactions to this lack of self-confidence was to 'clown' in an effort to win approval.

This, in turn, led to the sexual frustration that seems inevitable for most introverted intellectuals. He remarks that he almost envies Maslow for falling in love with his cousin Bertha when he was 19, marrying a year later, and then having a perfect mate for the rest of his life. He, Gabriel, lost his virginity at 25, 'about ten years after it needed to happen.' He also remarks perceptively that 'my increasingly heavy drinking in my late teens and early twenties was in part a symptom of sexual retardation.'

Here I am certain he is correct. I was certainly lucky in that when I was 19, and just out of the RAF, I was picked up by a 15 year old when I was working on a fairground, and promptly seduced. I have never ceased to be grateful to her for helping me to rid myself of years of emotional self-doubt and physical frustration. Once I knew girls were not averse to being undressed, I never looked back. And when I found Joy – when I was 22 – I settled down as happily as Maslow. Once my sexual and emotional needs had been taken care of, I felt I could give my full attention to writing.

But Gabriel had another problem: that he is a Celt. And the trouble with Celts is simply too much imagination. Larry Doyle, Shaw's Irishman in John Bull's Other Island, expresses it when he says: 'Oh, the dreaming! 'the torturing, heart-scalding, never satisfying dreaming, dreaming, dreaming! No debauchery that ever coarsened and brutalised an Englishman can take the worth and usefulness out of him like that dreaming. An Irishman's imagination never lets him alone...'

In other words, Celts suffer from a version of the problem that led me to write The Outsider: the sudden 'glimpse of meaning' experienced by so many romantics, and the frustration of not being able to re-create it at will. This, says Larry Doyle, is why so many of them find it hard to bear reality without the help of alcohol.

Gabriel set me thinking again about this problem because of a remark he made about a television programme on the sex killer Neville Heath, whose good looks and upper-class accent made him irresistible to women. Gabriel commented: 'He reminded me of someone I once knew who had the same kind of looks and charm with females.' He added: 'Although dear old Gerald was no sexual psychopath or sadist, just another fine mind destroyed by drink... I still remember a mutual friend calling me in the office in 1980 or so to say Gerry had been found dead in bed in a Salvation Army hostel, after choking in his own vomit in his sleep.'

Gerald, it seemed, was a gentlemanly Celt – a Welshman – whose father edited a magazine. An army officer at 17, he was adored by his men, and admired and liked by fellow officers, even though he broke all the rules and landed in endless scrapes. He got into a fight one night and severed a tendon in his hand which disabled his trigger finger; much against his will, he was discharged. He had loved the army and the sense of purpose and belonging, and found civilian life appallingly dull. Gabriel met him when he (Gabriel) was working as an accountant for an oil company and Gerald was a temporary clerk. When Gabriel produced an amateur Blithe Spirit, Gerald played the lead. And when Gerald joined an employment agency as a consultant, he asked Gabriel to join him, launching his career as a business consultant.

But Gerald was an alcoholic, and Gabriel was soon spending much of his time covering up for him. Then Gerald was poached by another agent, who soon realised he was an alcoholic. The agent finally had to fire him, although he told Gabriel: 'If we could have afforded it, we'd have kept him on for sheer entertainment value alone.'

And so Gerald ended in a Salvation Army hostel, drowned in his own vomit.

Gabriel added a postscript that intrigued me. 'I once said to you that some alcoholics have a kind of unfocused superiority that makes them totally unfit for routine life in any form.'

And this was obviously it: a kind of 'unfocused superiority', the kind of thing that made Sherlock Holmes explain to Watson that he took morphine because otherwise his mind was like a powerful machine, tearing itself to pieces for lack of anything to do.

Fortunately, Holmes's increasing fame, and the cases it brought, soon put an end to that problem. But Gerald never found an outlet for his 'unfocused superiority.' And nothing feeds the self-destructive urge in an intelligent person more than the sense of not knowing what to do next.

I have never ceased to believe that Gabriel will find it as easy to find an outlet for his own 'unfocused superiority' in the literary world as he did in the business world. Anyone who reads the present autobiography will understand why I think so.

PROLOGUE

I was born in Dublin in 1942. It was a relatively safe place to be born, just then, as Premier De Valera's policy of neutrality spared us most of the horrors of Hitler's War.

The Southern Irish Authorities did take the precaution of issuing gas masks, just in case... Although I seem to remember that most households in our neighbourhood were provided with a single appliance. Perhaps, in the event, we were expected to take turns.

As it was, the *Luftwaffe* occasionally skittered on Free State farmlands, whether to lighten their bombers for the run home or out of mischief (or malice) was never determined.

So, accordingly, the newspapers carried pictures of bemused rustics, pointing to fields ploughed out of season, by high explosive.

There was one tragic incident, when some Nazi bombardiers mistook Dublin for Belfast and dropped their load on the sleeping city. I remember my father telling me later that the Germans issued an apology. One deadly stick demolished a terrace of cottages in the North Strand area, killing or maiming a host of people. A blockbuster thudded on the Phoenix Park, narrowly missing both the Presidential Mansion and the adjacent U.S. Ambassador's Residence. The huge crater, he added, "later became a fine civic amenity", after being flooded and stocked with ducks.

"Oul Dev harboured no grudges" the Da concluded. "Indeed he went in person to offer our condolences to the German Ambassador on the demise of Adolf Hitler."

I never doubted him. He was also a policeman, after all. Which probably made him less forthcoming about the night that a German spy escaped from Mountjoy Prison. I heard that from my mother.

"Yer oulfella" she confided, "was on duty outside Mountjoy at the time."

* * *

With Ulster getting a regular dose of the real *blitzkrieg*, some Free State families did lose friends and relatives in the North – as well as those serving with the British forces, or in their U-boat devastated Merchant Marine. For them, neutrality was a theoretical issue.

However, I cannot recall an instance of the war touching our own relatives, friends or neighbours, in that respect, and indeed it was all over by the time I was of an age to understand such loss.

* * *

Otherwise, growing up in the post-war Dublin of the Forties and Fifties was an uneventful business, insofar as political or social upheavals mattered. Life in Ireland was never so slow to change and all of the old beliefs, customs and habits were still intact and seemed forever frozen in time.

But radical change was on the way and it seems to me that my own generation became its spearhead. With us the centuries old mould of Irish provincialism began to shatter, although it would take another 40 years to produce the relatively cosmopolitan Republic of today.

In the course of this volume I hope to recapture the end of the old times, and the beginning of the new. Or, to explain my title, the shift from sham hypocrisy to more open attitudes. Presaged by the raw music of rock and further generated by a flood of gritty realism in late'50s cinema, theatre and literature.

Preceded by three chapters devoted respectively to the boyhood impact of comics, radio and films, these advanced influences are detailed in chapters 11 and 12, with Dublin then a kind of Athens for bright youngsters.

Chapter 13 breaks the Irish mould, recounting a 1959 summer vacation I spent in London, working with school friends. There the new teenage subculture, abetted by immense social reforms in general, was in full swing.

Revelling in it all – not least in a sexual freedom unknown at home – we returned unaware that our mind-opening experiences were shared by other students on similar stints. Some, later rising to positions of influence, became key players in Europeanising the insular Land of the Shamrock...

Chapter One

SLUGS* AND SNAILS...

...And puppy-dogs tails. That's what little boys are made of.

A nursery rhyme apparently taken to heart by many teachers. For School, under the Christian Brothers, could be very hard in those days of rote learning and obedience or else. A few heavy slaps of a coin-filled leather contraption on petrified palms, after arriving late of a cold winter morning, was the measure of it for many. It was bad enough cycling to school with your hands frozen to the bone, without being lacerated for making the effort.

The Leather was a perpetual curse upon all of us; no one avoided it for long. Girls, under the nuns, got euphemistically 'smacked', with a wooden ruler.

Most of us, boys and girls, learned to live with corporal punishment – being often "skelped" at home as well as in school. As a way of maintaining discipline CP worked well enough, for the adults.

In the schoolroom, this, which Bernard Shaw memorably called "the pursuit of the child by Learning, cane in hand", inevitably led to abuse by low calibre teachers. Those who took their own inferiority out on their helpless charges – lighting on timidity or slowness as much as on a cleverness which only reminded them of their own stupidity. So you got whacked as much for being "stupid" as you did for being "too smart by

* A Dublin bowdlerisation of the original: 'Snakes and snails'.

half". No one was safe with them...

Okay, we may have been grubby little slugs and snails, with our bitten fingernails and snotty noses, but the teachers themselves (Brothers and laymen alike) were nothing to write home about. With few exceptions they were drab men in search of a quiet life, and often more interested in reading the sports pages, or picking their own noses, than demonstrating a vital vocation – let alone imparting the wisdom of the ages. While some Brothers were little older than adolescents themselves.

Such teaching, or beating, was not of course exclusive to Ireland. For example, 'Such, Such Were the Joys', the title of a bitter essay by George Orwell, describes his own experiences at an English public school, when he was immured in one at the age of Eight. He was still capable of rage in his Forties, recapping on how the dim bastards beat him for wetting the bed. It may have incubated the mentality that led to 'Animal Farm' and '1984', but adult Orwell would possibly have sacrificed the masterpieces for five minutes alone with any one of his tormentors.

Not to say that experience of maniacal, or incompetent, teaching is entirely ruinous. I survived both fairly well, as James Joyce earlier thrived among the thrashing Jesuits. But for every positive memoir, of school life, there are dozens in the mould of Orwell, constituting an unanswerable case against formally (ha ha) beating children – in the name of God, King, Country, or any other convenient abstraction.

There were some cheering moments: instances of fathers or older brothers bursting vengefully into classrooms, to berate or assault some bullying swine after he'd done the same to son or "baby bruder".

Another much-recounted incident related to a boy attacked by a Brother and cracked across the face. The boy had a detachable glass eye, which his tormentor did not know. Until his victim suddenly collapsed on the floor, clutching his face and howling: "Me eye Sir! Me eye!"

There in his pathetic little palm, the eye was ominously laid...

The shock quietened that Brother down for awhile.

Sometimes, maybe, we asked for it. As in my semi-final year when a classmate passed around a small bottle of strong poteen in the science lab. A few of us sipped a little in turn, just enough to bring on the giggles. The old Brother teaching caught our 'dealer' sniggering, correctly assumed it was directed at himself (we all had him for a slovenly fool) and went totally ape. After slapping the lad repeatedly on the face with an open hand he threw down and kicked him like a football. Then he marched him, bruised and bleeding, from the lab, bellowing "Get out! Get away now you cur!" Returning fuming to a numbed, totally aghast class.

* * *

Whenever I met old classmates in later life most of them remembered only the leather, with varying degrees of anger or bitterness, as if nothing good had happened during the long years of our schooling. A conclusive indictment, to my mind, of the obscene practice.

The convent-educated wife of an old friend, becomes apoplectic on the subject of nuns, and their mistreatment of girls. She particularly rails at and abominates certain "twisted bitches" who resorted to psychological forms of punishment, or persecution, and permanently ruptured the self-confidence of some of her classmates in consequence.

My own experience of the nuns, in Infant School – from the age of 5 to 8 – wasn't bad. But then I think I had only cosy lady lay teachers for my three years 'at the convent' – one of whom made me her pet because she admired my tie! The Convent was a sedate place where you learned to recite your ABC and your One Two Three and the worst that happened, if you were 'bad', was to be made sit among a class of giggling girls.

In my final year at school, I had personal experience of a Brother who, in the view of our entire class, was "not fit to teach". A bullying monster of the worst kind, given to snide jibes, he had a nasty penchant for hauling a boy out of his seat by the hair, or, even more agonisingly, pulling him to his feet by clutching the sideburns. All this for the most trivial reason and often for none at all; mostly, we knew, for his own sick amusement.

I deeply resented that kind of treatment, as a 17-year-old who had spent my last summer vacation working in London and seen a bit of real life. The second or third time he tried it on, provoked by traces of nicotine on my fingers, I hit back and stormed out of the class, for good.

A few days later, I was astounded when the man turned up at my home. Even moreso because he was sheepish and apologetic. My parents were out and I told him quite calmly that I'd had it. He saw that I was obdurate and just walked away, head bowed, visibly shattered. I still couldn't understand the change in him and remember feeling only icy relief.

In my innocence I did not appreciate the effect on him, on the class and on the school, of a promising scholar just quitting. I had done pretty well in my Intermediate Certificate and become marked as a boy who would do equally well in my Leaving and go on to university.

I have no doubt that the real cause of this minor tragedy was duly ascertained by the school authorities and that our unfortunate sadist got a real razing from the Head Brother. I was duly informed by former classmates that the bullying virtually ceased and that said Brother began to act like "a nervous man". So I had possibly done them a favour...

The story has a chilling ending, as I learned years later.

Apparently I was not he first boy to go 'off', in one way or another, because of such mistreatment. There had previously been a couple of nervous breakdowns under his tutorship, and other unpleasant incidents of a kind that worried his own superiors.

He was removed from teaching the following year and spent some time in a mental home. A wretched man, but with a lot to answer for. My parents were devastated by my decision. To them, I had simply thrown my future away. Had I stayed in Dublin that may have proved true. However, I moved to England, made the most of the education I did have, enjoyed the luck of the Irish for many years and prospered withal.

* * *

I must emphasise that (appropriately nicknamed) bullies and monsters were few and far between in relation to the majority of teachers.

I recall a few (too few) decent, admirable Brothers; fair-minded, even-tempered and good-humoured. These were the sort who set a good example and even inspired some boys to later follow a religious vocation.

Many Brothers hailed from country areas, to be dubbed "Colshies". To them, we were "Dublin Jackeens". Occasionally, this caused antipathy; more often than not it resulted in friendly banter – particularly when Dublin and provincial footballers, or hurlers, clashed in Croke Park.

A Park also notable as the locus of our annual sports days, when the stands were packed by parents and pupils for various athletics and gymnastics – flag-swirling and barbell-humping were regular favourites.

The Artane Boys Band (from a Reformatory) were always on hand to play martial music, as they did at every important 'match' in Croke.

Mention of the reformatory reminds me that orphans, or kids from broken homes, as well as truants and miscreants, were installed in such 'industrial schools', which were

5

rumoured to be very strict places indeed. Minds boggled: ours were strict enough.

School itself was organised into graded classes for each primary and secondary year. Boys in the A and B classes were expected to achieve high marks in most subjects, or several Honours in the Intermediate and Leaving Examinations of the secondary period – thus ensuring university entrance. A and B classes seldom exceeded thirty pupils. C, D, even E, classes often increased in size as the I.Q. fell, until as many as fifty or sixty were packed into some classrooms. (Morning Roll Call was an essential there!) I began as an A, before slipping to B, with one early year as a C.

Schools themselves were rated by their success in filling university places, provoking fierce inter-school competitiveness and uniformly crucifying scholastic regimens in the final terms.

Proponents of the leather might here have argued that 'it got results', in that it helped to produce one of the highest standards of tertiary education in the world. However, since CP went out, standards have not fallen at all. To the contrary, new centres of higher learning have been established, to cope with an increase in eligible students – only partly attributable to a relative increase in the school-age population.

Gaelic is also less compulsory a subject than it was in my day, when a working knowledge of it was *de rigueur* for the plummier jobs after you left school, in the civil service and nationalised industries.

The official aim behind the teaching of Gaelic, to create an Irish-speaking society, was never to be realised. *Bearla* (English) was too long and decisively established as the popular everyday language. Even so all road signs in Ireland are inscribed in both Irish and English. Route indicators on buses are often Gaelic only, road and rail terminals are bilingual. *Eire* on all postage stamps – no doubt to trumpet abroad that (Southern) Ireland is an independent republic.

Most of us came to resent being indoctrinated in "the Irish", as the equivalent of being flogged with a dead horse. The A grades got the very worst of it, being taught everything in Gaelic, even Christian Doctrine.

My own favourite subject was English – which they never quite figured out how to teach in Irish. I liked the English prose and poetry schoolbooks, with their snippets of great literature and immortal verse. Along with the stories of great Irish poet-heroes like Oisin (Ossian), Cuculann and Finn MacCool, or the kings of Tara, you picked up some good stuff from the English poets and writers. The Anglo-Irish were well-represented – Yeats being usually very 'easy to learn':

"Come away O human child!/To the waters and the wild/With a faery, hand in hand,/ For the world's more full of weeping than you can understand". Only matched for mnemonic ease by his 'Lake Isle of Inisfree'.

Milton and Shakespeare in the 'Sec'; no Dante, or Goethe.

Gaelic prose and poetry provided a trying balance, in terms of our struggling to digest it. Although in later years I often found myself repeating lines learned by rote, and appreciating their power and beauty for the first time. Great poetry makes its mark on the mind and never leaves us.

With hindsight, I can see clearly how much I owe to an Irish education, even allowing for the harsher methods of my own time. Neither, to be fair, was it all stick and no carrot. Prizes and rewards for scholastic attainment were also common and had their desired effect. So, at school, "we saw the two days", as the Irish saying goes – meaning that we had a bit of real happiness as well as the opposite. We even got out of school from time to time, on educational trips to museums, art galleries, the botanical gardens...or an excursion to 'see the planes' at Collinstown (now Dublin) Airport. In "Sec" we had an outing to John Players' cigarette factory, where blind eyes were turned when you were given free samples of the forbidden fruit. (The more enterprising having already filled their pockets.) I also remember a tour of Guinness's Brewery – free samples there being restricted to the Brother-In-Charge.

In Primary School I joined the Choir (a welcome alternative to P.T.) and sang with them on Radio Eireann. As a reward for our staid studio performance the choir-master – a "good stick" of a Brother – took us all to see 'The Robe' – "a fine Christian picture lads". The first film, as the blurbs had it, "in thrilling CinemaScope and all-round stereophonic sound". That was school at its best.

Sometimes, on a fine clear summer's day, a few of us got out on our own account, by "mitching" – playing truant. That would be just before or after the school summer holiday began or ended – two months for Primary boys, three for Secondary.

Those long glorious free days made up for an awful lot.

CHAPTER TWO

SUGAR AND SPICE...

...And all that's nice. That's what little girls are made of.

Boys who played serious Gaelic football or hurley seldom got a beating; more often became 'pets' in a milieu where many teachers venerated the G.A.A. (Gaelic Athletic Association).

Athletes in general were held up as examples of 'manly courage and purity' – the latter echoing a conviction of the celibate Brothers, that boys who burned up their energy on the playing field were very unlikely to play with themselves. Many of us detested Gaelic games and were, indeed, more prone to playing pocket billiards. Full marks to The Brothers there, who had us "pasty-faced sickly types" very well taped.

But we also knew something that they didn't – many a goal-scorer was no less fond of "a hand-shandy" than the rest of us.

Wherever there are schoolboys, or indeed schoolgirls, there is always a certain amount of smut and sexual innuendo. In those days we were all grossly uninformed on the subject and many kids seriously believed that babies were "found under a cabbage leaf", or a gooseberry bush. Nonetheless there was endless speculation among both sexes, as to why we differed in the nether regions. Dirty jokes were always at a premium, although the emphasis was lavatorial rather than sexual.

Among many boys, masturbation was a regular topic. Although few admitted to doing the "durty ting" themselves it was of course all too commonly practised. ("A tosser" was

9

always a derisive sobriquet in Dublin, and not only for those with Portnoy's Complaint; it meant anyone useless – "wanker" was equally used.) True boldness only came with puberty and the communal "wanking competitions", where he who spurted farthest got the garland. It was of course A Mortal Sin, which created terrible mental conflict at times – especially when you had to tell all about it in Confession.

"I..." squirm squirm, "I touched meself Fahder..."

"Touched yourself my son? How?" (They never made it too easy.) "Me"...gulp gulp, "me private parts..."

"I see."

"Yes Fahder...I'm very sorry." (Jayse, what'll he ask me now?)

"How often did you do this?" (The most dreaded question.)

"More than once, Fahder..."

"How many times, since your last confession?"

"Ab – about fifteen times...I think..."

"Holy Mother of God! Is that all you ever do with yourself?"

"I stole a pencil in Woolworths too Fahder." (Get him off the subject.)

"Now now, evasiveness or lies won't help."

At last...to stagger out of the box and stumble away under the accusing eyes in the nearby pews, with two long rosaries to 'say' for your penance and swearing to yourself that you'd never wank again. Or if you did, as inevitably you would...the cowed return in two weeks time. Later on, older and more devious, you exchanged confidences with other acolytes of Onan, with the result that there would be long queues of pasty-faced sickly types outside the confessional of the most lenient priest in the parish. He who seldom asked an embarrassing question and 'gave' no more than "two Hail Marys', or "a confiteor" (short prayers) as "acts of contrition" – mere peremptory penitentialities.

It was such a friendly priest who, after chiding me lightly for the sin, asked me if I knew how babies were born. I didn't? Well why didn't I come round to the presbytery later on and he'd explain. I duly turned up, more curious than embarrassed, for the revelation. Sat in an ante-room by his housekeeper, I jumped up to greet the beaming arrival. Why was I there? (He'd obviously forgotten.) Oh that...

"Well now" he said, "do you know about the bulls and the cows?

"I...I tink so, Fahder..."

"Well, there you are!"

There I was. That was it. End of lesson. (Or Epestle.)

* * *

There are those, learned in such matters, who extol the psychological value of the Roman Catholic vocalis. They might well have cause to revise their views in the light of its petrifying effect on schoolboys conditioned to sexual guilt.

So sex for us was a dirty-sweet business, which could easily lead to eternal damnation. Generating in turn a confused mind-set, carrying forward from childhood and puberty to young adulthood, where it became impossible to know right from wrong in the matter. It was no help to be told, then or later, that 'sex in marriage' alone was permissible, when your stiff little mickey was "gummin for it".

Even the streetwise boys who knew what he really wanted – "you stick him in the woman's hole" – never got beyond bragging about it.

* * *

Girls were even more confused by sex, becoming fairly unapproachable - beyond the odd fumbling game of doctors in primary schooldays. Or much later, up for a sly 'feel' in the back row of a picture-house.

Even then all they usually said was "Don't" and "Stop", or nearly amputated the hand that got too high up between the

11

hams. The nuns did an excellent job there: "no man will respect a girl who plays Jezebel..."

The Story of Maria Goretti was The Great Example for girls, as told to us all, by tight-lipped Brother or Nun. An Italian peasant girl, Maria had been "stabbed repeatedly by a scut of a boy who wanted her to be immodest". And had "given her young life before she'd give in to him".

If girls 'wanked', as they surely did, it was a well concealed secret, probably even among the girls themselves. For the most part, they believed what they were told – that sex was for having babies, full stop.

That part of their genitalia was for reproductive purposes only and certainly not for pleasure – perish the mere thought of it. They were mere receptacles for sperm. How they reconciled this with their first discovery of the clitoris, one can only surmise.

No doubt, if some nuns had their way, clitoridectomy would have become another means of moral sanitation and enforced accordingly. So, the girls had the asexual worst of it. (Boys only knew, vaguely, that girls "got hot".)

* * *

But...there were some little girls who took their knickers down easily enough for you. Some even told the odd dirty joke – like the one about the girl who cried "never never never" when "a man asked her to get in the bed." And kept repeating it with his every advance until "he got on top of her and asked her when he should stop".

"And what did she say?"

"Never never never! Ha ha." *Quad erat demonstrandum...*

I remember a very unfunny incident when two boys tried to get my pocket money, under threat of telling my mother that I'd deknickered one of their sisters. I wouldn't budge and they posted a note to the effect through our letter-box. Oddly enough I saw it lying in the hallway and couldn't bring myself to seize and destroy...a piece of factual truth, before the Ma swooped.

It said something like "Your precious angel took down" So-And-So's "knickers". (I was an only child and often branded as a mother's boy in my early years – thence the angel, Gabriel.)

Anyway, my mother was, as they say, "flippin" and caused further ructions by confronting the boys' parents with the evidence. We all had red bums afterwards, including the girl. A prime example of the sheer hysteria that sex aroused in many parents.

At the same time even 'good' girls were a bit afraid of being "too hard" and ending up like the unfortunate Spinster – a much maligned figure – particularly when they got to an age when the hormones began to leap.

But The Scandal Of Nurse Cadden was also burnt into susceptible minds; that had made headlines in its time (c.1950), in a way no child could miss. It was known that Nurse Cadden had "done somethin really durty at her nursery in Hume Street". (Read clinic for nursery.)

The most informed knew that the durty ting, related to "a dead baby bein found in the gutter". ("Are you coddin?" we'd ask them. – "No I'm cadden! Ha ha.") Apparently "abortion" was the real word for it and it could never happen to the girl who stuck to the principles of purity – as terminally practised by Maria Goretti. – Principles known to psychiatrists under another name: 'negative reinforcement'.

Positive reinforcement prepared a girl "to become a good wife and mother", or took their minds off sex by encouraging certain approved premarital careers – preferably in one of 'the caring professions' or the civil service. Aer Lingus was included among those, largely because many girls dreamed of becoming air hostesses. Modelling was regarded as respectable – women being women some nuns followed Fashion, vow of the cowl or not. ...Any girl who showed signs of a religious vocation was separately prized and nurtured.

* * *

For the boys, negative reinforcement related particularly to what our mentors obliquely damned as "the sin of Sodom and Gomorrah".

A boy must never, ever 'interfere' with another boy. It was the very worst of sins. Boys who did, more positively reinforced their tendency with gleeful reference to certain stray examples given them from the adult world. Every neighbourhood had at least one "Browny" – a man who 'interfered' with you, if you gave him half a chance. Some boys even boasted about such 'encounters' (which others of us later found 'epiphanised' in the uncannily true-to-life short story by Joyce.)*

"We all knew him", a reader of the story once conceded to Joyce.

As to heterosexuality, I recall an eye-widening conversation with some very clued-up youths – one of whom had attempted to "do an Erroll Flynn" on their family maid at the age of Twelve.

They also spoke knowledgeably of "a durty oul browny in Ellesmere Avenue", who "paid ye to go with him". But you didn't do so "if you valued yer arse", because they also knew of a boy who had "gone wit yer man and ended up wit his bum bursted wide-open."

So, we first learned about sodomy.

On a more humorous note, another of these 'lads' got "a larrupin from me old man", after said parent once found him loitering by an unsuspecting sister, with a small mirror ingeniously fixed to the toe-cap of his shoe..."so I could see up her dress, between her legs".

* Based incidentally on a personal experience of JJ the boy.

Gold medal stuff that, to salivating young devils like ourselves.

A regular denizen of the Phoenix Park preyed on boys and girls alike. And he went a lot farther than Joyce's paedophile dared to go, in that restrained fictional account. It was also well-known to the streetwise that Brownies en masse congregated in The Park, in an area of dense shrubbery called The Furry Glen. The amusing aptness of name was not lost on us. Men you saw starkers at bathing holes had pubic fur galore.

All this resulted in a highly ambivalent attitude to sodomites: a mix of prurient curiosity, crude wit – "'Je hear about the two Scottish brownies? Ben Dover and Phil Macavity" – joke disgust, or horror…

Mutual masturbation in the teens was conveniently disregarded as "not reely what the brownies do". They kissed… and much much worse.

I only knew of one such among the Brothers, to give some credit to that sexually-suppressed fraternity. With never a whiff of it from any lay-teacher. The Brother, inevitably nicknamed The Brown, became the butt of schoolboy humour, providing you hadn't been a victim. …Stories of injured footballers miraculously scrambling to their feet and legging it, on sight of The Brown bearing down upon them, with a First Aid kit.

Priests were universally regarded as Far Above Sex – justifiably so my own experience, with a sole exception: In my teens I was completely flabbergasted when a close pal confided that his mother sometimes slept with his uncle – a country parish priest - when that worthy was in Dublin. It didn't bother my pal in the least:

"She never sleeps with my old man anyhow, they fight like cat and dog." Besides, "he" (the clerical lover) "always gives me a few bob to go to the pictures. And to get me outta the house!"

At least he didn't sleep with his brother, the father.

The incidence of experimental homosexuality among boys

was predictably a lot higher in boarding schools – modelled on the English system, with juniors 'fagging'* for seniors and prefects. Most of us, non-boarders, indulged in little or none of it until our own hormones started to leap and sexual curiosity got hotter in a girl-elusive environment.

Before that, we were generally more interested in wanking to the corset adverts in our mothers' magazines, sometimes wearing a pair of ('modest'!) directoire knickers, pur-loined, in a double pun, from her underwear 'drawers'. If the Mammy ever got to know about that...but you were safe enough in the days before semen.

Apart from taking a slide-rule to erections – as we tried a bit of comparative measurement – or 'having a shandy' with my pals, I had one experience which taught me a weird lesson about the strange power of the sexual impulse. This related to letting myself be seduced, by a boy.

* * *

I must have been Thirteen or Fourteen, for I know that I had started to 'wet-come' at the time of the incident in question. Indeed I had spent a dismal grey wet afternoon alone in the house investigating the phenomenon and spent myself in the process, when I broke off to answer a knock on the front door.

"Ken I come in, Divvy?" – My nickname.

There stood a youth none of us liked. He was generally joked about in my own circle, as a stupid slob without any redeeming feature.

His total obsession with sex was legendary; equally the butt of humour. Here he was on my door-step, leering at me, as if I'd just told him the latest dirty joke. About to refuse entry, I

---

* From the standard dictionary definition, as 'toiling' – which sometimes included being buggered and may account for the otherwise extraordinary coincidence that a fag is a homosexual, in American slang.

suddenly had the weird feeling that he knew exactly what I had been up to: wanking.

Before I knew it, I was inviting him in and consenting, with little reluctance, to take down my shorts while he did likewise. Even to sitting on his erection, while he tossed me off...to gush again, for the third or fourth time that day, with a bizarre excitement.

Part of me didn't want to. (This wasn't like a lark with one of the lads; more a contamination.) But I did it all the same... with a mixture of disgust, horror...and pleasure. I was behaving passively in all this, like a girl, letting myself be dominated. He knew it and, I suspect, revelled in the notion that a 'smart' stuck-up kid could be cut down to size (or levelled by Sex) so easily. Sex is Power and above all, The Great Leveller!

Afterwards I felt nauseated and tormented by guilt. I was, I felt, worse than a Browny. If anyone got to hear about this how they'd laugh at me, mock me, ridicule me...before shunning me thereafter.

(It would also be hard to make malicious fun of brownies from now on, when I had learned, from first-hand experience, a little about the need for outside sympathy, compassion and tolerance in such matters.)

No doubt I duly confessed the 'encounter' and got no more than a severe penance – I have no memory of being threatened with eternal damnation. Which may have emboldened me to confide my humiliation to a close friend. He only laughed uproariously at my "prudishness".

"But..." I faltered.

"But me arse" guffawed my pal, "we've all done it with him. Even" – he went on to name two girls we all knew. "He has the tool of tools."

I guess I was blessed to have friends who were a lot smarter and thick-skinned than my hyper-sensitive self. So I hadn't behaved like a degenerate after all, I had merely joined an exclusive Club. One in which the other members regarded their seducer as a sick joke.

Enabling us to continue to make fun of him a few years later, when he would parade the floor at local dances with the tool of tools massively rampant beneath his buttoned flies. What we couldn't figure, then, was how he always managed to pull a pretty girl, and have her kissing him passionately on or off the floor. Boor or not, he was streets ahead of us in basic sexual matters, which often have little to do with thought (or conscience) and everything to do with decisive action.

* * *

Mention of my canny pal reminds me of an earlier incident.

There was in our neighbourhood, the (inevitable!) Much Older Boy, cloaked permanently in a mysterious aura of strange tension, who preyed merrily on us younger boys (and girls) for years. One day, I must have been Seven or Eight, he invited me into his house to see his...stamp collection. Alone in the house with him, the albums open on a kitchen table, he suddenly asked me: "Does your tossil ever get hard?"

I didn't know what to say. I knew instantly what he meant. It did, regularly, but I was most reluctant to tell him so. I stared hard at a blurring page of stamps, pretending I hadn't heard. I sensed, infallibly, that this went way beyond the usual kind of peer curiosity; furthermore that it could easily lead to something really unpleasant.

"Take down your h'rousers" he commanded suddenly, in a voice thick as cold porridge.

Turning slightly I was truly horrified to see he had opened his flies and had it in his hand – an enormous hairy purply atrocity.

"Take them down" he growled again. "Or I will use brutal force."

I legged it. Out of the kitchen, down the hallway, grabbing

18

for the front-door knob-latch, praying it would turn for me, expecting any minute to feel a hand on my shoulder...hauling me back, from one knob to another. I got out and belted for dear life. Still panting, I met with the above friend and another boy, blurted out my experience.

They fell about laughing, especially at the words "brutal force". He wouldn't have harmed you, they pealed, "he only wanted to feel your bum and pull your wire". Only! Oh yes... they'd been there themselves before...several times in one case. I was being a cissy.

But I couldn't see the funny side. Later I was still so upset that I complained wimpishly to my mother...that So-And-So had 'frightened me'. She played it down, saying only that she thought very highly of his mother and wouldn't want "to worry her". I much later discovered that several local parents knew precisely what was 'going on', in the house of philately, but chose to ignore it, from a similar sense of neighbourliness. Or, as they'd have put it: "for peace and quiet".

Obviously, between that and the later incident retailed above, I'd shed a few inhibitions and begun to change my sexual spots.

*　*　*

Junior girl guides were also called Brownies, which led to some very strange jokes at times.

Schoolgirls themselves had the usual 'crushes' on classmates or friends from time to time, which may have become erotic in some instances. But lesbianism as such was seldom a word anyone heard and the proclivity itself was largely unknown, to child and adult alike. In the main, Irish people then, especially the women, were extremely innocent, sexually, of anything beyond a narrow conventional band.

Certainly no one could have imagined, in their wildest dreams, both the public acknowledgement of female homosexuality and an open declaration of it, by a young Irish lesbian – daughter of a distinguished university professor – on a Dublin television chat show in the Eighties.

Compared to that, my generation had all the unscrewing to do.

CHAPTER THREE

"The common Dubliners amaze us
With their frequent use of Jaysus.
And it leads us to the notion
That it's not always from devotion."
                                    – Oliver St John Gogarty

I had a very long-lived Great-Aunt, Bridget, on my father's
side, known to all and sundry simply as "Aunt B". She survived
well into my own first marriage, in the Sixties. I always
remember her as very old, from the day we first met.

She was a really lovely lady, big-busted and genial, with
never, as they said, "a bad word for anyone". She doted on me
of course and a visit to her house meant "a few ha'pence, to
buy yerself a few sweets", and often a pile of foreign stamps, to
encourage philately...

Foreign stamps because, out of her tiny terraced home in
Carnew Street, Aunt B conducted an incredible regular
correspondence with Irish Missionaries abroad. A Practical
Christian of the best kind, she was also an indefatigible
hostess to visiting clergy, from "the land of the poor heathen,
God bless and protect them." Legendary throughout the
Foreign Missions for her hospitality, she was never without a
nun or priest, lodging.

Father Colwell wasn't a missionary, but a priest who Aunt B
had earlier 'adapted', as a novice, and helped financially on the
road to ordination. She had a good eye for promising talent
there, for he proved an enormous boon to his Order in due

course, not least by raising, as she said, "pots of money for them", on trips to the USA.

I could understand why the Americans took to him, with his amazing personal gusto and charisma – I never heard a man who laughed so heartily. When, for example, he'd ask, me if I wanted to be a priest and I'd reply earnestly that I'd "start as a Bishop", to save time...he'd roar with mirth...and maybe slip me a couple of shillings...while Big Aunt B burst her corsets in the wings, tickled to tears and invoking her favourite Gaelic phrase: "Arra Musha!" (Roughly: I'll be darned.) "Sure the child is a janius! Holy God – a bishop!"

Father Colwell was very popular with the ladies. Noticing that he seemed to spend far too much time in the company of women, Aunt B once took him to task. Much much later she told me how "he cut me right down to size. By reminding me that Our Lord Himself revered all women and often seemed to prefer theirs to the company of men."

I know that I was totally enraptured by Father C, and if the Catholic Church took in boys of Five or Six as acolytes, like the Buddhists do, I might well have been readily recruited by him. ...With possibly consequences for myself (and the Church) that defy conjecture.

Father Colwell threw himself into his vocation with the same gusto he displayed in the parlour and, I suspect, literally wore himself into an early grave as a result. I heard in later years that he had become Lord Abbot of Kilnacrot Priory... later again that he contracted cancer and had one leg amputated from the hip, then the other...Then, that he was dead.

Recently completing a critical study of the French Jesuit Palaeontologist, *Père* Teilhard de Chardin, I sometimes thought of Father Colwell, as a comparable example of the very best kind of Priest.

But the missionaries I met at Aunt B's weren't far behind, in the common humanity stakes. I was in fact meeting some of the finest and best of the true Soldiery of Christ – nice in the true sense and with a curious innocence about them. I remember those quiet, 'resting' nuns and priests as childlike in their piety, serenity and harmless enjoyment of simple things – like a certain serious little boy who sang like a crow.

For about that time, my mother had a mind to making "a drawing-room boy" of me. After the goal, she groomed me mercilessly "to entertain", at Aunt B's *soirées*.

My talent was presumed to be vocal and I can recall figures in black (or missionary white) beaming over their dainty tea-cups while I stood up, face scrubbed and dressed for a wedding, to 'sing' (after Bing): "An American landed on Erin's Green Isle...How can I buy it he asked with a sigh..." Reprise reprise: "How can I buy Kill-ahr-ney." Go on now Gay: give it to them. "Howwww can you purchase a fond mother's smile... How can you buy two blue Irish eyes...How..." And how.

On one such howl the best linen was out for a Bishop and I got to kneel and... kiss his ring, after he'd wiped it clean of my mother's spittle.

* * *

Nothing pleased an Irish parent more, than to "rear a child for the Church" – meaning particularly the elite priesthood, but hardly less excitement over an aspirant Brother or nun. Males who looked like they had the makings were inducted to assist at Mass, as altar-boys. – An attempt to make me one foundered on my inability (or reluctance) to master the Latin responses.

Two of my cousins entered the priesthood. One went to South America with the Missions. I always liked him a lot and was greatly saddened to hear that he also died of cancer, in his prime, many years ago. He remained very civil and friendly to me, whenever we met in later times, although he well knew then that I had "given up The Faith".

The second cousin, of whom I was no less fond, found that out for himself nearer the event. Having once motored me up to the Dublin Mountains, when I was Thirteen or Fourteen, to try and persuade me to become a priest, he was predictably gutted a few years later, to meet a young Buck who had only become "like James Joyce, and the rest of them". Indeed we had a heated debate of the Dedalian kind.

* * *

The upshot of all this is that I never had reason to 'hate' the Church, or to dislike its representatives; less so for knowing many of the best of them.

But there came a time when I decided that Roman Catholicism, or indeed any branch of orthodox church religion, was simply not for me.

Correspondingly, I came for awhile to regard it as a part of my boyhood which was shed and buried.

Before, that is, I began to realise that no one ever completely 'sheds' their early 'brain-washing' – be it religious, political, or otherwise. Whether you are brought up to believe in God, Karl Marx, or Mammon, it leaves impressions that can never be entirely erased, much as you may later profess to the contrary.

The best you can do is acknowledge the residual influences, respect their power and take account of it. – Joyce never underestimated the effect of a Jesuit education and sometimes thought of himself as a kind of obverse Catholic, or a reactionary (latterday) Aquinas. (One of his critics has observed that he continued to <u>think</u> like a Jesuit.)

The same, in a way, could be said of Shaw, who became in his time as messianic as any Prince of the Church. (Reviewing 'Blanco Posnet' in 1909, 27 year-old Joyce knocked him as "a born preacher"!).

We Irish seem to have The Druid in our genes...

* * *

In my pre-pubertal years I totally believed and accepted the whole Roman Catholic caboodle, lock, stock and barrel, no less than every other child of the Faith. Indeed many aspects of the Christian iconography were exciting and credible, for much the same reason that Santa Claus or the Arabian Nights were exciting and believable.

You had a veritable pantheon of admirable saints and terrible sinners, with a supporting cast of heroes and villains that put Hollywood to shame. Jesus, Mary and Joseph were readily identifiable models of saintliness, goodness and heroism (of sorts). Herod, killer of babies, was both sinner and villain supreme, while "Pontius Pilate, the Roman Governor" was "a terrible reppe" (reprobate). You only had to look at the pictures of Judas in the church to know what he was. Boo.

Regular Saints were remarkable people who flew, talked to the birds, tamed wild animals by just looking at them, and prayed a lot. It was all too good to doubt and – I am not merely trying to poke fun at things that greatly enlivened our minds here – led you to believe, also, that you were part of a fairy tale world where miracles abounded.

In that sense religion appeals to the sense of wonder, in every child.

You only began to go off it when the catechising began, or when they tried to make a saint out of you. But you never deigned to protest, let alone doubt. Besides, anyone who dared to question or doubt Sacred Doctrine was soon enough terrified back into the fold.

There is a famous passage in Joyce's 'Portrait', where a stern priest inveigles on Hell and Damnation, which sums up the forceful imagery that could be exerted against doubt. Faith was Obedience, enforced by Fear.

Billy Graham (who once did a revivalist gig on a bandstand

in the Phoenix Park) had nothing on the domestic 'Missioners' we heard proselytising in Season. I first heard the name Wilde used by a missioner in full flight: "Oscar Wilde, wretch of a reprobate and madman, screamed for a priest on his death-bed!" Even then that struck me as a bit of a *non sequitur*. If, whoever he was, he was mad, that was hardly a great testimonial for the sanity of death-bed conversion?

Women flocked to such fulminations, loving every minute of them; kneeling on dainty white hankies to avoid laddering the nyloned knees. "Me Ma wet her knickers listenin to the missioner" a pal once confided, adding with unconscious sexological perception: "Just like me sister did at the Johnny Ray concert in the Royal." (Ray, the Rod Stewart of the day, had indeed generated such female hysteria during his appearance at that Theatre that, it was well-rumoured, "the youngwans flooded the seats".)

Us youngfellas occasionally flooded our own seats in some cold chapel, when it was impossible to leave before whatever protracted 'devotion' ended. My worst memories are of being bored out of my tiny mind while hymns were sung, altar-censers were swung, or some ponderous old priest ground on endlessly in the pulpit. Ecclesiatical echoes of prolix pomposity...

I did come to detest the endless ritual and it was most agreeable, at about the age of 15 or 16, to 'drop' the Church and all it stood for. Although my decision may have been partly prompted by the knowledge that I would no longer have to confess...various dark little sins... there was also a less puerile motivation, based on burgeoning intelligence and cold commonsense...which I never later had cause to revise.

* * *

In boyhood then, you simply learned your Maynooth Catechism "by heart", followed the rules and did what you were told. Visiting priests and nuns from the aforementioned Foreign Missions sometimes brightened the school day; talking of the African jungle, showing us enormous ostrich eggs and collecting pennies for "the black babies".

Blacks in general were regarded as lovable heathen who, by God's Grace and evangelical zeal, might all yet be Converted to Christ.

Witch-doctors were a menace.

Your First Holy Communion was a big day, tasting the wafer for the first time and being afterwards given the kind of treats you usually got for a birthday, or "from Santy". Confirmation Day meant a Confirmation Suit, with long trousers and maybe even a snug waist-coat – "making a man of you". "No less than than the Jew-Boy after his barmitzvah". (Confused chronology there; you were confirmed at 10 or 11.)

'Early teens you went on weekend "Retreats" at some monastery or other, kept vows of silence ("sez who?"), slept with your pals in a dormitory (guzzling Tayto Crisps and passing around a bottle of stout, after lights out). – All "more like fun than religion"; but far too little of it.

More sombre memories included High Mass – "a whole hour of it, in the name of Jaysus" – sitting through The Stations of the Cross in Lent, mumbling responses to The Rosary, when your parents remembered that "the family that prays together, stays together"; singing hymns among wheezing coughing congregations, or being press-ganged into some Sodality procession – to trail on pebbled paths behind scapulared Children of Mary and flint-eyed Pioneers (members of the Total Abstinence Association – teetotallers); dipping your fingers in an icy holy water font on the way in and watching pious old biddies lighting prayer-candles to the suppurating Sacred Heart, "for an Intention".

It was a great Good Friday when a few of us felt old enough and bold enough to leave The Faithful at it and skive off irreverently to the Dublin Zoo – where I seem to remember we mirthfully watched rodents copulating. We were very bad boys indeed, by then.

* * *

However, if we had begun to regard ourselves as 'priest-ridden', there never seemed to me any reason to make a meal of it – as so many of our talented exiles did. Although Joyce later became "grate fun" for the way he lampooned and berated, as did Shaw, on "Pauline Crosstianity".

However, as I duly discovered, religious bigotry is not an Irish trait; it is universal. In England for example, it was often taught, under another guise, as Chauvinism. I'll return to that in my next chapter.

A brief note on two other Beliefs:

There was a tiny Jewish community in Dublin, which kept to itself ("all agog in the Synagogue"), as far as most people were concerned.

Money-lenders were all "Jewmen", Gentile or not.

Protestants, or "Proddies", were far more in evidence, with several families in my own locality. They also tended not to 'mix' with us Catholics on the whole and went to their own schools – which further favoured the informal apartheid.

In my experience relations between differing denominations were generally excellent in Dublin, where tolerance has always been rule above exception in matters of creed, race and colour. (The touch of Anti-Semitism in 'Ulysses' being far from characteristic.) I hasten to add that this applied mainly to those native-born into other religions, or to foreign residents, students and tourists.

An indigenous Roman Catholic who reneged met with little tolerance – which does largely explain the bitterness of so many of our writers and artists, often driven into exile on that account.

(The North was a far country then, with minimal interest

for the majority of Southerners. Republicans who wished to end partitition always had their caucasus, both in the Southern Establishment and among people of the poorer and rural classes. Almost everyone I knew in middle-class Dublin was apolitical on the matter. At that time the Catholic minority in the North had not yet found the voice to air their grievances.)

Chapter Four

Work is the curse of the drinking classes.
 – Wilde

Harking back to my reference to chauvinism...Although we were often told to be proud of "being Irish", few mentors harped on patriotism or nationalism, to anything like the extent that they dinned in the religion.

It seemed to us, conversely, that the English were obsessed by their Britishness, particularly their upper classes. Witness the English public school boys we read about in some weekly comics, or saw in the film 'Tom Brown's Schooldays'. – In consequence, I think that chauvinism became confused in our minds with Class.

And apart from being fed King and Country up to their teeth, the little lord fauntleroys apparently fared even worse than us in the chastisement stakes; perpetually bending over for caning by sadistic prefects and masters. – Caning in Ireland (as well as euphonious 'pandying' with a ferule on the open palm) was also reserved for the elite, who went to the home-spun equivalents of Eton, Rugby, Harrow, etc.

Reading the Fleet Street comics however, we often envied the English, with their toffee-nosed attitudes and monthly postal orders from Pater...cane or not.

* * *

In actual fact, Ireland then was no less class conscious than England; a truth well-mirrored in the Irish education system.

Broadly demarcated: the working (labourer and poor farmer) classes went to National Schools, to be taught by lay-teachers.

Lower middle to middling middle classes (on a broad run from white collar to small trader) attended The Christian Brothers Schools (CBS). Upper Middle to Blue Blood (another broad run from publicans and bookmakers, to professionals, entrepreneurs and landed gentry) attended The Priests Schools. – More Anglo than Irish those – places where soccer, rugby and cricket were the sports, as opposed to gaelic football and hurley in the mainstream.

Money crossed the barriers however and a prospering farmer or plumber, butcher, baker or candle-stick maker, could 'send' his boy to the best. (There were also elite convent schools for girls.)

Exceptional scholarship crossed the poverty barrier. De Valera for example started as a humble national schoolboy, but completed his secondary education at upper tier Blackrock College, before graduating from University College Dublin. – Dev was a rare example of an improvident American emigrating to Ireland. Born in New York he was despatched in infancy to poor farmer Irish relatives, began to shine as a scholar and never looked back. (Dev had it every way, in that the British later spared his life, as a ringleader of the 1916 Easter Rising, fearing repercussions from his American birthplace.)

James Joyce, despite having a Mister Micawber for a father, went to exclusive Clongowes Wood College from 6 to 9, until the parental purse gave out. Doomed* for 2 years to the Christian Brothers, he was eventually taken back by another Jesuit School, Belvedere, on a non-fee paying basis, by a sympathetic S.J. who knew his father...to graduate in turn

* In his scrupulous biography Richard Ellmann notes that "Joyce chose never to remember this interlude with the Christian Brothers in his writings", mainly because "he shared his father's view that the Jesuits were the gentlemen of Catholic education, and the Christian Brothers ('Paddy Stink and Micky Mud...') its drones."

from (Jesuit-administered) UCD.*

In Joyce's time Irish schools were still under British jurisdiction and compromised accordingly – no Gaelic then and only English games. The British discouraged religious studies at Newman's Catholic University, which had three other colleges in Cork, Galway and Belfast, as their governing Royal University examined only in secular subjects. – There was small dividend in anyone studying theology for its own sake. When the Jesuits took over in 1893, their rector formally toed the British line, leaving it to a faculty composed substantially of priests to exert a considerable informal influence on behalf of the Church.

The Irish got their own back after Independence by banning Catholic students from attending Protestant Trinity College – where the offspring of that (predominately affluent) Anglo-Irish minority mixed with 'the best from abroad', after a spell in their own private schools.

In my own time the system was extremely curious in that the official line then was that Irish children should study their own Faith and language at school and play only Irish games. The priestly Orders running the 'best' schools knew better apparently. Although they did not neglect the religious instruction they were more pragmatic, or expedient, in cultural matters.

They certainly appreciated that the best kind of future career plan took account of English Folkways and, more to the point perhaps, they understood the true significance of the Pound Sterling in Irish economic affairs. The result was an anglicised model of the pedigree Irish Boy, who could slip with equal ease into the upper echelons in Dublin or London. There to take his place, among the type of the gentleman amateur, as an aristocrat who ruled by fiat. Below him

* *Founded as the Catholic University by John Henry Newman in 1853, as part of the British Royal University.*

swarmed the mercantile *canaille* who lowly administered, manufactured, produced and generally dirtied their hands with – distasteful word – trade. In this latterday Feudal System, accent distinguished the best.

"There are no flies on the Jesuits" said Joyce, meaning that they never forgot the little practicalities of life. And usually found a way to satisfy their own interests accordingly, like the above Rector.

* * *

Still speaking broadly, National boys did the menial jobs, CBS put you in line for the "cushy" clerical jobs in government departments and industry/commerce – university entrance and/or executive possibilities depending on both your CBS grading and final examination results. ('A' boys often became accountants, doctors, lawyers, university men.)

Even a poor scholar from the likes of St Pauls, St Marys, Blackrock or Castleknock Colleges, could still climb pretty high on family connections; the best became leading lights in the national life.

The poorest university degree was often an open passport to the centres of wealth and influence, if one had 'the right breeding'. Just like England. (Indeed if you remember that breeding equated intimately with money, our two educational systems weren't fundamentally all that different from those in any of the other capital-driven democracies.)

In Ireland (much more than Semi-Socialist England) however, you were immovably fixed in your place at the bottom end of the social hierarchy. Lowly born and bred stayed poor and peasanted; a labourer had no hope, while a clerk often filed away or totted the cash book for years, because that was "all he's good for". Like it or lump it. Small wonder that emigration, especially to the more meritocratic States, became a common-place recourse. The nearest a bottom rung boy could get to the bigger kitty lay with his ability to 'learn a trade'.

A notable exception, in rural areas, being the children of 'small' farmers for whom education was a bit of a luxury anyway. They often 'worked the land' from virtual infancy and, like a cousin of mine who became 'Man of the House' at Ten or Eleven, when his father died, had little time, energy, or need for 'book-learnin'. For them, Robbie Burns applied: 'Give me a spark of Nature, Squire/That's all the larnin I require'. You could live comfortably enough as a man with 'a nice little spread'.

In fact some of those hard-working souls deservedly got a bit of the big kitty when Southern Ireland's admission into the European Economic Community, in the 1960s, sent prices for live stock and dairy products through the thatch.

Social stability, or knowing your place, as taught in the churches and schools, was solidly reinforced at home. The middle classes warned their progeny to keep clear of "gurriers" and "corner boys"; the upper classes often included the middle in that category. The lowest classes included a section of 'decent, god-fearing, hard-working and honest poor people'...who also 'looked down' on the Gurrier.

Gurriers..."came from the slums": the tenements of The Coombe, The Liberties, Sean MacDermott Street, or the new corporation housing estates of Drimnagh, Ballyfermot and Cabra West – the latter a stone's throw from ourselves, as we found out when we were occasionally 'raided' by stone-throwing hordes. They threw stones at the buses too. "The conductors on the Cabra run get danger money" was the joke there.

"Keep away from them" we were advised. "They are bad boys. They get their example in the home, with nothing but drinking and fighting."

They were poor and ragamuffined because they deserved to be. As a subspecies, gurriers per se had "no control over themselves" – a sly reference to breeding habits and families of 10 plus. They were ignorant stupid thieves and shysters. ...Barbarians, Communists, Bowsies (troublemakers). We kept well away from them alright.

My father, a onetime amateur boxer, came home one night with his face bloodied and his shirt in tatters, otherwise looking pleased with himself and smelling of drink. There had been trouble with bowsies in his friend Paddy Reilly's pub in Stoneybatter.

"We saw them off" was all he'd say. I felt like the kid watching Shane. ...As to the slandered Dublin Poor, it was a bitter irony that O'Casey, who might have been their Spartacus, only became branded as "a dirty Communist" in Ireland; while the very plays themselves, by their (easily misunderstood) coarse realism, exacerbated the inequality he sought to expose. It took that other 'slum' playwright of genius, Brendan Behan, to later remind Dublin that ignorance is never one-sided.

* * *

In Ireland, as in many other countries, there was another kind of 'class' division between city and country people (as in Dubliners and Colshies: 'city-slicker and yokel'). Peculiar to Dublin however was the aforesaid mild apartheid, between the majority of 'purebred' Catholic Irish and the minority group of Protestant Anglo-Irish. (A relatively amenable and pacific version of the situation in Ulster, with the ratios directly reversed and the two denominations never at ease and often at each others throats.)

* * *

The two sides of my own family provide a virtual Sermon on the above aspect of Irish Life. We had a clan of country-born True Gaels on my mother's side and a tendency to Anglophilia (albeit Roman Catholic!) among my father's Dublin-born brood.

As a joint entity they all belonged somewhere in the middle classes. Caught in the middle of the separate entities however,

I was well-placed to experience the four mentalities at work – urban, rural, Irish and Anglo-Irish. I think that the longterm effect of this was to teach me tolerance, as I could see good and bad in all of my relatives, irrespective of where they originated, or their politics. As a lesson that people should never be judged solely by hearsay, appearances, antecedence or inherited prejudices, it was both profound and useful.

...A final refinement – and that is the right word here – was provided for me by my mother's pretensions to gentility – I think that she always thought of herself as landed gentry, even without the land.

"I sing my own class" wrote Bernard Shaw*, "the Shabby Genteel, the Poor Relations, the Gentlemen who are No Gentlemen".*

His Shabby Genteel was my impossible mother, who never tired of telling me that I had the makings (not to say the blood) of a Gentleman, which was at least very agreeable and possibly further immunised me against the factional family surrounds – in that A True Gentleman should be Above All That. That we were, as a family unit, indisputably Poor Relations, will become apparent.

* * *

So, the Dublin-born Duffys inclined to English ways, while my mother's 'people', progeny of Roscommon and the rural West, were Irish with a capital I. As a result the two sides never actually 'related', in any social sense. I will look first at the former:

'Daddy' Duffy (my paternal grandparent) was a former Royal Irish Constabulary man. A widower long before I was

---

* In the hilarious autobiographical introduction to his novel 'Immaturity' – which should also be read, for essential balance, by anyone who derives their view of Old Dublin (or its Classes) from the descriptions contained in Joyce.

born, he died when I was still toddling. He sired eight: three boys and five girls, of whom six survived him. A daughter had died in the 1930s, of consumption, becoming my "late Aunt 'Benny'". Her sister Dora later married Dan, the widower – a bus driver. The other three girls, my aunts Cathy, Nell and Margaret, were all very Pro-British and far more interested in The Royal Family than the Pope. They never approved of Dan, who hailed from the North of Ireland, "talked too much politics"...and drank like a fish.

Cathy, first known to me as a prissy Skinster (single and skinny), maintained and decorated the Duffy Family Home in a way that I can only describe as English, without being able to put my finger precisely on the quality that made it seem so – to a boy who'd never been in England! Maybe it was the uncanny silence of the house, or the not a hair out of place interior decor, that jarred my slipshod Irish mind...as being, well, Stately Home. With purse-lipped Cathy as poised as The Queen Herself. – A little less prissy and poised, or a deal more homely, after she suddenly upped and married a silver-haired lodger, in her ripe middle-age. Apparently, long tall Cathy had a lot on the ball. But, as they said, not without envy, "you can't take it away from her" (begrudge her). "For Joseph is a perfect gentleman. Lovely manners. He used to be a monk." Cathy became a happy Lady, in his semenary.

As far as I was concerned, bubbly little Aunt Nell was mustard (nice hot stuff). She'd married early – an English butcher who died soon after, leaving her enough money to set up as a global adventureress, with occasionally stints as a teacher in exotic places, like Kenya and California. We became great pals and I looked forward excitedly to her Dublin visits, when she always spoiled me with trips to the cinema and seaside, or told me stories of safaris and Life in Hollywood. We later kept in touch and I was able to visit her in a Santa Monica nursing home shortly before she died, hot-spirited to the last. A real Indomitable, Dylan Thomas's poem 'Do not go gentle into that good night', could well have been written for Nell.

Margaret was more English than Irish, with a near Roedean accent which no doubt served her well as a long-standing hospital Matron in darkest Manchester. A classic example, in speech, bearing and conduct, of the 'capable unmarried career-woman', she proved another generous and affectionate Aunt, spoiling me in turn with boxes of marvellous English sweets — Spangles, Mars Bars, Penguins — comics and toys.

The eldest Duffy son, my uncle Bob, became a teacher and for most of my childhood was Headmaster of Marlborough Street National School. Whenever I met him I felt awed; he seemed to me A Great Man. But he was also a Family Man, with two boys of his own, and never slow to put his hand in his pocket and make your day, with a massive donation to "the pocket money fund".

Andy, the next in line, became a Garda Sergeant. He also died before my time, from a bout of pneumonia after a heavy drinking session. A chronic alcoholic, he was nonetheless revered in the Force as a natural poet and gifted 'fiddle-player' (violinist). My father often spoke glowingly of Andy and obviously missed him like a lost limb.

* * *

I had cause to thank Andy when, in my late teens, I made off on a stray bicycle, to pedal home from Town, late at night. I must have been really stupid with drink myself, to jump on a messenger-boy's bike, which has an enormous carrier-cage attached to the handle-bars.

A motor-cycle cop soon spotted this unlikely apparition and hauled me off to the cells at Mountjoy Police Station. After awhile cooling my heels, and sobering up fast, in a dingy six-by-four, the cop was back, towering and glowering under his crash-helmet.

"Your father is here" he growled. "But if it was up to him

or to me you'd appear before the magistrate in the morning. I'm only letting you go to honour the memory of your uncle, Andy Duffy, who meant a lot to us in this Station, God rest his soul."

My father just shook his head when he saw me. All he said was: "They got us out of bed. Your mother thought you were killed." Then we walked home together in silence, which startled me as I was ready for censure. I guess he knew that's what Andy would have done.

* * *

I was christened Patrick Gabriel and it was one measure of the rift between the two families that my father's side always insisted on the Patrick, partly because the maternal relatives insisted on Gabriel!

Absurd indeed, but there is no end to pettiness once sparked.

At the Duffys then, I was "Patrick"; visiting my mother's 'people' I was "Gabriel"; otherwise, at home and abroad, I was "Gay"...considered less obnoxious than the Angelic, at least to the average Dubliner.

Such ridiculous inter-family feuding has to begin somewhere. In this case I fear it began with my own parents, or more accurately, with the initial impression created on the opposite set of in-laws by each of them, as individuals.

To the Dublin Duffys, Babs Banahan, seemed a silly country girl. To the Banahans, Joe Duffy was a rakish city-slicker and far too fond of his drink, Guard or not. Babs reacted by putting on 'airs and graces' with the Duffys, while Joe just avoided Banahans – although he was happy enough to meet a Banahan 'on the batter' and 'buying' (drink).

There were enough of them to avoid, as my mother had eight brothers and sisters. Born Elizabeth she was always known as Babs, or Bab. And as if she hadn't enough to cope with from the snotty Duffys, her own siblings came 'to look down on' Babs, Joe and Gay, as the poor relations. Even if it often amounted to nothing more than patronage and a welcome hand-out now and then, the situation troubled her deeply.

Her eldest sister, Ciss, was married to an Irish Army Commandant. – Uncle M.J. had retired from army life and become Harbour Master at Dun Laoire for most of my own youth, with his family installed in the palatial Harbour House by the Mail Boat Pier. How my envious mother festered over Ciss at times!

* * *

A little sociological *en passant*:

About 25 years ago I visited Dublin with a lady-friend and parked our rented car outside Harbour House, driven by nostalgia to pop in for a look round the grounds. Most of the House was sealed off, apart from a couple of ground floor rooms, now being used as a snackery.

After tea and cakes we returned to find a car window smashed and my friend's hand-bag stolen. Reporting it to the local police we were told that such theft was epidemic along the Front. Some decline from my boyhood holidays there, when cars could be safely left unlocked, even with your wallet on the front seat. I had been foolish enough to believe that nothing had really changed, in long-sedated Dun Laoire.

At least, in my time, I'd stopped short at stealing a ride home...

* * *

A second Banahan sister, my 'Aunty May', married a prosperous baker. The relevant Uncle was a glorious character, to me anyway; I didn't have to live with him. For he drank prodigiously, backed, bought and raced the horses...until his thriving bakery business finally ran from wheat to chaff. Not before he also bought and sold a large farmhouse, where I spent a happy summer holiday or two. Uncle Ritchie was known as a Great Talker, in a city where talk is never cheap, on one side or the other. He'd lost two or three fingers in the bakery dough at some point and I had him summed up early as a splendid pirate of a man. Alas, like many a buccaneer, he ended sadly...alone and destitute somewhere in England.

Aunt Teresa was the only spinster of the group. She made her money running a hardware and toy shop, before selling out to go on a world pilgrimage – taking in Rome, Lourdes and Fatima in much the same way that the leisured English used to do a more secular European Tour.

She was held to be 'eccentric' and myself and cousins often made fun of her, at Christmas parties and the like. She also died poor and alone. Aunt Brigid lived 'down the country', having set up home with a farmer in their native Roscommon, near the town of Elphin. We only saw them occasionally, for summer holiday stays. When we alternatively stayed with my uncle Peter and his family, who owned a grocery store in the village where the nine originals went to school: Ballinameen. A second brother, my Uncle Frank, had remained in the nearby Banahan Family Homestead, married childlessly to a local woman (Aunt Dotie).

*   *   *

I visited that, touring with my pregnant wife and baby daughter in 1989, when we found Peter's widow, 'B.T.', still alertly alive and re-installed there. She at least hadn't changed, being the same hospitable, sweet-natured and good-humoured Aunt of my boyhood memories.* She died a few months later...about the same time that our second girl

---

* A temperament I still associate with childhood holidays in the West, where everyone you met was warm and welcoming.

was born.

No less than my wife – who grew up in Middle-American comfort – I marvelled at the idea of nine children being reared out of such a tiny two-roomed cottage. Where, we pondered later, did they all sleep? "We had a happy home" my mother often said, in praise of her ingenious parents...both of them dead and buried before I was born.

* * *

Back in Dublin, a third brother, my Uncle Paddy, had a hardware shop in fashionable George's Street. Even more fashionably, he had married into the Winstons – Martin Winston being a big name in the metropolitan rag trade, not to say *haute couture*, as owner of a modish Ladies Store. I have particular empathy with Paddy, as another incorrigible Dreamer who tried, with some success, to be a Businessman. Drink got him in the end, as it very nearly got me. His family never suffered for all that, at least in the material sense – which I suppose is something.

They lived by exclusive Palmerston Park and the children were all very well educated long before their frazzled father sold his shop and quit the fray. If my deprived mother found our occasional visits to their richly carpeted abode a trial (we trod lino), I revelled in the chance to play with two lavishy toyed male cousins. – The model railway alone filled a room.

The fourth, final and youngest brother, my Uncle Tommy, was another Army Officer – later an entrepreneurial factory owner. His family lived in another Big House, not far from our own little flat, and his wife, my Aunt Lucy, became very chummy with my mother. A beautiful woman of forthright ways she had so little of the snob in her that she regularly drank pints of porter (Draught Guinness) with the *hoi polloi*. I know that she often brightened my mother's dismal existence by 'treating' her to a few drinks. Tommy, breezy jovial, did as much for Joe. I enjoyed visits to them because the two daughters liked to play doctors.

"What you need in this life" Tommy once confided to smelly-fingered me, "is the aura of command." Not bad, not bad at all, Uncle Tommy.

* * *

Reviewing the situation, I was lucky in that each side of the family were very 'close' in themselves, with never a serious rift within the two camps in my memory. Apart from the usual sibling quibblings and petty rivalries, Duffys and Banahans alike stuck together fairly well and generally cared about and supported one another.

Certainly no one ever made me feel unwelcome or unwanted, very much to the contrary, and I am sure that this was very important in building up the self-esteem of a hyper-sensitive small boy. (The nearest I came to harsh emotional trauma was in my own home. I will discuss that later.)

Before we get too sentimental however, it must be said that I could be an agreeable, polite and well-mannered 'gossoon'. (From the Gaelic *garsún*: boy.) So there was no reason for anyone to take a hard line. For of course the real Sermon here is that many of my relatives were so set in their ways that they would have flared up at any sign of deviance from the set path, in matters of religious or social orthodoxy.

As long as you seemed to comply with their views you were safe and acceptable. Like so many people, they expected their children and the children of their 'own' to think and act like them.

Which, followed to its logical conclusion in my own case, would have meant cutting the Duffys because they didn't think like the Banahans, and vice versa. A dilemma I fortunately never had to resolve, by choosing one set of prejudices above the other.

Fortunately, as I hope to show in the following chapters, the child is never entirely at the mercy of fallible parents, guardians, relatives or teachers, insofar as preserving his own spark of individual intelligence is concerned.

As we will see, the kids of my own generation were enlivened, in that vital respect, by 'outside' influences which no priest, parent or tutor could dampen or suppress.

Class consciousness was a bit more problematical.

* * *

As regards my own nurture, I was well-trained to remember my own class, or to respect the authority of those whose fathers were more highly placed than a humble Guard. I came out of it all with an exaggerated regard for the Boss figure, which inhibited me in later life, both in promoting myself positively and in exerting authority without effort, when it was both earned and expected.

It is as difficult to give the orders, after you have been programmed to obey, as it is to abandon, refine, or transcend, the untenable beliefs and ideas that first formed your mind. Insofar as you do succeed in such matters, you begin to expose the idea of Class as an expedient sham, fostered by the favoured to protect their own narrow interests, at the expense of real, egalitarian, social progress.

* * *

In Ireland, that powerful early critic of the class-system, Karl Marx, was unlikely to make an impression upon us, as he was generally held to be an Anti-Christ of the lowest order. Roman Catholicism itself was set like flint against Communism, or Socialism for that matter. (The Irish Communist Party never extended its power base beyond the tenements.)

Young Joyce, a natural snob in many respects, barely touched on the subject in Stephen Hero, where Stephen walks through the Dublin slums and vaguely connects the horrible conditions to a Catholic upbringing.

Sean O'Casey would later make a literary campaign of exposing and attacking that whole rotten system, nearly being lynched by the Dublin mob for his trouble.

But it was Shaw, again, following Samuel Butler, who recognised that the problems posed by such socially divisive evils as family-bred class prejudice, could not be answered by political or economic reforms, however radical. For him the real problem was how to change, more fundamentally, the way we think – about ourselves, others, life in general. And that implies a more forbidding re-evaluation of our basic ideas and beliefs.

In England, Aldous Huxley and Evelyn Waugh impugned their class system from the top, with a humour that often blunted the point. While Compton Mackenzie's 'Sinister Street' would do so ambivalently, by exonerating the aristocrat who disowned his hypogamous bastard and generally equating the worst in human nature with *noblesse oblige.*

* * *

Happily, Class, at least as we knew it, is a star going nova in our own time. But that in turn has led to a fragmented society where no one knows their place anymore. Even in Post-Gorbachev Russia there are old people who look back with nostalgia to the relatively stable days of Totalitarianism.

So, if we lived in unfair times, classwise, we experienced a kind of artificial social stability that many children today are denied.

In particular, marriage was forever in those days, with the even (or uneven) tenor of family life seldom 'broken' by parental separation. (I cannot remember a single instance of 'desertion', as it was called, by husband or wife, in our own neighbourhood.

Although we did have a big orphanage nearby, and there were stories of 'common' men absconding.) Divorce was forbidden by Church and State alike. Women of all classes knew their place and men ruled the roost from hovel to mansion.

It took a very exceptional woman to break the mould of total economic dependence, which was the real basis of marriage – "a survival" (Shaw typically observed) "of the custom of selling women to men". Many contented themselves with that last resort of the strong-willed woman in a male-dominated society: covert matriarchy.

A lot of Irish sons were emotionally screwed up as one consequence of that development. – And many daughters: read Edna O'Brien for the female downside of Irish Family Life.

While Ibsen ('A Doll's House'; 'Hedda Gabler') and Shaw ('Misalliance', 'Widowers Houses','Mrs Warren's Profession', 'Getting Married') provide insights into oldtime marriage as legalised prostitution.

* * *

We now live in an age where women are finding their feet for the first time in human history and men are losing their hold in tandem.

In this melting-pot situation, affecting Ireland as elsewhere, stable family life of the old kind – Dad at work, Mum in the kitchen – has taken a hammering. While widespread juvenile dysfunction*, of a kind we never knew (drugs etc.), has many adults pleading for a return to 'old values'.

We also have Marshall McLuhan's "third parent": television; one primarily dedicated to converting kids to the brute values of Mammon.

For all its faults, the old class system wasn't exclusively plutocratic.

---

* Including a rising suicide rate among male youths, in Ireland.

CHAPTER FIVE

Only Imagine.
— Socrates

Socrates was exhorting his fellow-philosophers to retain the sense of wonder, the imaginative openness to new experience, that characterises the mind in childhood. That to him was the only thing worth having.

*   *   *

A far cry you may think, from childrens comic papers, the real subject of this chapter. Not in the least. Insofar as I have managed to preserve my own imaginative faculty (or obstinate ability to dream of a better world), I can trace the initial stimulus back to the illustrated pages of those 'fanciful' childhood diversions. In countering the mind-dimming effects of the prosaic everyday world, they equally fulfilled a basic function of all good poetry: mental enrichment.

Through my comics, I began to experience, albeit by proxy, a sense of the sheer variety of life and an awareness of the relative narrowness of the environing adult world-view, in comparison. I can only hope that the present generation of children benefit equally from the contemporary surfeit of cartoons, adventure stories and space-epics on television. But I doubt it somehow. There is just too much of it now. Often interspersed with links by nonsensical adults behaving like infants (as often for even more infantile vested interests), or by stroboscopic commercials perpetually pressuring in ways we never knew.

In my pre-televisual boyhood, comics were everyone's passion.

'Dandy' on Tuesday, 'Beano' on Thursday – the only two of them all still going, still produced in far Dundee, half a century later.

Almost everything else was composed and compiled in London and published out of Fleet Street. The overall output was simply prodigious with, I have no doubt, tens of dozens of childlike writers and artists working round-the-clock to fuel the cornucopia and provide for millions of young readers – not only in England and Ireland but throughout the British Commonwealth.

There were Fleet Street comics for every age – from Four to Fourteen. The majority appealed equally to boys and girls – with a few exclusively produced for either sex.

Most comics were of standard magazine size and format, with garishly illustrated technicolour paper covers, cleverly designed to catch the eye of any child. And there was nothing, nothing at all in the world, like the smell of a new unopened comic, fresh from the newsagents shelf, with its covers still glistening, and full of promise.

The earliest I recall were tabloid newspaper size, with large frame illustrations and text in clear big lettering, to appeal to 'Tiny Tots' – an actual example. That had 'Comic Cuts', 'Playbox', 'Chicks Own', 'Chips' and 'Rainbow' as 'companion' papers. I particularly remember Rainbow's 'jolly' Tiger Tim, as the kind of richly-striped soft-toy you'd love to take to bed, with your Bunny. A gloss-cover 'Mickey Mouse Weekly', with all the great Disney characters, completed the kindergarten set.

Such comics were strong on 'lovable' animals and completed your elementary education in comparative zoology, extending the temperate zone of nursery rhyme and fairy tale

– moo cow, baa lamb, nanny goat, 'friendly' fox and 'naughty' wolf – into the equatorial domain of ebullient lion, tiger, elephant, croc and rhino.

No one ever got eaten in such comics; the 'wild' animals guzzled cakes and ice-cream, or threw snowballs, just like us.

'Korky the Kat' and 'Biffo The Bear' lured respectively on the front covers of 'Dandy' and 'Beano'. (Long since usurped by other characters; alternatively old 'insiders', or New Age.) Mischievous children in animal outfits as far as we were concerned. Very like us, 'getting into trouble' because of their gluttony, petty thieving, property-abuse or truancy. But always 'getting the better' of the forces of repression: stern parent or teacher; or besting some slyboots or bully, in a triumphant final frame.

Inside 'Dandy' and 'Beano' many of our infantile propensities became characterised in themselves: 'Hungry Horace' (gluttony), 'Dennis The Menace' (anarchy), 'Beryl the Peril' and 'Minnie the Minx' (female anarchy) 'Keyhole Kate' (voyeurism), 'Pansy Potter' (tomboyism), 'Desperate Dan' (raw strength/pugilism and monumental gluttony: he wolfed down whole cow pies, with twin horns protruding through the crust), 'Roger the Dodger' (evasion of boring chores/duty). 'Lord Snooty and his Friends' provided a multi-class mix of daft characters, hinting that we were all the same reely...

Minnie and 'Little Plum' (lovably rotund Redskin) were the work of a gifted young cartoonist from Preston, Leo Baxendale, who also gave us 'The Bash Street Kids'* in 1953.

---

* A later attempt to civilise, beautify and sanitise them, or generally 'politically correct' them, fell dead flat. "The Beano", reported the London 'Daily Mail' of 17.02.94, "has abandoned its new look Bash Street Academy in the face of hostile reaction from readers. ...The comic is restoring the Bash Streets Kids to their original Fifties design, including Spotty's spots, 'Erbert's glasses and Plug's ugly face." (The reformers having introduced a remedial optician and plastic surgeon.) "...We got over 2,000 letters and not one in favour', said a spokesman at Beano's Dundee HQ. 'We even had death threats.'" From who – kids?

What a chilling comment on the times we now live in...

A right bunch of slum-dwelling ruffians (smelly, eczematous, deformed), they specialised in tormenting their Teacher – drawn as a cadaverous drip in master's gown and "weird effin head-gear" (our slang): a 'mortar-board' hat. Designed to appeal to ruffians, they were to many of us on about the same level as the children of Wellington's "drunken scum" (who won him Waterloo) were to the Iron Duke. That is, we felt nicely superior, belly-laughing at the dumb louts, leaving it to the gurriers to emulate them. 'Our Ernie', "Mrs Entwistle's little lad", laid on for readers in the industrial North, gave you an idea of English working-class life, as endured in a dingy row of Wigan back-to-backs.

So, 'Beano' and 'Dandy' still survive unchanged, with many of the above characters continuing to get into timeless childhood 'scrapes' every week. The full extent of their equally timeless fascination may be measured by their frequent inclusion also in 'The Funday Times', a replica Forties/Fifties 'comic', produced as a regular supplement to the contemporary (London) 'Sunday Times'. (It was first inserted, even more piquantly, within the vaunted Literary Section.)

Although I will come shortly to George Orwell on Comics, I am driven here to wonder how the social reformer who wrote 'The Road to Wigan Pier' would have reacted to 'Our Ernie'. I suspect that he would have detested the strip, which basically caricatured the poor drudges who made England 'the workshop of the world', as a laughable bunch of slobs.

To us, Ernie's father was obviously an ale-swilling cretin, in his flat cap, grimy tunic shirt and hobnail boots. His massive blubbery mother was a slovenly whale, in curlers. So these were the people of the English North, eating and speaking tripe and inhabiting a starkly-drawn landscape of teetering railway viaduct, canal, mill and colliery head. Yuch! It may have been only a comic strip, but it put you off that kind of

English Worker for life.*

'Mike Dobson' featured on the cover of 'Knockout', providing a high fidelity representation of what it was like to live in a middle class English Suburb, in a detached house surrounded by picket fences. "They melted all the railings down for munitions during the War." True. Mike was Korky, Biffo and the rest in compacted anthropomorphism; a Boy after our own hearts he was bang up-to-date, with a new 'wheeze' every week. Inside you had another bunch of larger-than-lifers, including 'The Fat Boy' Billy Bunter, spherical twin-sister Bessie, and scoutish 'Deed-A-Day-Danny'(!).

'Radio Fun' had strips featuring all the well-known BBC artistes of the time, including young Petula Clark's 'diary' notes ('Pet's Schooldays'). Long before we ever heard them on the radio, their comic adventures made us fans of Jewel and Warriss, Issy Bonn, Donald Peers, 'Big Hearted' Arthur Askey ("Hello Playmates!"), and Cardew 'The Cad' Robinson. Here was a world where, in the words of the song, "a smile is your umbrella" and Fun always won.

'Film Fun' (appropriately produced in monochromatic black on white) did as much for the film comics we idolised: Laurel and Hardy and Abbot and Costello in particular. There were also strips on Joe E. Brown, Red Skelton, 'Old Mother Riley' and her daughter (Arthur Lucan and Kitty McShane) and "durty oul" George Formby, "with his little ukelele in his hand". – Some guessed what The Sly Wink was really getting at there! (A 'TV Fun', begun 1953, plugged 'box' stars like Diana Decker.)

There were a few other weeklies, including 'Lion' and 'Tiger' (with 'Roy of the Rovers' – Frank S Pepper's follow up to his 'Rockfist Rogan'), full of sports and adventure stories,

* *Strange irony that one of the most successful and long-running of all TV soap-operas, 'Coronation Street', would top the ratings by bringing 'Wigan' to the screen – albeit subtly altering the old emphasis to portray such sad people as unbeaten, and 'the salt of the earth'.*

appearing about 1950 with 'Eagle' – which proved a phenomenal success and merits a little digression in itself.

* * *

'Eagle', I now know, was the brain-child, or brain-wave, of a charismatic, chain-smoking English Vicar called Marcus Morris.

Appalled by the amorality and violence of many comic papers – particularly the American – he expressed his views in a short article, 'Comics that bring Horror into the Nursery', which was published in the London 'Sunday Despatch' (c.1948) and created quite a stir.

Equally aware of the potential propaganda value of the comic strip, Morris now resolved to hit back at the child-harmers with a new 'Christian' comic paper. After many trials and set-backs, 'Eagle' was born. Indeed, having obtained backing from the powerful Hulton Press, it was launched, April 1950, with a fanfare of publicity that was more American than English.

Thousands of free copies of the first issue were mailed to people concerned with children or youth work. Gigantic golden eagles were mounted on cars and driven round cities, towns and villages throughout the U.K., with representatives handing out tokens that could be exchanged for a free copy. Plans for Morris to parachute into Hyde Park and a national release of 200,000 'Eagle' balloons, were reluctantly shelved.

This unprecedented pre-publicity was wholly warranted in that the new comic itself was a minor masterpiece, in everything from design and layout to the quality of the strips themselves. The first issue of 900,000 copies sold out and it went on from strength to strength. An 'Eagle' Club drew 60,000 applications after the second issue and became the core of a nightly 15 minute 'Eagle' programme on commercial Radio Luxembourg. – Immediately followed by a 15 minute serial, featuring its flagship Character: 'Dan Dare: Pilot of the Future'.

'Dandy' was hard put to match all that!

Dan Dare – mercifully evolved from an early, more evangelical idea of Morris's: Lex Christian, Flying Padre of The Fighting Seventh – became a great Hero and, with his adventures on Venus, turned some of us in the direction of Science Fiction. He was written and drawn by Frank Hampson, a genius among giants at the top of that fertile profession, who created dazzling futuristic devices, space-ships and, in Mekonta, an other-worldly metropolis which would have made a Verne or Wells gasp.

In Dare's arch-enemy, the Mekon, Hampson gave us the very nightmarish personification of Absolute Evil: a tiny slime-green 'maneen', all ugly elongated head and no body: "My brain is far superior to your puny organ, Dare." Duly hearing his shrill sibilance on the radio, you made light of it to disguise your fear: "I yam The Mekon! Yuk Yuk."

Dare's batman, Digby, hailed from Wigan. The Green Belt.

'Eagle' did its share of pulpiteering, but with enormous style, backed by the kind of talent and intelligence that gives any Faith a good name. Hampson also contributed an absorbing 'strip life' of Christ, to a series which included Alfred the Great, Nelson and Baden Powell. When FH was ill or away Morris could count on others of his versatile creative team to 'do' Dare, or 'Tommy Walls' – the Hampson strip for Walls' ice cream. These included Chad Varah (later Founder of The Samaritans) and BBC radio script-writer Alan Stranks (who also wrote an 'Eagle' strip based on his top-rated police serial P.C.49). The great investigative journalist Macdonald Hastings was also on tap, to do some gripping 'factuals'.

Like 'P.C.49', the strip 'Riders of the Range' was based on a BBC radio serial – produced by Charles Chilton. As a typical piece of chutzpah 'Eagle' sent Chilton to Arizona, where he was made a 'sheriff' and filed the story for their readers. (More of him in Chapter Nine.)

'Harris Tweed, Extra Special Agent', contributed by an art master at Harrow school, was a clever blend of Holmes, Wodehouse and Sapper. The cartoonist Thelwell ('Chicko') also got his first break with 'Eagle'.

Last but not least my Global Aunt, Nell, had an article about life in Kenya accepted and lavishly illustrated, to my delight. They later published a composite drawing of all their characters, submitted by a 16 year old London schoolboy: Gerald Scarfe.

In time, this uniquely successful comic paper spawned three more of the same moral tone: 'Girl', 'Swift' and 'Robin'. Peaking in popularity in 1962, all were gone by 1970. An attempt to revive 'Eagle' foundered recently; praps they should have renamed it 'Phoenix'...

* * *

Even more than the prodigal flood of English weeklies we prized the gloss-covered wedgy American monthlies: Superman, Batman, Wonderwoman, Spiderman, Archie...the vividly drawn gangster and cowboy stories; cartoon comics included Little Lulu, Porky Pig, Hekyll and Jekyll (two black crows) and 'Looney Tunes' (the inimitable Bugs Bunny).

These 'Dell' and 'Marvel' comics, with their ads for bubble gum and air-guns, were known in school lingo as "fifty-two-ers", because they had 52 pages. Inferior copycat editions published in England had a derisive 36 pages – "thirty-sixers". There were also "sixty-fourers" – digest-sized 64 page westerns ('Kit Carson', 'Tom Mix' and 'Buck Jones'), issuing monthly from that amazing font of Fleet Street. – Not to miss a trick they also published hard-cover Christmas 'Annuals' of all the weekly comics.

Schoolboys have their own market sense and when it came to swapping and trading, values were strictly assigned in favour of the U.S. product. A "fifty-twoer" was worth at least two of any other comic. Inevitably, as no one (or no one parent) could afford to buy more than a fraction of the supply, all comics became a form of hard currency in themselves, with much regular activity on the school bourse. U.S. Horror Comics became the hardest of currencies, before they were summarily banned (c.1952), as totally beyond the pale of adult decency.

...An indication that many of your Yank 'Comix', with their adverts for Charles Atlas's* body-building system and products like hair-restorer, were also avidly read there by a sizeable population of subliterate or otherwise inadequate adults. (Indeed some Irish adults read our comics too, but they kept very quiet about it. They also had their own 'comic': the 'Punch'-like 'Dublin Opinion', which we often enjoyed.)

* * *

Marcus Morris had his echoes in Ireland, provoking an attempt, by some concerned educationalists, to counter the influence of 'foreign filth' with the establishment of a home-bred Catholic Comic. Colourful enough, that still got the thumbs down because it was produced in Gaelic, which we found hard enough to learn in class, without trying to follow a comic full of it. (An earlier attempt to match Disney and Hanna Barbara, with a more Celt-friendly cartoon character, Sean Bunny, proved equally ill-starred.)

A CBS bilingual monthly magazine, 'Our Boys/ *Tír na nÓg*' (The Land of Youth), was tolerated because of Kitty

---

* *His name became a synonym around Dublin for anyone with muscle. First frames depicted some "seven stone weakling" having sand kicked in his face by a beach bully, while a pretty girl sat by tittering. Final frame showed wimp transformed after using an Atlas Course to build the body by "dynamic tension", flooring bully while girl gasped admiringly.*

The Hare*, who told absorbing stories of Irish country life in the pidgin English of the West. That was distributed in the schools…along with two hard Evangelicals:

'Saint Martin's Magazine' and 'The Messenger of the Sacred Heart'.

Otherwise the Irish authorities contented themselves with continuing to impose a purchase tax of one penny on every foreign comic. A futile form of indirect 'censorship' that at least benefited the Exchequer. We coughed up of course, with a sigh of Oh to be in England, where your favourite read only cost tuppence or threepence a time…

* * *

The 'moths' (as we called the fair sex) had 'Girl's Crystal' (1935-1953) and 'Heiress' (1948-1956), which met competition when the pre-war 'School Friend' reappeared in 1950. Eagle's "sister paper" 'Girl' was launched in November 1951, with a typically Morris cover serial: 'Kitty Hawke' (!) 'and her all-girl air crew'.

Although no self-respecting schoolboy would ever admit to reading a girls' comic, in fear of being thought a cissy, there were times, like those when you were in bed with flu with nothing else to read, when need overcame fear in that respect.

'School Friend' was maybe the most tempting, with their scatty school-girl 'Dilly Dreem' and the secretive appeal of 'The Silent Three' (female Scarlet Pimpernels). Even 'Meg's Schooldays', 'True Romance', or the like, were far better than nothing…when the wind howled and you'd had enough of Biffo…

* Representing the old Irish 'Traveller', a kind of itinerant folklorist who still survived in turf-fire rural areas; along with poets (like the great Padraig O'Conaire), folk singers and 'Irish Fiddlers' (virtuoso violinists and often incomparable musicians, who, as emigrants, greatly influenced the rhythms and idioms of American Country and Western Music.)

Which reminds me to balance my previous emphasis on smut and sex with the observation that Romance itself, of the true-blue variety, was not entirely confined to schoolgirls. As boys we had our own innocent passions, often indeed focussed on the pixie-hooded heroines of our sisters comics. (Like John Betjeman, I had a crush on a heroine called Wendy.)

There was also a fair bit of harmless boy-girl puppy-love between ourselves and the girls, many a boy becoming lyrically fixated on some (usually unsuspecting) girl he knew – with the Virgin Mary in his mind rather then Mary Magdalen. (Loreto girls looked nicer, in brown and red, than the ones who wore navy-blue gym slips.)

That produced the kind of mind-set where women were either modest and chaste "like your mother", or rampant harlots, with no in-between. I remember, years later, seeing that strikingly illustrated in a John O'Hara novel, where a Good Catholic protagonist explains that he visits hookers because he wouldn't dream of inflicting his lusts on his wife (the mother-figure). As a schoolboy I would have understood and entirely agreed. Dirty jokes about your own mother were simply inconceivable, while the idea that our parents "shagged" – yuch!

* * *

Some newspaper comic strips were extremely popular and well-followed. Indeed 'Mutt and Jeff', 'Jiggs and Maggie', 'Mandrake the Magician' and 'Rip Kirby', syndicated in the two Dublin 'Evenings' ('Herald' and 'Mail') were probably our earliest exposure, in infancy, to this new kind of magic.

The three metropolitan dailies offered very little and you had to search through "reams a print" to find 'Count Curly Wee and Gussie Goose' (pretty dismal stuff after the age of four or five), or 'Rupert The Bear' – ditto dull. 'The Sunday Press' had an entire page of strips, including 'Blondie' (oh those multi-tiered Dagwood sandwiches!), enough to make that day. 'Sunday Independent' had 'The Phantom', who became my own favourite Hero for a time. My Aunt Dora took the English 'Daily Mirror' and got me hooked on 'Andy Capp' – who she adored. (I never saw the saucy 'Jane' striptease strip – presumably Dora was vigilant there.)

* * *

Wholly pictorial comics soon led, with developing literacy, to the appetite for those where you got a lot more printed text for your pence.

Fleet Street was still on hand, incredibly, with four 'serious', text-full comics, catering for the prepubescent sophisticate. 'Wizard', 'Rover', 'Adventure' and 'Hotspur' had many pages of closely printed material, featuring, weekly, 'gripping tales' of heroism and adventure.

Here, 'Beano's' Dennis The Menace had grown up, found a true outlet for his anarchic delinquency, and emerged as A Man To Be Admired: a 'Rockfist Rogan'. This F S Pepper hero stereotype – Patriotic Fighter Against Evil and Protector Of Women – re-appeared in various guises, or as the same character with a new name, in most of the stories.

In one guise he was 'Wilson, the greatest all-round athlete who ever lived', in others he was the best footballer (FSP's Roy of the Rovers Mark II!), mountaineer, boxer, runner, Channel swimmer, soldier, air-ace...

Doing in effect all of the things that enabled us to sleep safer in our beds at night. Confident that, out there somewhere was a rugged square-jawed fellow, with clean features and a sound mind in a healthy body, executing the kind of decent derring-do that made us all proud to be privy. He was of course as Snob-British as they come; for all that we lapped him up, and everything we imagined he stood for. Bravo for Bravery!

*　*　*

Those in Ireland who feared the 'foreign' comic as a subversive influence on impressionable young minds were not fools. English and American alike they did provide a flood of imagery that was as often disturbing as harmless. The English propagandised a way of life that was based on racial superiority and imperialistic principles*; while the Americans let us into another kind of counter-culture, based on racial intolerance (Black/Redskin/Mexican), greed and violence**. Both totally at odds with the basic Irish temperament of easy-going tolerance and let-well-enough-alone, as well as a flagrant contradiction of much that we were taught in church and school.

I remember, for example, a serial in the 'Wizard' which ran for many weeks and profoundly affected all who followed it. England had been taken over by a vicious, Japanese-like, 'horde from the East', the Kushantis. They had only beaten their way through Europe, to duly beat the usually unbeatable British, because there were so many of them. They bred like rabbits, lived like pigs and behaved like demented rats. In this they squarely reflected the political correctness of England in the Forties and Fifties, which was based on uncompromising xenophobia.

*　*　*

George Orwell, a profoundly perceptive observer of foibled humanity, wrote a famous essay, 'Boys' Weeklies' (1939), which reflected his own disquiet with those of the pre-WW1

---

* Notwithstanding a pre-WW1 series in 'The Marvel', which paired an Oxford Undergraduate and an American Trapper with a Zanzibar Negro.

** But I think we must draw a line through the two Latin-Americans who wrote a book impugning Donald Duck as a capitalist-imperialist lackey.

59

and inter-war years. More precisely, his disquiet with their two "basic political assumptions" – "nothing ever changes, and foreigners are funny" – which, to his mind, bred only complacency and intolerance in the young.

Orwell knew that this dumb attitude may well have led to the British Empire, in times when a gun-boat was all that it took. But, in a radically changing world it had become a formula for imperial collapse and an ensuing era of political and economic crises at home.

Orwell was something of a true Prophet too.

He initially concentrates on the 'Gem' and 'Magnet' (defunct by my time) which specialised in ongoing stories of "what purports to be public-school life" (Orwell), after the model of Eton or Winchester. He notes that, year after year, the pubertal characters and their ages remain the same – nothing there ever changes.

Marvelling that both of them sustained a 15 to 20,000 word story, each week, for nigh on 30 years, he surmises that a vast team of writers must be behind the "easily imitated...repetitive style". In a 1945 footnote he records his astonishing later discovery that all of this material is the work of one man! That at least explains its stasis, as the febrile output of one prodigious school-boy of the ilk: Frank Richards.

The stories, Orwell expands, centre on "horseplay, practical jokes, ragging masters, fights, canings, football, cricket and food". "Stealing" is avoided, partly because it might lead to expulsion and upset the writer's roster of established characters. "Sex is completely taboo, especially in the form in which it actually arises at public schools." – A deliberate move away, to him, from the older 'Boy's Own Paper', which "used to have its correspondence columns full of terrifying warnings against masturbation".

Mentioning that some of the "Fellows" get as much as five pounds a week in pocket money, Socialist Orwell grinds his teeth: "This kind of thing is a perfectly deliberate incitement to wealth-fantasy."

Also reflecting the fact that the status-conscious school story is "a thing peculiar to England". Promoting a stereotypicality, with boys sharply defined as athletic, rowdy, aristocratic, stolid, clever, eccentric ...or narrowly characterised as honest/dishonest, reliable/unreliable, sportsmanlike/mean – bully, liar, cheat, sneak.

The Boy Wrongly Accused who won't snitch is a popular favourite. Etc. There are also "Australian, Irish, Welsh, Manx, Yorkshire and Lancashire boys to play on local patriotism". And always a scholarship-boy, so that "boys from very poor homes" may feel included, as readers, in this privileged menage... "Fisher T. Fish (the money-grubbing American boy)", is "the old-style stage Yankee...dating from a period of Anglo-American jealousy".

The whole atmosphere is one of "pre-1914" Conservatism:

"England is always in the right and England always wins, so why worry?"

Moving on, he finds this being replaced in the newer comics (including 'Wizard', 'Hotspur', 'Adventure' and 'Rover' among the eight he names) by a trend towards "bully-worship and the cult of violence".

But even their "sock on the jaw" style is harmless compared to the "Yank Mags, 'Fight Stories', 'Action Stories', etc." which are read by many boys. "In the Yank Mags you get real blood lust, really gory descriptions of the all-in, jump-on-his-testicles style of fighting, written in a jargon that has been perfected by people who brood endlessly on violence." They appeal "to sadists and masochists".

He compares a 'manly' fight passage in 'Rover' to one in 'Fight Stories' – where "a clublike right" smashes into a face, returned by another "full on Sven's already battered mouth" and bits of tooth are spat out.

Compared to the worst of the English boys' papers, which still have "a moral code", he finds the average Yank Mag a cesspool of "crime, dishonesty...cynicism, corruption". Or veering towards crude pornography – as in a story where Nazis torture and kill "naked girls".

But they portend the Future too, because they are so compulsively readable! They seem to him to be part of an ongoing "process of Americanization" which will gradually replace toff and cricket-bat by thug and "rubber truncheon".

(Not, in the event, by comics, but by film and television.)

After a brief look at "women's papers" – 'Oracle' and 'Peg's Paper' – which seem to him to provide a form of wish-fulfilling escapism for the shop/factory girl or domestic help ("orange blossoms instead of machine-guns"), he turns back to the boys.

While admitting that comics as they are satisfy a definite "demand" in boys "at a certain age" (for vicarious thrills), he asks himself if anything can be done to counter their negative influence – as propaganda for "snobbishness...gutter patriotism" and "*laissez faire* capitalism".

Tracing ownership of 'Gem', 'Magnet' and five more of the current crop to Lord Camrose's Amalgamated Press* Combine, it seems to Orwell that their Toryism is not unconnected to that of his 'Daily Telegraph' and 'Financial Times'. The answer to that, it seems to him, might be "a left-wing boys' paper". – If it could avoid becoming an equally odious tract for sick-making Sovietism. An unlikely idea, he concedes, beset with "several difficult problems", before concluding:

"I am merely pointing to the fact that, in England, popular imaginative literature is a field that left-wing thought has never

---

* Which in fact originated with Alfred Harmsworth's (later Lord Northcliffe) attempt to counter the immoral effect of 'penny dreadfuls'! In his time, Northcliffe made Marcus Morris seem like a libertine; imposing a 'moral code' on his writers whereby cheats, liars, spiteful characters never prospered and smoking, swearing, or drinking were out. He topped it by a total ban on the word 'rotten' in his girls' papers.

begun to enter...The fact is only unimportant if one believes that what is read in childhood leaves no impression behind.* Lord Camrose and his colleagues evidently believe nothing of the kind, and, after all, Lord Camrose ought to know."

* * *

Meanwhile, we in Ireland, no less than the coming generation in England, were being stuck with many ideas and values that had already passed their sell-by date. Ideas such as White Is Right, if necessary backed by Might; related Christian Values based on the unquestionable spiritual, moral and intellectual supremacy of Western European Man.

What Orwell would have thought of the American Comics we read may be suggested from his attitude to 'Fight Stories'. I suspect that they might have had him envisaging an impending social crisis for that Society, when all it could think of was apple pie, dollars and ordnance.

The Kushantis may get them yet, if they don't watch out...

Times have certainly changed, in the world of comics as everywhere else. But if the future of Western Man, on both sides of the Atlantic, now rests with going to the other extreme – e.g. banning Enid Blyton's 'Noddy' as racialist, or contriving to include token Blacks (or Gays) in strips – like the scholarship-boy in 'Magnet' – I think that an Orwell might regard his specimens with far less revulsion.

A truly radical-progressive comic, boldly going where no comic has gone before and demonstrating to our kids that intolerance, greed and violence are things to grow out of, if

* No less true, as Orwell would duly demonstrate, of what we read as adults. It is arguable that his 'Animal Farm' (1945) and '1984' (1949) – after Koestler's 'Darkness at Noon' (1941) – did more to expose the true horror of Stalinism, and kill Communism for the West, than anything other than such literary subversion could have accomplished.

you really want to grow up, might well find a shelf-life – who knows?

....It might be said that childrens television now negates all this, with, at least, a marked turn away from overt snobbery, racialism and sexism. In its technologically-enhanced comickry however, it raises other questions and presents new problems for the value-theorist – e.g. the persistent emphasis on aggression, as a valid form of self-expression.

There is no doubt that television in general influences and affects our children, for better or worse, in ways that no printed comic ever has; generally reflecting also, a kind of social chaos, nihilism and despair, that my generation never knew.

Leaving it to the television producers to examine their own consciences here, I will rest my case with the printed comic for the moment, mindful that they are still available in profusion and widely read – as often nowadays by subliterate adults as by tot and teen. Both in traditional form and in a new guise, as 'graphic novels'.

* * *

Which brings me, briefly, to some of the books we read then.

The childrens library near our school proved a godsend in that respect, as pocket money seldom ran to the price of a book.

Beginning perhaps with soppy Christopher Robin, or other Nursery School characters in Georgie Porgie trousers and Dutch Boy hair styles, you soon gravitated beyond twee Enid Blyton to the hardcore urchinism of Tom Sawyer and Richmal Crompton's archetypal schoolboy scamp: William. (An attempt to rival him, for girls, by Evadne Price, with a series of books (1928-1940) beginning with 'Just Jane', had failed so miserably that I never recall seeing a Jane story.)

Then on to 'Ivanhoe', 'King Solomon's Mines', 'Tarzan the

Ape Man', (Captain) 'Biggles in the Orient' – Rockfist Rogan-type Brit shoots up little yellow men in his propellorised warplane. Here, the girls had 'Worrals' (Flight Officer Joan Worralson), for early Womens Lib. But it was a rare schoolgirl who got as far as H.G. Wells's model of The New Woman: 'Ann Veronica'. Mostly they stuck with the standard segregated school story, with its semi-independent type.

Many would live to see an Angela Brazil heroine become Prime Minister of Great Britain. Some girls found books useful as an aid to 'deportment', walking about straight-backed with a heavy tome balanced on their head.

Adults markedly applauded the kind of storyline that paired goodness with religious belief and morality with wet sanctimoniousness. (The more relaxed Protestant Ethic of 'Reader's Digest' was equally endorsed.) Aesop's Fables was/were okay. But so was Fu Manchu and other even more bloodthirsty adventure yarns...which the perplexing adult world apparently approved. Even 'Frankenstein' and 'Dracula' joined Lewis Carroll and (well-expurgated) Grimm in childrens' stacks. Sherlock Holmes was probably the nearest we got to real intellectual stimulation; 'Sexton Blake, Detective', less cerebral, suited the dunces.

Humour was in short supply and the funniest book I read in those days was John D Sheridan's 'The Magnificent McDarney', about a typical Dublin 'character', with a fondness for drink and lame horses.

* * *

On the Shavian principle that "fine art is the only teacher except torture", our comics and books indisputably gave us some idea of the former, both nourishing our imaginative intelligence and fortifying our minds for the tortuous didacticism of School.

Our other great sources of Art – fine and not-so-fine – were

Radio and Films. I will return to discuss them after a taste of Life.

* * *

Glancing over the childhood section of Goethe's Autobiography recently, I was intrigued to note that he affectionately recalls a kind of 'comic' which, with Robinson Crusoe, greatly enlivened his own boyhood.

These were the *Volkschriften, Volksbucher* (popular works or books), produced in 18th Century Frankfort. They featured stories of the Middle Ages ('The Eulenspiegel', 'The Wandering Jew', etc.). Goethe: "The enormous sales they met with led to their being almost illegibly printed from stereo-types on horrible blotting-paper". (Not unlike the earliest English comics.) But young Johann and his friends still "preferred the relish of these works to the taste of sweet things". Didn't we all!

CHAPTER SIX

Energy is Eternal Delight.
— Blake

Given the considerable deficiencies of light reading as a burner of real energy, we had the usual mix of active pursuits and hobbies; from long hikes in the Phoenix Park and longer cycle-rides in the nearby countryside, to marble-casting and roller-skating, to conker-bashing (chestnuts baked in the oven to harden them for the game) and ice-skating (makeshift slides of frozen tap-water on the concrete pavements).

There was also Summer fishing for "pinkeens" (minnow) on the Tolka River, or tadpole-netting in the phlegm-coloured quarry-water at Dunsink Observatory; swims in the sea, or the sea-water baths at Blackrock. In the cold weather we occasionally visited Tara Street Baths, where I once saw a begrimed boy soap himself all over before diving in, to take a bath in every sense of the word. That put you off Tara.

In your early years you fought little battles with father-made paper aeroplanes or boats (on a table-top ocean), backing up the toy soldiers and artillery. More advanced weaponry included the usual pea- (or barley-) shooters and home-made catapults.

A few "pellet guns" – U.S.:B-B – (air-pistols and rifles) were in circulation; although much curbed after the boy I mentioned in chapter one lost his eye as a result of an accident with an air-rifle. Another boy in our street was much envied because his teenage brother often took him out shooting rabbits with a real rifle. "A point two-two" he'd say proudly.

There were snow-ball 'wars' in Winter. We played cowboys and indians in the backs – waste land – and fought more realistic wars with 'bangers'. These were made at first out of a nut stuffed with cordite caps, then double-bolted and thrown detonatively on concrete. Later, we made "reely grate bangers" out of used bullet-casings, retrieved from the McKee Barracks shooting range – shaking our suburb with explosions.

The latter closer to Stephen King than Mark Twain, in that we often risked life and limb making gunpowder – ingredients provided by some unsuspecting local Pharmacy. Charcoal and sulphur were much easier to buy than potassium nitrate (saltpetre).

"What do you want it for?" asks the canny chemist.

Cannier urchin: "The fahder wants it to rub on his piles, or sompn."

Outside, with a packet of the deadly stuff in his hand, our buyer would nod up at the shop-sign, M.P.S.I. (Member of the Pharmaceutical Society of Ireland) and chortle: "monkeys' piss sold inside!"

Getting spent cartridges to pack and tamp was a doddle, at Mc Kee:

"Watch out for soldyers!"

"Feck the soldyers. They're drunk or asleep most a the time."

A libel not without substance, in that it took the befuddled garrison so long to rouse themselves on the night of the 'bad' German air-raid, that, it was said, the bomber was back in Berlin before their lone Ack-Ack opened up on an empty sky.

* * *

Girls spent "all their time skippin' or playin' hopscotch. Or wheelin' effin' dolls about in prams". They "cluttered up the pavements" with their "hoppin, skippin and jumpin". "One-Two-Tree O'Leary" they sang in-time as they swished the rope,

"One...two...tree...Oh Lear-ey".

Sometimes, out of pity as much as camraderie, we'd rope them in for a game of hide-and-seek or a variant: Kick The Can.

* * *

Writing this brings back the flavour of the times, and the memories:

One of the earliest being the funeral of 'Daddy' Duffy, my last extant grandparent. He 'kicked the bucket' (in defusive Dublinese) as aforementioned, when I was Four or so. ...Into a high black horse-cab with mourning relatives, behind the mysterious motorised hearse, for the slow sombre ride to Glasnevin Cemetary. There would be no more bars of black chocolate from the tall kindly old man with the whiskers...

...Walks with my mother in the Gardens of the Phoenix Park, perhaps to the statue of some long dead Hero (Wolfe Tone?), where you could drink cold fountained water from a chained metal cup. If you were lucky, she bought you a tuppenny ice-cream "wafer" from the Parkgate sweet-shop, on the way in (or out).

The rumours...in 1946...that Hitler was alive and well and "living incognito minus the ronnie" (moustache) in the outer suburb of Crumlin. Why not? they said. Sure Dublin was opening its doors to a stream of German refugees at the time. I even fell in love with one, Renata by name, who became part of a neighbouring family.

Buses, trams and steam-trains were magical things. (Guinness had their own miniature railway, running along the Southern Quays from within the vast brewery at St James's Gate; with tiny goods trains ferrying the big wooden barrels of Export Stout to long Guinness barges, which plied the shallow Liffey water to anchored barques in the docks: all-in-all a schoolboy's delight to behold.)

Taking the swaying double-decked Dalkey tram to visit Dun Laoire relatives was an event. The few remaining trams covered the southside coastal routes and 'began' from Nelson's Pillar – much later blown up by the IRA.

"Jayse have they nothin better to do" asked Dublin in disgust, "than blow the other arm off poor Horatio Nelson?"

(That also necessitated a major overhaul of indicator scrolls on whole fleets of buses – the familiar 'Nelson's Pillar' being tersely replaced by '*An Lar*' (The Centre). A victory for the Irish Language, if not for the bothersome boyos with the really big bangers.)

In those days the National transport company, C.I.E., ran most of the city bus routes; a fleet of double- and single-deckers in bottle green livery. A British company, G.N.R. (Great Northern Railways), ran trains to the North and the buses to our favourite seaside places – Howth Head and smooth Portmarnock Strand. Climbing aboard their cream and blue diesel-driven double-deckers meant A Day At The Sea. A day of sand-dunes, sandwiches and sunburnt paddling in the shallows.

In Summer, I boarded the Ballina bus on the Quay's. A single-decker to country enchantment, with luggage stored on top beneath a huge tarpaulin sheet that flapped with excitement in the slipstream. Long sunny days in Roscommon with my mother's 'people', which I remember as vividly as Hemingway did his boyhood days in the Michigan backwoods.

Country life meant virgin fields enclosed by hedgerow or low grassy ditches, crystal streams and brown bogs, where a boy could play and fantasise to his heart's content. It meant small snug thatched cottages with flagstone floors, where water came icy-fresh from a well and candles still lit the house after dark. It meant rich creamery milk, the smell of butter in a lidded wooden churn, the dry taste of buttermilk and morning eggs still hot from the cluck-hatching hen.

It meant bulls and cows and other animals, which did (*pace* my Confessor) help to give our country cousins a headstart in learning 'the facts of life'. There were certainly enough birds and bees about.

Sometimes we went by train, puffing and whistling along by the weedy old canal to Mullingar, crossing the mighty Shannon River at Longford. Then a pony and trap from Boyle Station, on narrow winding roads as old as the hills, until you smelt the farmyard ordure in the very air and a collie barked Hello.

A meal of home-made brownbread and chicken pickings with the cousins and into a big feather-bed to swap stories of your town and their country. Idyllic was the only word for it. The West then was a place of gentle easy people; all-in-all the very essence of innocence.

* * *

Returning to Dublin late-summer meant only school, porridge again for breakfast and bread by Kennedy...Boland...or Johnston Mooney & O'Brien. "Bread and jam" were staples, with cups of sweet "tay" or tumblers of Merville Dairies milk. When times were hard you got hot crisp "dripping toast" – slices of Small Pan fried in dripping – or "French toast" – ditto soaked in raw-egg and fried; mmm! Plenty of eggs always – boiled, fried, poached or scrambled. A hard-boiled was "a bullet".

In Ireland, the war brought a certain amount of food rationing, with a scarcity of fresh fruit from the tropics in particular. I must have been Four when I saw my first orange and I clearly remember the first time I handled that real novelty – a banana. (Tales of dockers being fatally bitten by tarantulas in the bunches.) Kelloggs' corn flakes and wheat flakes only reappeared about 1948.

As my father liked a drink and a game of cards we were

often obliged to buy our own food "on tick" (credit). I was sent "to get the messages" (groceries), as a kind of decoy, when the tab was overdue. I was never refused, presumably because "a polisman's credit" was good indemnity in itself. If only they knew my rake of a da...

Occasionally, to spread the debt, I was despatched for victuals to Miss Dawe of the Dee Creamery – a hunched old 'huckster' in sack-cloth and sashes, with a hairy wart on her chin; she frightened me to death. (In my youth Dublin was full of such shops, run by childless balding old women with facial protuberances; generally united by total devotion to The Church and with pictures of the (haemorrhaging) Sacred Heart and (fra angelical) Blessed Virgin well-displayed about their dismal premises, competing with age-yellowed adverts for detergents. – No washing machines then; all was hand-wash, with Persil or Rinso.)

Rashers, eggs, sausages and fried tomato for Sunday breakfast indicated better times, as did roast beef for "dinner" – lunch in England.

Fish was Friday – a Fast Day when meat was forbidden by the stern Church. Fish 'n' chips from a "chipper" (chip-shop) was the nearest we got to junk-food Valhalla; no Wimpey, Burger King or MacDonald's then.

Cakes were rare treats - cream-buns ("from the Monument" Creamery) a benison. Figrolls were the biscuit. ...One day a year for pancakes, another (Halloween) for the "barm brack" - a big currant cake which always contained "a gold ring" for one lucky child in their slice.

Halloween also meant "apples and nuts" and you and your pals went door-to-door begging for them, in Halloween Masks so no one knew you. Or so you thought. They'd know the voice. But they'd pay up, laughing. Easter meant those enormous (hollow) chocolate eggs, after six weeks of Lenten frugality.

Sweets were precious, although you could buy a stick of

liquorice, a handful of jelly babies or "nancy balls" (aniseed balls) for a penny. It was "like Christmas" to be given a golden Crunchie, a Kit Kat, a cylinder of Smarties, a tube of Rolo, an Aero Bar, or a slab of Cadbury's Milk Chocolate. All of these Anglo-Irish confections remain name unchanged (except for price) today. Branding is forever in the deathless sweet trade apparently.

Christmas itself meant open boxes of chocolates on the sideboard, cake galore, Thwaites Lemonade and American Cream Soda till it came out your ears. Even ice-cream – normally available only in the hot weather. Hunks of fruity Christmas Pudding in yellow clusters of Bird's Custard. Who needed roast spuds and Turkey?

The spud itself was, in Ireland, as rice to a Chinaman. Old people told us how lucky we were to have plenty of spuds, reminded us that The Potato Famine of the last century "halved the population by starvation and emigration". Spuds were also Murphys and anyone of the surname drew the former as nickname. Spud Murphys abounded.

Old people were always respected and listened to then; most families would die rather than abandon their sires to an old people's 'home'.

That is one bit of tradition we might have done well to retain.

* * *

Christmas also meant TOYS. The Stocking, crammed with sweets and treats. A clockwork mouse...a board game...a set of watercolours, a conductor's ticket-punch...a Jack-in-the-Box...a (politically incorrect) Golliwog...Including, maybe, your First Bike, with maybe a brand new cowboy-outfit to make a horse of it. Not forgetting the two pearl-handled six-guns which you spent the day learning to fast draw. Just like "the chap" (hero)...in innumerable cowboy pictures.

How "Santy" got the bike down the chimney you never knew, or cared. No less than you cared, in the weeks before Christmas, how the same Santa presided over all the big store toy departments. "Going to see Santy" was heaven itself. You saw him, Ho Ho Ho, in the course of one long happy day...in Clerys, Pims, Todd Burns, Brown Thomas, McBirneys; repeating each time what you 'wanted' on The Night. And each time, the omnipresent profligate presented you with a grand gift-wrapped Christmas Parcel. (Paid for behind your back by the mammy.)

Toys were few enough and prized accordingly – modern kids are spoiled rotten by comparison. My own children, bless their stinking cotton socks, could stock a small toyshop (or kiddy video store). I usually counted my treasured possessions on the fingers of one hand.

My parents always made sure I got something I really wanted, even if it meant that they put themselves in hock. My first bike was bought "on HP" (hire purchase) and took a couple of years to pay off.

My mother pawned her wedding ring to buy me an electric train set. (Not for the first time – the ring, she'd joke weakly, "was in and out of uncle's like a yo-yo", in support of many a good or necessary cause.) The pawn-shop itself was class-segregated, with a big open room for gurriers and a small private annexe for 'genteel' patrons – of a kind who run up their credit card accounts instead, nowadays.)

I wish I'd kept my mint Dinky cars, which now fetch hundreds of pounds at auction. The manufacturer of my Bayko Building Set has long bitten the dust. My train-set was a 'cheap' Tri-Ang, inferior to Hornby then – an elite brand later acquired by Tri-Ang, to its detriment. But they couldn't harm the great Hornby-made Meccano construction outfits, which still survive intact. Oddly enough, it was German train-sets like Marklin Electric or Trix that everyone wanted – but they were as expensive as they were superb. All you could do was gape at them enviously, displayed or laid-out in Helys of Dame Street.

A local greengrocer had a whole room above his shop devoted to a Marklin lay-out. But we were warned against being lured to view by our parents, in that the old batchelor was deemed to be "a bit queer" – they meant only strange. In fact there was, in due course, a bit of trouble between him and the police, on Browny business. Until one of our neighbours, a policeman who liked the old roue, intervened and "got him off with a caution". He sold the shop and left the locality soon after.

Life was never far away from us and our toys.

Apart from my own father, we had several other *Gardai* living locally. A real boon when some passing rookie 'arrested' us for playing football in the street. A summons to appear in Court was always "quashed" accordingly, at the behest of the fathers of the goalie, the centre-forward, the ref...

And...an occasional boon in Autumn if we were caught "boxing the fox" (robbing an apple-orchard). "A few words" to the irate householder, from Sergeant So-And-So, would oil the boil.

The Irish police then were a clanny and clan-protective species. And as *Gardai Siochana* (Guardians of the Peace), they did so with minimum fuss and bother; before a new age of armed robbery, drug addiction and police-baiting 'joy-riders' duly changed all the rules. (*Ban Gardai* (female Officers) were non-existent until, I think, 1964.)

* * *

Soccer was the favourite street-game; sometimes hurling, seldom Gaelic football. Several Dublin soccer teams were followed closely: Shamrock Rovers, Bohemians, Tolka United...Dalymount Park, the nearest soccer stadium, was the real home of football to us – not Croke Park.

Stanley Matthews and Danny Blanchflower were our heroes, and, at a pinch, the great hurler Nicky Rackert. A lot of Dublin kids wore black arm-bands after an air disaster in Munich (1958) decimated the Manchester United team – (manager Matt) 'Busby's Babes'.

Summertime we played a bit of cricket. I needed stitches in an eye-brow after one bout of bad wicket-keeping. I gained a certain respect, by proxy as it were, after my cousin fielded for an Irish Eleven that beat the fabled West Indians. No truth in the foul rumour, he later assured me, that we got them drunk on Guinness first.

Looking back on it, I was more interested and involved in sport than might have been indicated earlier, by my dislike of Gaelic games at school. Never a terrific participant, I nonetheless got caught up like everyone else, in 'following' everything from boxing and motor racing, to running and mountain climbing – after the Ascent of Everest fired us all. Roger Bannister's four minute mile had us all at that. Moreso, after Dublin harrier Ronnie Delany created a sensation by winning a gold medal in the Olympics. Girls generally played tennis...

Joe Louis, "the only boxer ever", got two of my neighbours in gloves and gum shields for awhile. Stirling Moss and Fangio were the racing idols. (Dinky Cars did a nice line in Formula One replicas.)

We collected and swapped sporting cigarette cards – one in each packet of 10 – driving our relatives to lung cancer in the process. Some avid collectors even "chipped in" to buy the occasional pack, thus becoming "scuts who puffed butts" in the eyes of the irate adult. Smoking was very daring. Not to say paradoxical, begun in pursuit of a sport-linked hobby. (I only took to it in my late-teens, over a pint.) If you got hooked you could buy Woodbines in packets of 5, moving closer again to real vice, in that you were "on a hoor's smoke". For some knew that soldiers and sailors often paid for sexual services with the brand, and that unacceptable lotharios got the wry put-down:

"Take your hand offa me leg – here's your Woodbine back."

Stamp collecting was a much safer bet – 'the king of hobbies, the hobby of kings', as your album had it. Well, some kings perhaps. Card playing began as a similarly innocent 'hobby', while I'm on the subject, until Old Maid got deflowered by our discovery of stud poker.

...As to racing, we got a first-hand idea of that from a flash young man who drove "a Jag"(uar) and knew how to make a boy's dreams live. "Get in" he would invite a pack of us to fill the cabin, before taking off for the Phoenix Park and hitting ninety on the wide straight parkway. So this was how Fangio must feel...in the Ferrari.

Another chipper youth took up stock-car racing and would ferry a few of us to watch him dare-devil at Santry Stadium. It was as much fun driving there in the roaring bar-fendered stock-car, as it was to watch the ensuing mayhem on the sparking cindered track. Bliss!

(Any car was a novelty in those days, being far beyond the scope of most family budgets; we had a single Ford Prefect owner in our own street.)

We left going to the greyhound and horse-racing tracks to the adults; many of whom literally went to the dogs, putting their shirt on either animal. Horse-betting predominated, with bookies dens almost as numerous as pubs in some areas – operating under the hilariously grand aegis of Turf Accountants. The 'shops' of P.J. Kilmartin were ubiquitous; as my ever losing father's bookmakers they flourished.

We stuck to dogs as pets – the most useful of all in that they chased cats. Although it took a hare of a terrier to catch a Dublin cat. One mongrel who farted frequently and loudly was very popular. Your own cat could be interesting, in pursuit of bird or mouse. Our tabby learned to live with a Yorkshire Canary I acquired from a friend who had an aviary. Another pal bred rabbits and gave me a fierce black animal. 'Clarence' feared nothing and used his thumpers on any dog or cat that came within range. Breeding greyhounds and racing-pigeons was never our thing; gurriers did that (or Colshies).

Loosely apropos: living in a street of Dublin Jackeens my Colshie mother developed a trace of paranoia in that respect. "They look down on us" she'd say of the neighbours, "because I come of decent country stock." Then a haughty sniff: "We're better than any of them."

Personally I never experienced any prejudice and lent a deaf ear to her moans, not least because she got on famously with most of the locals, whatever she might have thought. As far as I was concerned pals were pals and we were all the same. We even looked the same, with our close-cropped heads under our conical school caps, our patched short trousers and 'jerkins', our crepe-soled shoes and falling down socks. Shirts and ties were always worn, under a 'ganzie' (thick woollen jersey) in the cold weather. Our big belted overcoats looked like rugs. All the more with a thick woollen school-scarf wrapped around your neck.

* * *

I mustn't forget to mention circuses and carnivals, which came to every Dublin suburb at least once a year.

I only got to see the eponymous Duffy's Circus once or twice, alas, but I seldom missed a Carnival. Earliest memories: riding the carousel of hobby-horses, with the Mammy aboard to forestall a fall. Later: in the Ghost Train or on the 'bumpers' (dodgems) with your pals, stuffing yourself with great hairy pink blobs of candy-floss the while. A few pennies bought an exciting Lucky Dip. A sealed packet containing 'novelties' – a few sweets, a whistle, a paper-hat, a magic wand...

Carnivals were all 'well-up' on the latest pop music, with Rosemary Clooney, Teresa Brewer, Guy Mitchell, or the like, blaring out from ubiquitous loudspeakers. No less *au fait* with the latest fad or craze, the barkers touted Hula Hoops, Davy

Crockett "bearskin" hats, or anything else the kids were currently into, to turn an extra penny...

They also provided the nearest thing we had to Spectacle, only excepting the annual St. Patrick's Day Parade.

* * *

As far as indoor entertainment went, we were always ready for a Party. Although there were some little get-togethers during the year, to celebrate a birthday or Feast Day, like Easter Sunday, I must come back to Yule for real revelry. Nothing held a candle to Christmas Parties.

In my experience they were always closer to vintage Dickens or Sterne (or Dylan Thomas's 'Christmas in Wales') than, say, the dreadful adult affair in 'The Dead'. James Joyce was indeed preaching sombre Ibsen or dour Chekhov there, as far as the jolly festivities of my own memory are concerned. (December snow was a rarity in drizzly Dublin too; I recall very few White Christmases.)

Later carrying that wearisome, fractious (and so untypical) kind of confrontation forward, into the Christmas Dinner of 'The Portrait', Joyce has the children banished to a nursery. That was also completely at odds with my own experience, where children were always included and indulged to excess, at the main table.

My mother's family and their own families usually congregated at one of the largest houses available, to group around a long laden board, pull glittering Christmas Crackers and generally let the hair down, no holds barred. Upper case Fun was the order, in a riotous holly and ivy atmosphere of seasonal goodwill, with a tight truce on all bickering, rivalries, or petty quarrelling, for the duration.

We often attended a Banahan 'do', as it was called, and my most vivid memories are straight out of 'The Pickwick Papers', with the adults in party hats and pulling the crackers with you;

generally roistering and giggling no less than ourselves.

Except we mostly got our background carols from the wireless, with 'Come All Ye Faithful' or 'Adeste Fidelis' played morning to night on Radio Eireann. Interspersed by repetitions of 'White Christmas', 'Rudolph The Red-Nosed Reindeer', and the rest. Culminating in the late afternoon and evening, with variety programmes featuring such stalwarts of Dublin comedy as Jimmy O'Dea, Maureen Potter, or Danny Cummins.

The radio was only silenced if some piano-playing relative started to tickle the ivories and encourage vocal accompaniment. Until almost everyone was roaring away the refrain to a comic song by Percy French...

When Dinner was almost ended, with several uncles "well on the way" (my own father keening "Oh if I had the wings of a swallow") and several aunts hoping it wouldn't be hers that "disgraced himself" – by doing a header into the trifle – the kids slipped away to play. In time, some of the uncles would join in, by then hardly needing a mask to play Blind-Man's-Buff.

When we got rid of them, again, we'd maybe settle down to play one of the popular board games – ludo, snakes and ladders, tiddly winks, dominoes, draughts, Monopoly...(Chess never caught on in Ireland.)

There would always be someone to torment the girls with a water pistol or pea-shooter, or to drop a stink bomb under a puritan. A bit of 'magic' perhaps, from someone else given a conjuring set by Santy, before spoilsport mother appeared with your coat and hat.

But never mind, there would be more parties ahead, on St. Stephen's Day certainly, and well into the New Year. There would also be PANTOS (like comic papers come to life), several of them, with the aforesaid O'Dea, Potter and Cummins hamming it up for rapturous full houses. O the sweet brassy sound of the band in the pit! ...The fire curtain, covered with display ads for Dublin merchandise, would slowly levitate from the footlights and perch high above the Mansion-polished sliver of stage, to reveal another, sumptious velvet curtain, swaying with promise. A great cheer when that went up. And a greater gasp when you beheld the half-lit set designers Wonderland behind it.

Aladdin, Hansel and Gretel, Robinson Crusoe, Cinderella, Sinbad The Sailor, Ali Baba...A thigh-slapping Principal Boy (or "princeable girl", if you know your Joyce) with legs like a thoroughbred mare, and a gorgeous face that you dreamt about for weeks afterwards. A Villain to Boo until you were hoarse. A timid shy Simple Simon who you wanted to see "gettin" the androgynous Principal Boy. "Gwan now Buttons – give her a kiss!" Booming Jack Cruise in blazer and yachting-cap, cracking topical jokes. 'Dame' Cecil Sheridan, hilariously beshawled in the ragged drag of an 'ould Molly' from Moore Street Market. A Giant mebbe, who roared until you screamed with terror...

All this taking place in the palatial interior of The Royal, The Queen's, The Gaiety, The Capitol, The Olympia, while you sank into plush red seats that rolled up in curving rows from gallery to ceiling.

Up there, great glass chandeliers that blazed like heaven itself, until they slowly faded and snuffed and you were left with the cloistered dim yellow sidelights, glowing EXIT signs...and that yawning deep open cave of Stage. A shadowy figure stumbling on from the wings, keening:

"Oh Dear Oh Dear Oh Dear...I'm so unhappy!" To "Aws" from kids.

Enchantment...

* * *

Less enchanting were our own infrequent attempts to entertain. As well as singing under my mother's shot-gun for the clergy, I was drafted into a school of Irish dancing for awhile – one of two or three mortified boys in a gaggiggle of girls. Reels and hornpipes, your face burning.

After that, I was enrolled at the Dublin School of Music, to learn the violin...until my tormented music teacher eventually pleaded with the devastated Mammy to take me away – please. I missed the Theory classes, run by a delightful Beatrix Potter of a woman: "Here is Sammy Semibreve! Now what is Minnie Minim doing under Charlie Crotchet?"

I really wanted to learn the piano but we couldn't afford one. I began to slide off the short-list for likely drawing-room boys. As a last resort, the Ma got me into an Irish Club, full of Gaelic-speaking types in white roll neck wool sweaters; hoping, I believe, to at least make a Decent Irish Boy of me. All they did there, as far as I could see, was sit around imaginary camp-fires and lustily sing 'She'll be coming round the mountain when she comes', accompanied by a bald little elf of an accordionist. I remember one day-long 'nature ramble' in the Dublin mountains, which nearly killed me. Finis.

"So" my father asks, "if ye don't want to mix with decent boys and girls and enjoy the outdoor life, what do ye want?"

This led on to "what dye want to do with yerself" (in life) – a question every adult kept asking you for that matter. Uncle, aunt, teacher or priest, they were all at it: "What dye want to be?"

"A dust-man", was a hot favourite among the youngest. The idea of driving a tipping dust-cart like Joey (the local garbage collector), being very attractive indeed. "Back away Joey!" we'd shout, directing his side-filling Tipper as it reversed onto the waiting pile of dust-bins.

It is no wonder that some utopian philosophers solved the problems of waste-clearance in their ideal societies by having the kids shift the shit. On the principle that every infant loves a dung-hill, or a wallow in effluent.

...Although I never knew a pal who wanted to be a coal-man, put off possibly by the thought of shouldering huge sacks of the stuff. (I had enough trouble fetching buckets of coal from a snow-covered slack-pile in Winter.) ...Nor a junk-man - because, as you learned on your mother's knee, they belonged to the lowest Irish class of all: the abominated, feared and dreaded Tinkers (mendicant travellers who did often disgrace the good name of the true Gypsy) – "the durtiest teeves, and murderers in creation", etc. Come to think of it, even the hapless gurrier had a patsy there. (The 'Honest' Tramp was positively tolerated, as "a poor man down on his luck", by comparison.)*

"A bus conductor", or a "train driver" came later. Then a doctor, because of the beguiling stethoscope; a dentist, so you could pull your own teeth instead of suffering at the Dental Hospital; a pilot for flying, a sailor for freedom, a priest for a pat on the back, etc. Never, a teacher. (I only knew one youth who later entered for the Christian Brothers.)

Trades and professions were seldom mentioned – in primary schooldays most of us hardly knew what the latter did – apart from party politicians, who we mostly held to be boring old bullshitters.

Class consciousness determined our attitude to the trades. Plumbers, carpenters, electricians and the like issued from the national schools, where suitable candidates went on to learn their chosen craft "at Tec". Our Secondary Education was their stint at Technical School. "City 'n Gills" (City and Guilds) exams were "all they did".

* * *

That Ireland was a predominantly agricultural country was

* Even Shaw, who wrote a glowing Introduction to W.H. Davies' 'Autobiography of a Super Tramp' (a book my father liked), once dismissed Gypsy-loving author George Borrow as "a born fool" (for romanticising their lifestyle). He may have there been thinking of the worst of the Irish breed.

evident to all in my own locality every Wednesday. That was Cattle Day and we lived adjacent to the vast stockyards on the North Circular Road.

You had to watch yourself, going to school through the herds of cattle being driven down the Old Cabra Road, before you took more than the shine off your shoes by walking into an enormous cow-pat. Or you could have a (literally) dirty skid off your bike if that was the transport.

Everywhere you looked some dopey looking heifer was lifting the tail and spewing a stream of light brown dung. While the herders cursed and swore blue murder, at the herd, at the weather, at man, beast, or boy. (Enough to give any utopian pause for thought.)

Occasionally a lorry-load of bleating sheep or honking pigs would add to the confusion, the driver leaning out of his cab to barrack the herders: "Use yer stick on them! Make way for Jaysus sake!" The herders would lift their long knotted cattle-sticks and barrack back: "Dye call that a lorry! Get down and milk it and it might fuckin move!"

But herders were popular, as 'characters'. One such, who had been caught in congress with a spring lamb, earned his pints in responding indignantly to the taunt, "Hey fuck the pig", by snapping back, cleft-palated: "Wa'n't a pig, was a sheep!"

(I much later heard stories of soldiers in country areas having their flies inspected for traces of sheep-wool on return to barracks...)

*　*　*

Dubliners will forgive a character anything and it was always rich with them. Bang Bang, for example, travelled the buses free, repeatedly shouting "bang bang", to the delight of young and old alike. Johnny Forty-Coats was an ancient hairy tramp who never went without the price of a drink to put in one of his many pockets. Characters wandering aimlessly about in animated soliloquy were a common sight.

An early character on the grand scale was the barrister Sodomy Cox (so named for his support of Wilde), who lived in a room framed by one O of the huge OXO (beef extract) advertisement in Lincoln Place. A tiny room which once led a claustrophobic visitor to remark: "If you'd close your fly, Cox, and open the window, we might be able to breathe." A covert heterosexual of catholic tastes, his main hobby was touring public lavatories to photograph the graffiti.

Cox's visitor was the poet Seumas "Dublin is full of spoiled Prousts" O'Sullivan, who famously accused a freeloading fellow poet of "drinking beyond our means". That was Padraic O Conaire, who travelled everywhere with a goat...

Dublin regarded poets in general as "terrible men" – the apogee of characterhood. But they were respected too, if sometimes in an odd way.

For example, my father told me that the *Gardai* in his home neighbourhood had orders "to leave Paddy Kavanagh alone, unless he tries to kill someone or exposes himself to a girl". All the more 'Parisian' as that undeniably worthy Poet, who spent his awful final years staggering the banks of the Grand Canal in a stupor, detested anything in a uniform and made no great secret of it.

They later had similar orders to 'cool it' in any affray with Brendan Behan. However, once Brendan got going, there was no cooling anything.

*　*　*

The annual Horse Show at Ballsbridge reminded you that we bred some of the finest equines in the world. Going there, as to the earlier Spring Show, was a great treat. Apart from the sleek animals there would be loads of commercial display stands in the Great Hall and you came away with a pile of glossy brochures on stud-life, farm implements and fodder. Or, at the Spring Show, with piles of pamphlets on divers subjects, from bedding to high fashion. Your mother would be lost in admiration and envy at the ongoing parade of *haute couture* (which sounds so much better in French). The women went to town at these Ascot-like events, swanning about in "the last word" from Grafton Street, and items of millinery that a Martian would take his hat off to.

The only privates on parade I ever saw were those at a Military Tattoo in the Phoenix Park – when I was five or six. I remember being lifted onto a massive tank and trying to climb on the gun-barrel; a ride in an armoured car and being Kodak-snapped by a piece of field artillery.

Briefly back to toys, I had my share of tin soldiers in boyhood, usually busbied British Guardsmen, standing stiffly erect – no residual *double entendre* intended.

To my mind the fact that Irish schoolboys played happily with English soldiers (and Windsor-style castles), and virtually depended on England for all their toys*, made a mockery of extremist attempts to divide our two peoples.

Or, of affirming Irish Independence in all things, when an export ban by the stronger economy would reduce the Republic to chaos in no time.

* * *

My earlier mention of OXO reminds me of beeftea, which was given as an elixir whenever you were "under the weather" – a term used selectively for both childhood illness and adult drunkenness – and which put you, as picturesquely, "under the doctor".

I am thinking now of health in general.

And, for the most part we enjoyed a great deal of it, being

---

* *Even the tiny American G.Is we acquired were 'Made in England'.*

well-nourished on the basics and equally well-clothed against the East Wind from the Irish Sea, with all the rain and sleet it brought in season. Colds of course were as common as the full name.

Having your tonsils out was the worst that happened most of us.

Enough nonetheless to put you off hospitals for life. I remember, still, being held down by several people in white coats and fighting the horrible wad of ether with every ounce of strength in my writhing body.

Afterwards they showed you the testicular tonsils, pink blobs in a little kidney dish, chiding and telling you that that was all the great fuss was about...All indeed – they hadn't been half-smothered.

Doctor Masterson was our G.P. and a lovely big rugby player of a man he was, with a rich smell of cigars on the deep pile staircase as you climbed to the surgery. He always gave you a sweet, after having the tongue out for a look, said "you need a tonic" and sat down behind a big polished desk to write a prescription.

While your mother simpered at him, like she did with a priest, until you didn't know where to look. "Oh thank you Doctor!" Three bags full Doctor. What a pity you're not a bishop or I'd kneel down to kiss your ring. Mothers were the limit.

'Larry' Masterson, I learned years later, was decapitated in a car crash, rushing out in the middle of the night to tend one of his patients. I hope he's in Heaven. News of his death reminded me of the night when a teenager was decapitated in a similar car crash, mere yards away from Masterson's house. We knew one of the survivors well and he afterwards described the sobbing doctor's efforts to cope with the carnage, after our friend had staggered from the wreck and found him running across the road, black bag in hand, still in his pyjamas.

That was the worst accident ever in our neighbourhood. My

own experience of such things was mercifully restricted; except for one chilling visit to comatosed Uncle Dan in hospital, just before he died. He looked surprisingly peaceful and unscathed, for a man who'd come off a speeding motor-bike, head-first and helmetless. I couldn't believe he was going to die, as they said. Surely he'd open his eyes and wink?

I remember also being taken to visit a tubercular cousin, on her death-bed, and coming away thinking how serene and saintly she seemed... 'T.B.' was still a common killer in those days, only matched for parental dread by meningitis. Most of us, fortunately, got nothing worse than mumps, measles, scarlatina, chicken-pox or whooping cough.

My mother was taken hospitalised for major operations on several occasions. I only clearly recall one such instance, when I was old enough to be told that she was "havin her gallstones out". I have no direct memory of the time when, as she later divulged, "I lost your baby brother". Unless that was the day I came home from school to find my father alone, blowing his nose furiously and obviously agitated, struggling to make a pot of tea.

"They carted your mother off to the Mater Hospital today" he finally got it out, "for treatment. We'll be on our own for a little while now."

Like so many families, nothing brought us closer together than crisis.

Although my own feelings were mixed, in that I almost liked those times when she was incapacitated, at home or away – for reasons that will shortly become apparent. So that all her being in hospital really meant to me was time off from school...to visit her, propped up post-operative and pale, on a trolley-like bed in a big open ward.

She was at her best then, plying me with fruit and sweets, slipping me a shilling or two to buy comics. While my father sat awkwardly by the bed and dragged on a fag, dispelling the smell of formaldehyde.

Apart from the tonsils, or the occasional bread-poulticed whitlow* – when you hoarded the lost fingernail as a grim trophy – I never had much to complain about, health (or accident) wise. I got kicked by an un-shod horse once, in the face, which may have scrambled my brains a little. Otherwise I traded on being a 'delicate' mother's boy and fell 'ill' to avoid school on the slightest pretext.

If I was lucky I got a glass of Andrews Liver Salts, which tasted like lemonade. Unlucky, I got a dose of Angier's Emulsion, cascara or syrup of figs – "to open yer bowels" – or one of Larry Masterson's bitter tonics. Anything was worth it to be snug in bed on a wintry day, having a stray relative calling "to see how ye arr" and bringing sweets, a toy, or comics. Come night, 'Knockout' read cover to cover, you could 'play' yourself to sleep.

If the Ma came "to kiss you goodnight" and caught you at it you lied.

"Why are you all hunched up like that under the sheet – are you alright."

"I'm alright Mammy. I'm just playin camels."

It should have been dromedaries: the beast with one humpback.

* I recall showing one such sore to a boy who'd had ringworm. He told me about a local woman who had a tapeworm (another kind of ring-worm!) and had me in stitches with a story about her husband. – "Standin by her bare arse with a pair a scissors, waitin for it to show its head." "Ye have ta get the head" he added.

89

CHAPTER SEVEN

Spare the rod. Pleese!

Yes indeed, Sex was never far away, in one form or another. I know for a fact that sexual frustration played its part in altering my mother's behaviour for the worse, when I was about Five or Six.

* * *

We rented a two-room flat on the ground floor of a semi-detached house.

One of about forty such (or eighty semis), forming a small Drive in the northern suburbs. Snaking to link two busy main roads at the top end, the Lower Drive terminated in a semi-circular cul-de-sac. It was all-in-all a fairly traffic-free place for us kids to play then.

Our flat was classically 'modest'. The front room served as dining-room and lounge, duly trebling as single bedded sleeping quarters for me, when I outgrew my cot in the back (bed)room. A kitchenette led out to 'our' back garden, a lengthy plot of arable land where my father grew potatoes, cabbages and rheubarb, with a few bushes devoted to blackcurrants and gooseberries. (The Ma made scrumptious jams in season, selling what we didn't eat to a local grocer.)

The useless front lawn was rented with the flat above us. In compensation perhaps, they had sole use of the upstairs bathroom and toilet. We used an outside water closet and washed in the kitchen sink.

Knowing nothing better, I never minded having to piss and shit in a converted coal-shed. Besides it was snug enough with the door pulled shut (even in the coldest weather), and often the only place you could be sure of a bit of privacy – to reflect, read (at night by candle light), or, now and again and if you felt the urge, to invoke Onan.

* * *

In my infancy, we had a Protestant family 'upstairs', with two children of about my own age as playmates. The parents were a warm, friendly pair and my mother got on well with Mrs B. Indeed I think that she was largely responsible for introducing my own to the solace of alcohol, by often dropping down of a night, when the men were out, with a little worry killer. For one thing, they had in common that we were the only two families in our street who shared a house – everyone else having their own little Semi. (Possibly mortgaged to the hilt, but theirs.)

There in fact was the original root of my mother's despair and frustration, in that she was also the only one of her own family without the full bricks and mortar. She desperately wanted her own house and had hoped that the flat would be a temporary expedient.

It mortified her to be asked, by the better-off siblings: "Any hope of a house yet?" The longer it went on, the more embittered she became with my father.

But it seems that there were times, earlier in the marriage, when she also 'hated' my father for leaving her alone at night to play Patience, while he drank or gambled elsewhere.

"There was one night" she told me years later, "when you were a baby and started to cry. I got so mad about everything that I picked you up out of the cot and began to shake you like a rag-doll. I could have killed you the way I felt. But I must have been shouting or screaming too, for Missis B came running downstairs and flew at me. Anyway she calmed me down and insisted I take a glass or two of sherry with her... And she told me if I ever felt like hitting you again, to call her immediately."

So it began...Mrs B's valuable samaritanism duly proving a tainted benison: ensuring my infant welfare at the expense of gradually turning my unfortunate mother into a chronic toper. Alas, Mrs B would be far away when I later again needed that kind of neighbourliness.

For we would remain closeted in the flat long after she and her family moved on. (We only moved, to Bray, in 1962, where we rented a house in Martello Terrace...virtually next door to where the Joyces once lived...and where the Christmas Dinner in 'The Dead' was set...) They were followed, over the years, by a varied succession of lodgers.

I affectionately remember two liberated party-giving air-hostesses, who lavished the sweets and toys. One of them had an unconcealed affair with the landlady's son, mildly scandalising my strait-laced parents. 'Jean' nearly gave my mother a heart-attack on one occasion, by taking off her blouse, with me in the room, to show us where "Jack" lanced a boil on her back. I was mesmerised, only wishing that I was Jack. It was a lovely back. And she had gorgeous pointed diddies too, beneath that taut white bra.

I guess, her prudery aside, that the sight of a pretty young girl in love must have turned a screw in my mother's heart at the time, for beauty and love were fading features in her own tormented existence.

Soon after the genial Proddies moved into a house of their own, she really began to nag my father, about getting himself promoted, so that we could afford to progress likewise. He did his best, poor man, but duly failed the oral of his sergeant's exam because of 'nerves'. He never sat again and I think that their relationship truly plummeted from that point. As the only child I caught the brunt of my mother's anger and frustration, when the prospect of home ownership decidedly vanished...with, I guess, most of her old romantic feelings for my father.

As is the way of life at such times, he took increasingly to drink, the horses, and staying out 'till all hours' playing cards with his cronies on the Force.

My mother, to her eternal remorse in later life, 'took it out' on me.

So I got beaten for his sins, usually with a long thin cane on my bare legs or backside.

That was also how she first tried to explain, or excuse, her behaviour to me, in later years. But by then, even she suspected that there was more to it than that. Until she finally worked herself up to an admission nearer real truth: "I think I liked beating ye at times."

As such, it was a gradually acquired taste, beginning with her 'smacking' me in infancy – a few slaps on the bare botty – when I was "bold" (naughty). For example, I had a bad spell of bed-wetting soon after I came out of nappies. That literally pissed her off and she began to spank me 'dutifully', to try and cure me of it.

Then she took me to see Doctor Masterson and very nearly got spanked herself. "He was furious with me" (bless him). "He told me that beating you was no solution and that I should put down an oil-sheet, until you grew out of the habit." I remember that oil-sheet – urine-coloured itself. ("That had the queer smell" – Joyce inimitably recalled his own experience of same in 'The Portrait'. Spot on.)

When exactly she changed her tune, from "I'll give you a smacking" to "I'll give you a real thrashing", I cannot precisely determine now. But I do remember my terror when the cane appeared and my begging: "Please Mammy! No Mammy!"

I recall her expression: wild staring eyes, clenched teeth, as it began.

I remember her breaking a cane on my arse on one occasion, then despatching me to Carton's of Manor Street to buy a replacement, with the chastisement being ritually terminated on my return.

And I remember a truly terrifying incident when, with my backside still burning, she seemed to flip completely – filling the kitchen sink and ducking my head under, screaming she'd drown me...while I wriggled and fought for breath. As suddenly she stopped, threw herself on her knees and hugged me, begging me to forgive her. While I veered from pure terror to bewilderment and back again.

I suspect that the beatings – which were mercifully as sporadic as they were unexpected – may have eased off considerably after that. She must have terrified herself then and maybe glimpsed her real sickness.

Nonetheless the scourging persisted, until I was Eight or Nine, or big and bold enough to spot the signs and fly the coop; finally, too big to hit. It was then that she began to turn increasingly to drink, whenever funds allowed, becoming pretty much an alcoholic by the time I finally left for England. No less than my father and later again, me. "Why did I beat you?" she'd groan in her dotage, "sure no better child ever lived. You were good as gold. ...I must have been mad. I've beaten all the spirit out of you..."

She may have had a point there. But I can't be certain, as I was always a curious mixture of gregarious boisterousness and shy timidity. For example, from as far back as I can remember, I always wanted to make people laugh – by playing the clown, pulling faces, telling jokes – and had no trouble doing this with close friends or family.

When it came to playing the comedian or entertaining more formally however, I became mortally shy and tongue-tied; stage-fright. (About Twelve, after reading 'Frankenstein', I acquired a limited vogue among my peers as a horror story-teller.)

Now my mother sometimes actively encouraged me to play the fool. As, weird woman, she herself often did with her close friends and family - many of whom saw 'Babs' as "an absolute scream" and fell about accordingly. I'm sure that none of the people she so amused could have remotely imagined her as any kind of sadist – let alone to the child she so obviously doted over. Only she and I knew about the 'mad' streak.

Except for one really weird/scary instance, where I remember her actually pointing out the marks of the cane on my thighs to a neighbour's daughter (a few years older than myself) and taking great pleasure in detailing for her just how she beat me. (Here was a scenario very close to that of Joyce's 'Encounter', with my own mother cast as the perverted flagellant...)

I was also very anxious to 'please' – as I had often wanted only to please her, despite the beatings – and always desperately needed to be liked. Correspondingly I feared and dreaded rejection, by anyone, and for all my couldn't-care-less attitudinising, I tended to suck up to anyone in authority. I was also slow to stand up for myself if physically challenged, or generally engage in healthy confrontation.

As another aspect of this, although I grew up able to think or act quite independently (or rebelliously) at times, I would as readily revert to bourgeois middle-class type and become a deferential, sycophantic, ass-licker if the social chips were really down – for example if keeping an office-job meant meekly kowtowing. So much so that a good friend could justifiably remark to me, in my Twenties, that I still had "the longest forelock in town".

Needless to say I also attracted a fair bit of bullying in childhood, as a drippy little goody-goody, from those who found no merit in my clowning. Whether the beatings at home did anything to form (or deform) my character in the above respect, I just do not know. I do know that I came though my teens without worrying about my lack of machismo – which I anyway often equated with brute stupidity – and concentrated on projecting myself as a cultivated, Gentle Poet. I could even foster a compensatory self-image with stuff like this:

> An Only Child, a lonely child
> Who lives in love, his face a smile
> A smiling face, a love so blithe
> Derided like a lump of shite.
> For to the crowd the poet's line
> Is ever but a plaintive whine
> Comparable to bowel's lament
> When de-embracing excrement

– It went on, justifying a possibly defensive element in my clowning:

> Eventually his sentience
> A nimble jester it presents
> Amuse the bully is his answer
> Accommodate that boorish laughter
>
> Thus Nature's accident of wit
> Saves his strength for later years
> When even greater human fears
> Upon him dart, against him pit.

Although it sounds like I must have been reading Shakespeare on the lavatory, there is an odd bit of sense to it too!

Anyway...what I may have lacked in terms of physical aggression, I made up for in mental drive – a blessed kind of drive that I can clearly trace back...to...my mother. For in many respects she was an otherwise intelligent and considerate woman who really belonged in a different place and time.

On reflection...I suspect that what she really needed was a

creative outlet for her energies, for she loved poetry, song and dance and had (with her own 'clowning') more than a touch of the actress. She also had charm and a shrewdness in dealing with people, which I also inherited – only getting myself into trouble, in later life, whenever I failed to exercise them purposefully. She most certainly wasn't cut out for the grinding routine domesticity that fate meanly provided.

There are people who need to develop, in themselves, and know no peace unless they experience a sense of forward movement in their psychological lives. Robert Service caught some of this in the lines: "There are some men who don't fit in/Their feet are never still/They leave their homes and kith and kin/To roam the world at will."

We are nowadays, after 8,000 years of civilisation, becoming aware that there also women of that type. My mother was one and, I think, had she been fortunate enough to see, say, 'A Doll's House' in her youth, with Ibsen's Nora solidly slamming the door on wifely servitude in the last act, it just might have given her the idea of real independence.

Before a rakish Guard who could waltz and box was billeted in her hamlet...at a time when she was happily managing her own little shop.

But then, I wouldn't be here to speculate.

It only remains to say that such people, when nurtured against their real nature and denied any creative outlet – for needs they seldom even recognise – can as easily become poisoned by their own self-ignorance, to turn mean and nasty. Indeed the 'failed artist' who becomes a drunken neurotic or psychotic dope-fiend is a well-known type.

My mother couldn't have explained her own bouts of sadism in such high-falutin ways, but she was able to work out eventually (too late for my benefit alas) that she needed help.

"If only I'd told your father" she'd repent on a different tack, "about the beatins...He'd never have condoned it."

True, he never once laid a finger on me, as a stereotypically

97

gentle pugilist outside the ring (or a pub full of bowsies). And he would certainly put any foot he had left with her down, hard, at the idea of child abuse.

But she never told him and it never occurred to me to do so (or to 'grass' on her). I guess he was generally too self-preoccupied to notice the fine stripes on my legs.

As for me, I'm afraid I lost a lot of my own feeling for her and in that sense she killed the love we both needed. For it is a great misfortune all-round when ties of blood become clotted by fear, mistrust or the like, until a kind of emotional gangrene sets in. So it became.

She 'lost' me – with all the bitter self-recrimination that duly provokes in any parent. While I lost that sense of emotional security which later makes it very difficult to form trusting, loving relationships in life.

As we all know, a spoiled mother's boy – only child or not – often makes a lousy lover/husband/father. Even moreso, when he is alternately cossetted and brutalised, by a Jekyll Mother and a Hyde Dominatrix.

He can easily end up roaming the world without much will, looking for a motherly woman with a malacca cane in her portmanteau.

Although I never retained a taste for being thrashed, I was never averse to older women...Herr Dokter. Spoiled girls have similar problems.

So...although we all learn to survive our screwier parenting it leaves a lasting effect on mind or heart, that we could well do without. Mother-in-law jokes have a hard basis in unpalatable fact.

On a more positive note, I developed, possibly through mother's fierce pride in her own (albeit thwarted) intelligence, in her family and, indeed, in me (as overall apple of the eye) – there was as much coddling as caning – a similar sense of my own superiority. That proved a mixed blessing, in an intemperate young man who also had his head full of dreams;

proving often as problematical as the opposite sense – of inferiority – in coping with everyday humdrum.

At least I duly fostered some idea of my own 'destiny' and owed her for the mind, nature and education that enabled me to pursue it, however fitfully. I won't belabour that issue here; we'll have enough of it later.

I certainly grew up so intellectually arrogant that it never even occurred to me that this abuse had anything to do with a final descent into alcoholism. Looking back with hindsight however...my rejection of church and school, my own teenage bohemianism (and drunkedness), my initially callous rejection of hearth and home and my *wanderjahre* to England*... cannot have helped their situation in the slightest. By the time I began to put something back in, it was too little too late.

Even then, I offered financial help only, treating them with studied politeness and acting out of a belated sense of filial responsibility, that had nothing of sincere affection in it. Of course they would have sensed that, in their aged misery and hopelessness.

I had no real feeling for either of them and they knew it. While my mother would have detected in me a lack of feeling for <u>anyone</u>, but myself, and no doubt attributed it to her own handiwork.

It just may have been, but I think not. For I wanted to be "a grate riter" then and what she really saw was the cold selfishness of raw ambition.

They were both dead and gone before I knew how I should have behaved, or what I should have said, to bring them some warm comfort. I meant well enough, immaturely expressed as it was, but acted in a way that only paved their hell with my patronising good intentions.

* * *

* *Maybe all this was <u>revenge</u>? – see next chapter.*

I find this very difficult to write about, even now, partly because it brings home to me afresh, the yawning gulf between youthful folly and later experience. O that we could appreciate sooner that parents make us, far more than they ever break us. - And let them know it, before they die, or when they desperately need to hear it from us. I suspect that many readers will understand this kind of regret all too well. "They fuck you up/ Your mum and dad" wrote poet Philip Larkin. Only, it seems to me, if you choose to ignore a lifetime of benign formative influences, and waste your own life brooding over the deformative few.

Balls to that. Screw The Past. Learn from it. We live in the Now.

Neither of them ever blamed me for anything; like most parents they blamed themselves. My father died a broken man, pleased only that, at last, I seemed "to be making something" of myself.

She became wise in her old age, and only wished that had come years sooner. It was then that she confided her most intimate past problems to me.

"Oh If only I knew as much about life then. And" she'd cackle "about sex. Sure your father and I were like two children in such matters."

"But tell me" she'd squint up at me from her nursing-home bed, "it wasn't all bad was it? We had many happy times together?"

Did I remember her remorse, for example, after "a bad beatin"? When she would hug me and say she was sorry...and take me off to the Carlton Cinema, to try and make amends.

"I must have confused you terribly. Mad one minit, lovin Mammy the next. Can you ever forgive me?"

Long forgiven old girl and, I hope, largely forgotten.

But not before a series of problems, in coming to terms with life (yes, and sex) that might have been avoided but for the... confusion.

Who knows? Or really cares.

Life is finally, tritely, what we make of it and there are no simple excuses for failure or collapse – least of all those based on "what me mammy did"...In my view anyway.

CHAPTER EIGHT

"Oedipus Schmeidipus! All a boy needs is to love his mother."
– Archetypal Jewish Mother, laying down the law on Sigmund
Freud.

* * *

A mere 24 hours after completing the last chapter, I find the
statement about forgiving my mother and forgetting the
beatings just too pat, or saccharine, for comfort. For an
instance why: I snapped tetchily at my wife earlier tonight,
because she complained that I was again over-feeding our
(grossly overweight) golden retriever.

While she stormed off to collapse, after a long hard day
coping with our two hyper-active girls, I finished cooking and
eating a meal. I felt better after eating and at first attributed my
temper to low blood sugar, thinking, nice man that I am, I'd
give her the apology.

As suddenly it occurred to me that my blowing it had more
to do with all the psycho-analytic dredging I've been at here.
So I went and put it to my wife that I possibly barked at her
because her nagging reminded me of my mother. Was it
equally possible, I suggested, that I had not forgiven my
mother, or forgotten the thrashings...but that, deep down, I
still resented her...to the point of hatred?

I'm afraid that we agreed it was a lot more than possible...
"Whenever you have mentioned your mother" my wife
observed, "or those "beatings, you seem to change..." (From
the benign to the malevolent.) "...You do seem full of

resentment...of hatred for her."

So I guess maybe I have been carrying it around all these years, which might explain a lot about my more neurotic personality traits...from the self-destructive alcoholism to a sense of personal and emotional insecurity that bordered on paranoia at times.

Any competent shrink could link symptoms to underlying syndrome here – as the turning inwards of a hatred that I could not cope with consciously, partly because it conflicted with my later idea of myself as a positive, creative type – one who felt largely uncluttered, or unconditioned, by the psychopathogenic influences of my childhood.

If that is the case it makes partial nonsense of my professed feelings (at the end of chapter seven), as a form of wishful thinking at odds with the actuality. Put bluntly, it implies that I was screwed up by the Mammy, far more than I'd like to admit. If so, I have matured, insofar as I have, in spite of that. And if I do have hatred in me, at least I have never lived merely to feed it.

To the contrary, my disposition, if not exactly loving, has always inclined towards helping, rather than hindering or harming, others. – A far more common trait, I believe, than our self-lacerating Culture ever realises. Most of us mean well!

In attempting to do so, we may always safely assume that some parts of us (natural or nurtured) incline to the opposite, and try to take account of them as our enemy. In the final analysis, we can all only try, in this life – not least to discover, acknowledge, confront, or transcend our faults, foibles and afflictions, as inevitable concomitants of any human Being. The more we can learn to know ourselves, accordingly, the better our chances of effectively using our mind and will to take fuller control of our lives.

Incidentally, you will find a lot more of the above kind of positive thinking in the books of Abraham Maslow (1908-1970), who was, for my money, one of the greatest psychologists of the twentieth century.

He promulgated a psychology based on his studies of mentally healthy people – while Freud *et al* were concerned only with extrapolations about human nature based on their treatment of the mentally sick.

(I realise that words like 'healthy' and 'sick' in this context are nowadays loaded and deemed suspect as highly relative terms – but few could disagree that happiness is preferable to misery, if you want to switch and match words here.)

However, Maslow is more relevant in present context as a man who greatly overcame his own faulted family nurture – as well as his persecution, as a young Jewish boy in New York, by anti-Semitic Irish and Italian Roman Catholics.

His mother seems to have been close to raving lunacy.

He remembered her, in a snatch of autobiographical reminiscence, as "the type that's called schizophrenogenic in the literature – she's the one who makes crazy people, crazy children..." He goes on: "I was awfully curious to find out why I didn't go insane. I was certainly neurotic, extremely neurotic, during all my first twenty years – depressed, terribly unhappy, lonely, isolated, self-rejecting, and so on – but in theory it should have been much worse."

Casting back, he realised that he owed his sanity to an uncle, his mother's brother, who lived nearby and "took care of me...He may have saved my life, psychically..."*

Reading that kind of thing also helps one to put one's own experience into objective perspective. My own mother, with her random streak of madness, was pretty anodyne in comparison. As I have indicated, she had her sound maternal qualities too, which would have been my own equivalent to the above avuncular influence. There was, in a word, Love. At least enough to keep me from losing too many marbles.

---

* *Cited in 'New Pathways in Psychology', by Colin Wilson. Gollancz. 1972. p.131. (Wilson also played me Maslow's tape of that.)*

* * *

I cannot kill this troublesome topic yet! It seems that everything they say about rigorous self-analysis as traumatic in itself applies here.

I am surprised myself at the extent of my personal turmoil, after rummaging around in the roots of my character, motivation and personality. But it also seems to be true that, once you begin such self-analysis, or try to be really honest and unsparing with and about your Self, the process become self-catalytic, and it is as if a dam bursts somewhere deep in the Psyche...triggering the release of even more deeply repressed memories...and not without even more intense mental pain.

In my own case, having, as I imagined, said all I needed to say and finally completed the chapter – with the above then tacked on – I started the next (on Radio) with manifest relief. But apparently my unconscious, or subconscious, mind, having been so stirred up, determined to seize the opportunity to express itself more resolutely.

I began to sleep badly and experienced some febrile dreams.

Then I began to feel 'persecuted' in a way that I haven't since distant bouts of post-alcoholic remorse. Going for my daily swim I imagined that the pool attendants were laughing at me – totally absurd, as I know them far too well for anything of the sort.

What the devil was the matter with me?

It took me a few days to realise that I had, in the jargon, somehow 'regressed', as a consequence of the self-analysis, and that I was again reacting defensively to my environment as I had in my early years. Then I gradually began to really remember...

* * *

I remembered that my mother had given me a gleaming little

pedal-car, when I was Four or Five. I remembered pedalling out of our front gate, very pleased and proud with my new toy. Then, another child appeared, told me they wanted the car, and simply commandeered it. I gave it over without any protest and just stood there watching mutely as it was 'driven' away...

My mother comes bursting out of our house, swoops on the little thief, hauls them out...before escorting me and car back home...Then...she is shouting at me, telling me I am ungrateful, spineless, a "little coward"...before she takes down my trousers and canes me angrily.

She beats me for not standing up for myself, for not fighting back.

My mother hates "a coward", irrespective of age. That, I'm almost certain, was when the beatings first began. She began to mark me, to try and make a man of me. (Later on, just for the hell of it.)

The scenario repeats itself, whenever I am being victimised or bullied by other children. They begin to know that my mother is always watching out for her "little angel", from behind the curtains and make a game of tormenting me, for her reaction...She never fails to come dashing out to 'rescue' me and it is great sport to see her...and to run away from me (and her) with peals of laughter.

I get beaten repeatedly for being such a hopeless case. As a result, if I am shy and timid to begin with, I now become more and more so...to the extent that I begin to feel permanently on guard, defensive, persecuted. I spend half my time waiting to be taunted, mocked and generally laughed at. This must have gone on for a very long time and been so emotionally damaging that I could not bear even to remember it later...so I buried it, for all these years. It explains an enduring streak of fearfulness in my nature, a residual sense of defensiveness – it used to be a feeling that something unpleasant is always about to happen – a cloying distrust of certain (always 'non-artistic') people (more intelligently confined today, and that rarely, to their motives); a preferential need to humour and placate others, to make them like me...and above all that cowardly tendency, which took me years to decisively dispel, to avoid open confrontation at all costs.

I remember now that the other kids used to jeer me because my mother gave me hot milk at bedtime! They obviously found out somehow and regarded it, for whatever reason, as the perfect proof that I was in effect a milk-sop. How those jeers made me squirm in misery! And no doubt equally 'petty' jibes – but never of course petty to the child who is victimised.

It got so bad – my peer image! – that kids of my own age began to avoid me; to be seen even talking to me branded the talker as another cissy; to 'play' with the Mamma's Boy was right out of line. So I had to find my friends among younger children...where oddly enough (or fortunately for my otherwise devastated young persona) I became a Leader. I organised a little gang of infants, stuck with that and got some kind of relief!

I remember another incident. Christmas. I am given a lovely pair of six-guns in a holster. I go for a walk, feeling like Hopalong Cassidy. Down in Annamoe, among the Corporation houses, two gurriers threaten me, or effectively 'mug' me (the eternal mug) and take the guns and holster. I finally return home, to confess my crime (in being so easily robbed). Pandemonium. A caning. A futile search of the entire neighbourhood, hand in hand with irate Mammy, with no sign of thieves or guns. Confirming anew my gormlessness, my inability to 'stand up'...

* * *

But why then – I ask myself, much as Maslow asked himself above – did I not grow up (in my own case) a complete namby-pamby, or a terminally dispirited twerp? With no courage, no spirit, no ambition – wanting only to hide and cower...

More memories. She pestered my father to teach me how to box. He gives me some lessons. My heart isn't in it, but I do my best to learn. I must have learned something. For one day, I am Nine or Ten, a boy picks on me, as usual. Now I have always known, that I am not a coward. This time, again for whatever reason - possibly the last straw reason! – I hit back. The kid recoils. Other kids sense infallibly (as kids do at such times) that something is up. The angel is not backing off, or running away – more hilarious, he's trying to look tough! They crowd around us, egging him on – "do him!" (meaning me), "do him!!". I still square up. I am not afraid of him. I am if anything desperate to prove something here. And I know again, deep in my heart, that if I give in now...my life will be forever hell.

I hit out, punching him on the chest, just a little gratified to see the surprise on his face. He hits me back in the stomach. The gang cheer. I don't care. I'm beyond caring as I'm beyond fearing. I hit out again.

Then, as the others are cheering him on harder than ever, almost hysterical with delight at the thought of my getting pasted, a boy of my own age, one of a large macho family down the street, shouts: "Give him a chance! Give Gay a chance! COME ON GAY!!"

I glance at him with a look of gratitude bordering on love. He is on my side. He wants me to win! I positively go for the other kid. He comes back hard. He's no coward either. And I sense respect. He now knows that he has a real fight on his hands. We really start to slug. Something snaps in the gang too - one or two of them begin to cheer me on, adding their come on Gays to those of my original champion.

My mother comes rushing onto the scene. "Stop it!" she howls, "stop it at once!" We stop, still glaring at each other. The others shuffle about awkwardly. But no one is laughing or jeering now. Someone says: "It's all right Missis Duffy. They're only sparrin."

I stare at her. She's looking at me oddly.

Someone else says: "Make up lads. Shake on it."

I shake hands with Joe Louis. We half-grin at each other. My mother is turning on her heel, sniffing, bidding me follow her home. But for once I don't. I guess I know I mustn't. I dawdle awhile as the audience breaks up. There is a smell of sportsmanship in the air.

"Tanks for cheerin me on" I say to the kid. "Ye're a pal."

He shrugs: no big deal. Like hell it wasn't.

He and me became good pals after that. And I'm pretty sure that the bullying ceased and that I began to be accepted increasingly by the peers as a result. By Eleven or Twelve I was certainly one of the main gang.

Relations with my mother were never the same again. Whether because of that incident, or (as I said previously), partly because of my age and growth, I do not recall any more canings afterwards.

*   *   *

Now the set above will be familiar to any young man of the world! There are times when physical self-assertion is the only way to win respect. And it never fails to impress – even if you're beaten a point is made.

Unfortunately I didn't learn from the experience.

So although I was henceforth free of bullying in my home neighbourhood, I continued to suffer and be victimised by bullies at school. The trouble being that I wasn't only naturally shy and timid (unless really provoked) but I also had the essentially pacific temperament of a born dreamer.

I wanted a quiet life and the experienced school bully is a past master at exploiting such mildness. He is adroit at persecuting on the sly and knows precisely when to back off, or change his tune, to leave you floundering in humiliation. I suffered agonies at the hands of such snide characters at times. If only I'd known that this kind of bully is invariably a coward and that he pulls back at the first signs of real anger. Not because he is smarter (or indeed stronger) than you but because he fears real confrontation a great deal more than you do! A dose of the above hard medicine will stop any such bullying dead in its tracks.

There is a section in 'Borstal Boy' where Behan comes up against a young bully in his first days at the borstal. This little miscreant makes Brendan's life miserable, with all the usual sly ploys and taunts, leading the other 'offenders' to see BB as soft; they begin to walk on him also. Behan stops it by walking casually up to his tormentor in a workshop and tearing his face open with one slash of an awl.

Behan gets a spell in solitary. But no one bothers him again.

By the time I read that I had finally learned my own lesson. Or had it rammed down my throat, long after I left school alas, when I turned on a workmate who plagued me, lost my temper with him, challenged him to fight...and been absolutely winded when he went pale, backed off and practically kissed my arse thereafter. I'd laid that ghost forever.

Indeed, one night in a Dublin pub I met a sly young man who had perpetually bullied and tormented me in my first two years of secondary school. We got to drinking and talking and he said he was "amazed" to see me in a pub. After saying he was sorry he'd "pestered" me added: "I always thought you were such a goody-goody – such a molly! You used to infuriate me because you acted so superior and never hit back."

"What if I had hit out?" I asked.

"I'd 'a run a fuckin mile - that's what!"

Enough said!

* * *

So if we dig back to what finally preserved me from total wimpishness in later life, it probably goes back to my first experience of standing up for myself. But it is not always necessary to resort to fisticuffs, or physical violence in general, to do that. It is often enough, as I went on to learn – as my final example above indicates – simply to show temper – or to "lose your rag", in Dublinese. Which leads me to conclude that the most valuable lesson you can teach any shy timid kid is – <u>how to lose his temper</u>.

I always thought there was shame in it, that it was the mark of an inferior nature. It is not. To the contrary, there is nothing like losing your temper for clearing the air when warranted. While there is nothing quite so effective as losing it deliberately and creating a controlled explosion! Real development is bringing yourself to a point where you become a person who is obviously capable, a: of losing your temper and b: of following up physically if necessary.

Some people are born with this knowledge - not many I fear.

* * *

Anyway, the contemporary sense of persecution went as I delved into the childhood anew and began to make notes for the above section.

While it lasted, the paranoid state of mind made me grateful that I no longer booze – not least because my benders had begun to result in self-lacerating hangovers of a kind one couldn't pin down – taking one dangerously close to nervous breakdown and mental collapse.

I found myself thinking of Evelyn Waugh's terrifying 'classic' account of such dreadful depression – as applied to a heavy drinker (based on Waugh himself) in 'The Ordeal of Gilbert Pinfold'. And going on to wonder if perhaps the terror, fear and persecution mania of such states, is partly based on an alcoholic (or post-alcoholic) state of mind that actually reflects the buried psychic residue of childhood trauma.

Considering that such buried humiliations often contribute to a sense of inferiority that drives a person to drink in the first place, it is not unreasonable to suggest that the inhibition-shattering action of alcohol also dredges up the horrible repressed memories, in a vague and confused way...voiding them through unsettling hallucinations and overstressed emotional feelings. 'Pinfold' is frightening as the record of such an 'irrational' affliction, which seems beyond the reach of any known psychotherapy and thus very close to that most irretrievable mental condition: complete insanity...total madness.

In which case excessive drinking does not make us mad, but uncovers the madness we all harbour, to lesser or greater extent, as a consequence of our worst experiences in early life...

* * *

Deep self-analysis may provoke the same shattering emotional effect and expose the cherished self-image we have cultivated as a sham, a travesty of our real nature, a mask set upon the fearful, vulnerable, child within! It does have the great advantage, over drink or drug-induced states of mind, in that it is a deliberate controlled attempt to attain self-knowledge, within a fundamentally psycho-therapeutic framework.

For example, in a recent biography of him, John Cleese is quoted as saying that his first sessions in rigorous self-analysis reduced him to a gibbering, persecuted depressive for a period of ten days or so. He persisted in tearing his Psyche open nonetheless, working closely with an excellent professional psycho-therapist, to finally 'break through' and attain a new insight into his Being.

He thus discovered that you can confront your buried Self, emerge the better for it, and begin to accept yourself in a new way – as well as liking yourself more justifiably, despite the newly-discovered warts of character or personality! There is a great benefit in seeing ourselves for what we really are, or even seeing ourselves as others see us, as part of any exercise in self-discovery and self-improvement.

* * *

As to what we were, in our childhood innocence, as we attempted to cope with our surroundings then...it can be most instructive to remember (or rediscover) that little 'person', in analysing how we became the person we are now. Much of what we do in later life is greatly determined by those early experiences. What are we trying to prove, for example? Are we, in our adult thinking and behaviour, 'compensating' in some way?

In her autobiography, Enid Starkie recounts a happy upbringing in upper middle class Dublin. She remembers "a mamma's boy", Willie Teeling, as an effete Christopher Robin who later "surprised us all" by becoming a famous adventurer and explorer in desert climes. Was Willie 'compensating' and proving 'something'? Perhaps. (I realise that in this context, persecution can become, paradoxically, a spur!)

Enid herself, 'a nice respectable Dalkey girl', later produced the best ever biography of that archetypical diabolical: the poet Arthur Rimbaud. We wonder Why? To conclude only that we are all highly complicated and always liable to develop, whatever our upbringing, in divers ways.

Incidentally that great modern explorer, Ranulph Fiennes, tells us, in his autobiography, that he was sometimes bullied unmercifully as a boy, and, contrary to what you might expect of such a courageous man, would have done "anything to stop it", or placate the persecutor.

However, if we cannot predict The Adult from The Child, there are limits to what a child can endure before he is marked

113

badly for life. One thinks of Oscar Wilde...dressed as a girl in his infancy. Or the unhappy German poet, Rainer Maria (!) Rilke (1875-1926), similarly humiliated – his mother calling him "my little Sophie".

I think that both of these men (understandably enough) buried their earliest memories, shied away from too much self-delving as adults and never fully realised just how much of their childhood misery inhered...to taint and maim. For as Jean Jacques Rousseau (1712-1778), who started a whole movement for 'fearless self-revelation' by his 'Confessions', remarks therein: "It is not what is shameful or humiliating we hesitate to confide, but that which makes us ridiculous."

It therefore took tremendous courage on his part, to work up to a point where he could confess, publicly, that he used to expose himself to servant girls as a sexually frustrated young man. Even then, he was 54 before he could begin to attempt to expose everything, and it took him four hard years to complete the book and show the world what he really was – or 'where he was from', as the Americans say. The book is a sad tale of criminally stunted growth at times and contains a powerful indictment of Christian Education, both as Rousseau endured it and as a causative factor in the coarsening of a fine character.

Fortunately for him perhaps, it was published after his death, as the unending tale of persecution skirts the territory of outright insanity and would have made it impossible for a live author to avoid a lot more of both.

Yet it directly inspired such a great spirit as Goethe, both to write his own masterly memoirs and to say that that "the greatest work of all literature would be a truly honest autobiography". One can but try...

Happily, unlike Rousseau, or Goethe, we live in times where frank openness is increasingly accepted and true honesty is not regarded as ridiculous. But it has taken two millennia for the words of Heraclitus to sink in: "I am a man, therefore nothing human can be strange to me."

* * *

I remember that I occasionally tormented Tibby, the family cat, pinning it down and hitting it with hard cushions...much as I was tormented by my mother...Just in case you think that I never merited a thrashing.

(There displaying the kind of behaviour that can turn abused kids into adult monsters. Fortunately my temperament was not essentially sadistic.)

...I also remember a day – I cannot have been more than Six or Seven - when I was playing in Carnew Street, near my great-aunt's house. I had a kind of vision and the definite conviction that I was 'different', and that I should never let myself be influenced too much by other people.

I think that greatly explains why I never, finally, took anyone too seriously, or caved in because of anything they did to me...or, in due course, held blindly to everything they believed in or followed slavishly, when my own intellect or best instincts revolted.

Of course I was different. But we all are. And we should never forget it, never forget the little kernel of true individuality that is our common inheritance as fundamentally free-thinking, diverse, idiosyncratic, uniquely self-constituted members of the human race.

If we do that, we also have a way of dealing with any thoughts and feelings to the contrary – including those based on our subconscious retention of fears and self-doubt, as a result of childhood intimidation or negative acculturation.

Correspondingly, more aware of our individual right to be different, we are less likely to remain gunged or dispirited by those who have browbeaten or bullied us in our vulnerable childhood – from a deranged parent or malicious playmate to all of those officially sanctioned ignoramuses who told you what to think and how to behave, in their own interests or for 'religious', political, or social designs.

*   *   *

But Amen, to the deadly dredging. There is more to life than Egotism!

...Almost time now, to go to the cinema. – 'Coming Shortly', in the words of the old Trailer, after we first listen to the radio.

CHAPTER NINE

"Wakey Way-key!"
        – BBC Bandmaster Billy Cotton
Thus he opened his Sunday Lunchtime 'Bandshow' – Time To
Get Up!

*   *   *

The Forties and early Fifties were indeed Radio Times – the
title of that longstanding BBC weekly magazine which listed
programmes; it is nowadays equally devoted to television,
including commercial and satellite.

*   *   *

In that pre-transistor era we listened in on valve-fired sets
which took awhile to 'warm up' and the big wooden radio
cabinet was our television then, with only the facetious BBC
Goon Show going out "in glorious colour".

The overall effect of Radio on us was incalculable.

Cosy evenings in darkened rooms, illuminated only by the
yellow light from the tuning strip; fiddling between light,
medium and shortwave and hearing English, Irish and foreign
accents in turn.

You could get Radio Eireann and the BBC clearly at any
time, while reception from places farther afield was a matter of
luck and atmospherics.

Listening in to most of the foreign names displayed was
near nigh impossible on the average receiver; we soon gave up

trying to get Hilversum or Kalundberg, although you could always pick up Radio Moscow on the Short – during a broadcast in English if you timed it well.

It sounded just a bit like the BBC. We concluded that Paris, Berlin, Vatican City and the rest were emblazoned on the station guide panel just to fill the thing up a bit. No loss – who spoke French or German anyway? (To us "Sessy Bonn" was, like Issy Bonn, a BBC comedian.)

So, you had Radio Eireann, morning, noon and night only – off the air when decent people were all out at work and gone again by 11pm, when decent people went to bed. The BBC Home Service came on for the farmer at 6am, carrying on through the day till 11 or midnight. Forces Radio, later the Light Programme – the only reason you needed that Wave – came on when a Gentleman awoke, about 9, and stayed with its audience in time-tandem with the Home, until the butler climbed to his eyrie.

The BBC Third Programme began in 1946, but I never bothered with it until I was well into my teens, as a specialised service dedicated to intellectuals and classical music lovers.

Turning into the teens I discovered that (commercial) Radio Luxembourg, AFN (the American Forces Network) and The Voice of America were all readily tunable in Dublin. More of them as we go on.

* * *

My very first vivid memory of radio was the BBC's 'Listen With Mother', which you did every weekday just after lunch. That also provides my first musical memory: 'Polly Put The Kettle On'. "Suki took it off again".* Naughty. After the Song, the Story. Avuncular and avauntular voices: "Are you sitting comfortably?" Yes, I yam. "Then we'll begin!"

* Still with us, on kiddy video.

118

Schooldays began with Radio Eireann in the morning. All the morning and lunchtime programmes had sponsors and ran for 15 minutes, interrupted by the boring old News, at 9am and 1.30. – Next News at 7.

Some later Big Name entertainers and actors, who 'made it', often in England, began our mornings on RE. Eamonn Andrews, Milo O'Shea and his wife Maureen Toal spring to mind. 'Milo and Maureen' being a very tightly scripted fifteen minute sit-com, with the emphasis on comedy.

Lunchtime provided a twice weekly saga of a soap opera, 'The Kennedy's of Castlerosse' – 1 to 1.15 – sponsored, I think, by Fry Cadbury's (chocolate). Many other sponsors I do clearly remember, with their little slogans dreamed up the Irish version of Madison Avenue – an incidental longterm vindication of the power of advertising.

You had Donnelly's "skinless sausages – never burst or break on the pan"; the Imco Dry Cleaners, Merrion, jingle – "a cleaning and a pressing and a dying for you" (dye becomes die: cute offer); Mitchelstown Creameries, "the home of good cheese"; a special blend of 'luxury' tea, to be drunk "down to the last golden drop". Waltons Irish Music Shop sponsored fifteen minutes of "the songs our fathers loved".

The announcers were generally graduates of some elocution academy and there was a Radio Eireann 'voice', as there was a 'posh' BBC.

The majority of the programmes featured "popular recordings", interspersed with the commercial message, and this is as good a place as any to look back at the popular music of the time.

* * *

My own earliest musical memories correspond with many of the songs and tunes remembered by Woody Allen in his movie 'Radio Days'. Although some of those American hits from the late-Thirties and early-Forties continued to be played by RE and the BBC well into the Fifties.

'When You Wish Upon a Star' for example, made a long-standing impact, as the closing music for the last sponsored programme of the day on RE – the Irish Hospital Sweepstakes half-hour – see also below.

A lot of Glenn Miller...and Bing (from 'Trade Winds' (1940) and 'McNamara's Band' (1946) to 'Galway Bay' (1948); his 'Silent Night' and 'Jingle Bells' helped 'make' many a 'White Christmas'...'Don't Fence Me In', with his 'pals', The Andrews Sisters)...Hoagy 'Ole Buttermilk Sky' Carmichael, Nelson Eddy...Judy Garland's 'Over the Rainbow' and 'Trolley Song'...the first bursts from Perry Como (1946) and Doris Day (1947) – much later crowned Queen with 'Que Sera Sera'. ...Some virtual 'standards': 'Lili Marlene', 'Paper Doll' and 'You Always Hurt the One You Love' (both The Mills Brothers), "Money is the root of all evil" (emphasis by the solo Andrews,), 'Begin the Beguine', 'Alexander's Ragtime Band' (Bing and Al Jolson), 'Glow-Worm', 'Buttons and Bows'...

A song called 'The Fat Man' (1948) I never remember hearing played – by rock-herald Fats Domino.

(I must have heard Bing sing 'How Can You Buy Killarney' in '46 or '47, for I'm fairly certain that I was 'covering' that, for the clergy in my great-aunt's parlour, long before the Lee Lawrence hit of 1949).

Much-played English pops of that era, included those from the war years: Vera 'We'll Meet Again' Lynn and Gracie Fields; 'Run Rabbit Run' and 'We're Gonna Hang Out the Washing on the Siegfried Line' by Flanagan and Allen; the pre-war 'A Nightingale Sang in Berkeley Square' and art deco period orchestral numbers by (Bert!) Ambrose or the lush Mantovani string ensemble - a big '47 hit with 'Hear My Song, Violetta'. In 1946 Issy Bonn was singing 'Let Bygones Be Bygones'. He melted many a lady's heart in '47 with 'May I Call You Sweetheart?'

By the turn of the new decade we were well into the best days of the American 'Crooner': King Bing, Sinatra, Vic Damone, Tony Bennett, Perry Como, Eddie Fisher, Nat King Cole; moon, spoon and June. Not to forget Al Martino, the first Number One when UK pop charts began.

On the borderlands of croonerdom and somewhere else, Johnny Ray, Frankie Laine, Tennessee Ernie Ford and Guy Mitchell became virtual icons. 'Cry', 'Jezebel', 'Sixteen Tons' and 'She Wore Red Feathers and a Hula Hula Skirt' were the kind of songs that wowed the aficionado. Rosemary Clooney shook your shingles with 'Come on-a My House' and we sang and hummed it for weeks. – Its folksy lyrics, I later discovered, were the work of Armenian-American writer William Saroyan, whose short stories became a passion in my teens.

More diverse pop memories include 'Tzena, Tzena, Tzena' and "Balleree, Baller-a-ha-ha-ha" (a kids choir sing the Alps), pumping 'Sugarbush' (Day and Laine), voice-thrashing Teresa Brewer, Kay Starr's 'Wheel of Fortune', Lita Roza sobbing through 'Allentown Jail', vamping Eartha Kitt, Sincere Dinah Shore, Miss Patti Page ('Tennessee Waltz'), Jo Stafford ('Shrimp boats are a comin')...Danny Kaye's 'The Ugly Duckling'...'The Galloping Major' ("I'm riding on my charg-er") and a convulsive 'Laughing Policeman' (who just couldn't stop his ha-ha-ing).

The Chordettes 'Mister Sandman' played interminably, as did 'Vaya Con Dios', by Les Paul and Mary Ford – whose 'multi-track' guitaring later inspired almost every hep-cat who picked up a twanger, from Presley to The Beatles and Hendrix.

There were Novelty Groups like The Ink Spots – "will ye listen to that bass – jayse he must have a larynx down to his boots". There were novelty songs, proving anew that a 'catchy' tune needs no lyrical coherence: 'Does a Puff-Puff Go Choo-Choo?', or (still playing, Woody): 'Maisy dotes and Dotsie dotes and little lambsy divey' (??).

We had Singing Cowboys like Gene Autry and Roy Rogers

– "A four-legged friend, a four-legged friend, he'll never let you down" – with Trigger whinnying off-mike. Anne Shelton or The Luton Girls Choir were a letdown after Roy. As was Ronnie 'In a Monastery Garden' Ronalde, who yodelled like a Swiss and mimicked birdsong. – "'Je hear about the preg-ant sparrow Ronnie? She opened her legs for a lark."

Waltz or schmaltz seemed to soothe my mother's schizophrenia* and we often listened together harmoniously. 'Blue Tango', 'Swiss Rhapsody'...her great favourite was 'Greensleeves'. (Father favoured John McCormack.)

Many of the Broadway Show-stoppers caught on mightily from the late-Forties, as well as those from customised Hollywood Musicals. E.g.: Show Boat, New Faces (sinuous Eartha Kitt), Oklahoma!, Kiss Me Kate, An American in Paris, Annie Get Your Gun, Seven Brides for Seven Brothers; all with hits from master lyricists. Doris Day was good as buckskin cowgirl Calamity Jane, belting it out bravura in The Golden Garter Saloon.** We (boys) went off her when she went coy as unfingered virgin in buttons and bows, gingham-singing soppy songs in even soppier pictures. (While Astaire and 'Singin in the Rain' Kelly were "dazzes".)

Billy Eckstine, Sidney Bechet and Louis Armstrong ('Mack The Knife') brought a first whiff of Jazz, which would become an interest in itself after we saw the Eddy Duchin, Benny Goodman and Glenn Miller biopics.

If Ellington's drummer Louis Bellson got you going with the hit 'Skin Deep' (1954), a year later every boy in Dublin was beating dustbin-lids after watching Gene Krupa stormin' away for Goodman, in fabled Carnegie Hall. That he was rumoured to be "a drug-addict" only enhanced his glamour.

---

* *Whether she did have a touch of that or not, it is apparently the case, writes Brenda Maddox in a biography of Nora Joyce, that modern Ireland has a rate three to five times more than most western countries.*

** *"Gentlemen and Gentlemen", the MC memorably addressed its patrons.*

We also had some local Eckstine and 'Satchmo' imitators, as well as a few Nat King Coles and Frankie Laines.

Such themes as 'High Noon', 'Shane' and later, 'The Man With The Golden Arm' became big hits long before the films were released in Dublin – providing in effect the best kind of advance publicity.

Although British film themes, like Larry Adler's score for 'Genevieve', or 'The Dambusters March', achieved equal popularity, you seldom got the same buzz from English Pop as you did from the slicker Yank performers. – Notable exceptions being Eddie 'O Mein Papa'* Calvert ("the man with the golden trumpet"), and virtuoso pianist Winifred Atwell ("queen of the keyboard") – who duly found world stardom through Radio Luxembourg. Pure-voiced Ruby Murray ('The Belfast Rose') hit big with 'Softly Softly'. The less said about 'Little Red Monkey' (obstreperous radio comic Jimmy Edwards toiling to appeal to tiny tots), the better. Jimmy Shand and his (Accordion) Band were played interminably, until you went right off 'foot-tapping Scottish Airs'.

Dickie Valentine, David 'Cara Mia'** Whitfield, Frankie Vaughan, Ronnies Carroll and Hilton...headed a cosy of Brit Crooners. Sassy Survivor Jimmy Young both doubled for Guy Mitchell and covered some Frankie Laine hits. In general and although we wouldn't know a record production value if we saw one, there was a broad consensus (as with the comics) that American product was best.

'English' Traditional Jazz, as played by the Chris Barber Band, was "out on its own" and comparable with any from New Orleans. A mix of Trad and Mainstream by the Humphrey Lyttleton outfit was equally esteemed. 'Humph' had his pop-ularity crowned with one enormous hit, 'Bad

First ever instrumental to sell 3 million-plus worldwide.

That topped the charts in the U.S.,where he also became the first British male vocalist to sell a million. (We still didn't like it.)

Penny Blues', which used boogie-woogie piano to maximum effect and appealed to even the tone-deaf. The great Ted Heath big band scored another bull with 'Swingin' Shepherd Blues', trilling all and sundry at a later time (1958) when rock and roll was otherwise ruling the roost.

My own conversion to a newer form of jazz was the result of a spaced out little girl playing me "a fantastic record" she'd just bought: Johnny Dankworth's 'Experiments With Mice'. Soon after I heard Mel Torme's 'Mountain Greenery' and was hooked to become a 'modernist'.

Indeed I remember we had quite a few jazz fans in our locality and a sniffy kind of musical snobbery grew up between 'cool' modernists and 'square' Trad buffs. A friend baffled me by liking both.

* * *

Staid Radio Eireann had no problem playing the occasional bit of jazz, which they seemed to treat, quite correctly, as a musical improvement on the average pabulum of Pop. The station's own Irish Hospital Requests took over from the sponsors on Wednesday lunchtime and usually included a couple of "Jasmin" (as Colshies said Jazz Men) in their play list.

Transmission closed for the weekday with the Irish Hospitals Sweepstakes half-hour, possibly reflecting its importance as a foreign currency earner. Oddly enough Guinness, the most important commercial concern in the country, never used radio; presumably, in that case, because they knew that their customers needed no encouragement to drink.

Radio Eireann became unlistenable when they remembered their basic Charter and put out programmes in Gaelic, or otherwise broadcast Gaelic games and events of limited interest to the average schoolboy.

I was nearly put off Synge and O'Casey for life by being

forced to listen to their plays on Sunday afternoons, long before I could understand a word of it. For some reason the adults pretended to like this stuff; although, truth be told, they only listened for a laugh at the expense of peasant or gurrier (while ostensibly celebrating Irish Literary Art).

High Mass was broadcast on Sunday morning, but easily evaded on the basis that you attended Low Mass (the short one) anyway.

Apart from that I do not recall much religion 'on the radio', or any pestering to listen to it. The Angelus Bells were tolled twice a day, at Noon and 6pm – you 'blessed yourself' and said a quick prayer. (It must already be apparent that Catholicism was never my own passion.)

As I come to the polymorphous diversity of the BBC, I am reminded of a bit of competition from RE in the detective serial stakes: 'Meet Michael Sullivan'. You met him two or three nights a week. He was a Dublin Private Eye, domiciled in exclusive Merrion Square and spoke in the best kind of clipped tension-filled English. A Raffles without the Bunny, or a Batman without the 'ward', he consorted less ambiguously with a silken-voiced woman who we all fantasised about – boys and girls alike. A sterling thief-catcher too; I forget when or why they took him off – possibly because they ran out of storyline.

And, as I come first to BBC Comedy, I recall also a brief Sunday series on RE, 'Living With Lynch', featuring Joe Lynch in comic scenes from Dublin life. Inclined to brash street-humour, it had its moments, but clashed with superior fodder from across the Irish Sea.

*   *   *

Anyone who sat glued to their set on Sunday lunchtimes, in those truly great years of Radio, will forever celebrate the wonderful, bountiful BBC – just on these weekly hearings alone. That was perfect product.

Forget the Billy Cotton Bandshow, which came on about Two with cockney songs ('I've Got A Luverly Bunch Of Coconuts')*, 'swinging' Sousa marches, and an awful jokey atmosphere, between bandleader Cotton, lead-singer Alan "Breezy" Breeze and various "drunks" – as bumptious BC called his sidemen. That signalled a mass exodus of kids, before their elders switched over to Radio Eireann and corralled them for some even more diabolical GAA sports fixture.

The real listening began much earlier, around Noon, with 'Two-Way Family Favourites', one of the best record programmes then on the BBC. Here the Light remembered its roots as the Forces Programme and 'linked' live with Germany, to play selections requested by troops in occupation for their extended families in England, or vice versa. The BBC always did their best to be 'with it' then and you were sure of hearing the liveliest pops, a bit of good jazz, and a comedy number or two.

The high was between One and Two, as the family ate their Sunday Dinner, when there was always one and usually two, of those inimitable 30 minute comedy programmes. 'Take It From Here', with Jimmy Edwards and (Ted) 'Ray's A Laugh' introduced you to a kind of universal humour that was, no less than Trad, "out on its own".

This was Music Hall, after Dan Leno and Max Miller, 'made safe' for family listening – notwithstanding many risque double entendres – and brilliantly scripted by comic geniuses like Muir and Norden. (Think of tv's 'Cheers' as a measure of the consistent humorous quality.)

* *One, nonetheless, of a stream of smash hits by the ensemble.*

Their real brilliance – *pace* 'Cheers' – was a kind of balancing act, as writers, between light sexual innuendo and exaggerated rectitude, and the related transformation of 'everyday situations' into, often hilarious, comedy events.

It was all totally inoffensive, appealing both to children and the child in every adult, and expertly delivered by consummate comedians - masters, above all, of 'timing'.

The basic formula, of snappy joke-filled dialogue, catch-phrases and zany characterisation, provided the impetus for a series of such 'varieties'. Even when written around a major comic figure and titled accordingly – as in 'Ray's A Laugh' – they invariably featured a wealth of back-up talent, many of whom became as popular – often, later, more successful – than their Prime Mover.

Thus in 'Educating Archie', ventriloquist Peter Brough and his Dummy, Archie, became later eclipsed and forgotten, while their Stooge, Max Bygraves, went on to top the bill at the London Palladium and generally achieve a durable stardom. – He is still 'pulling' today.

We liked Archie well enough, and his friend Veronica – the role which gave Beryl Reid her big break, into major film parts etc. We enjoyed 'The Navy Lark' (Jon Pertwee/later tv's 'Doctor Who'). Popular double acts included old Hall troupers Jimmy Jewel and Ben Warriss, and a pair of fledgling newcomers: Eric Morecombe and Ernie Wise.

(Tony) 'Hancock's Half-Hour' (with Sid James and Hattie Jacques/the 'Carry On' film series) launched that Chaplinesque genius on the ugly twisted brick road of early fame and terminal alcoholism.

Dropping his marvellous writers, Galton and Simpson*, who took him to the pinnacle of popularity, was rather like The Marx Brothers discarding Perelman.

---

* *Moving on later to television they achieved, with 'Steptoe and Son', viewing figures of 20 million-plus - seldom since bettered.*

The humourous family sit-com, partly utilised in 'Take it From Here', otherwise got off to an indifferent start with a slow series about 'down-to-earth' Londoners, 'Meet The Huggetts' – although it gave coy Petula Clark the breaks. ('The Clitheroe Kid' and 'Al Read Show', playing on crude Northern English working-class humour, only baffled in Ireland.) The genre really took for us when 'Life With The Lyons' began, a not so everyday story of a scatty American family living in London.

Indeed that ran so successfully for several radio seasons as to warrant two feature films about their comedic domestics. Unerringly scripted by Bebe Daniels – who wrote herself in as addle-headed housewife – it used a dour Ben Lyon* as foil for his 'crazy' wife and children, with a razor-tongued Scottish house-keeper, Aggie, for added spice. Guest appearances by comic Vic Oliver, to spar with Ben, adroitly used the old Hope-Crosby routines.

(I suspect that young John Cleese learned a few lessons from Bebe and The Lyons when he came to drafting his inimitable 'Fawlty Towers'.) In England, the Lyons had earlier earned their spurs, by refusing to hightail it back to the States during the war. (Ben even becoming an ace pilot in the RAF.)

* * *

There is no doubt that Monty Python began with the Goon Show; a debt acknowledged when the Pythons fondly recruited Spike Milligan for their celluloid Goon Show, 'Life of Brian'. No one who did not experience it first-hand, at the age of 10 or 11, can possibly understand what that mould-breaking comedy programme did for us on a wet Sunday in Dublin. "What is this go on show?" drawled a toffee-nosed

* Often credited as the man (home in the US as a Fox executive in 1946) who revamped Norma Jean Baker as 'Marilyn Monroe'.

BBC Executive when they were angling to go on (the air). "Sounds damn silly to me."

So it was. Gloriously, insanely, silly, in a way that took nonsense light years beyond Edward Lear and Lewis Carroll, and seized our pristine imaginations more than the anarchic Marx Brothers ever had. E.G.: "There's someone screaming in agony."/"Lucky,I speak it fluently." Milligan, Harry Secombe, Peter Sellers and Michael Bentine (in the early series); they seemed to us, the four funniest men alive. All of them later big stars, with Sellers of course taking the world by storm. R.I.P.

The Goon Show was basically intelligent, in a way that any quick-witted kid could appreciate, but which often left the brain-deadened adult cold. In mocking The Raj and generally making fun of imperial conceits, the Goons also reflected a burgeoning state of mind, in England, that would duly find devastating expression in John Osborne's 'Look Back in Anger' and the attendant 'Angry Young Men' movement.

('Mad Magazine' prefigured a similarly radical trend in the States, which would take serious form in their 'Beat Generation'*.)

'Beyond our Ken'/later 'Round the Horne' provided a kind of nonsense that catered for bright and dull alike. 'Hosted' by an urbane English Gentleman-type, Kenneth Horne, it provided a splendid vehicle for the hilarious Kenneth Williams – a quite extraordinary mimic of dull officials and weirdoes. That broke new ground with a regular spot featuring Williams and Hugh Paddick as a gay 'couple'** and, by a witty mix of the ripe and innocuous, probably defused a great deal of our

* When I met Lawrence Ferlinghetti a few years ago (one of the original Beatniks, with Kerouac, Ginsberg and Burroughs), all that he wanted to talk to me about was…Monty Python and Fawlty Towers.

** Writers Barry Took and Dick Vosburgh were emboldened to do so by Sir John Wolfenden's Committee (1951-1957), which came out in favour of liberalising the laws against homosexuality in the UK.

prejudice in that area. – Brownies could be very funny, deliberately.

The late Marty Feldman, whose bulging eyes and Goon-Python antics made him a star on both sides of the Atlantic, also started out scripting for Horne.

* * *

So, the BBC Light Programme, Sundays, became an addiction.

Many comedy programmes featured a just-bearable 'musical interlude', by some wholesome singing group – even the Goons admitted a three minute harmonica player (Max Geldray) or Mayfair Club Singer (Ray Ellington). By the time the station had regressed, through Cotton, to more typically 'light' music – Mantovani, Geraldo, Semprini Serenade, 'Sing Something Simple' – we would be somewhere else. Graduating with age from playing cowboys and indians, to playing pontoon or poker, to taking a girl to the pictures.

For most of the week The Light was "a dead loss". If you happened to be at home you had 'Housewives Choice' or (factory) 'Music While You Work' – a relic of the War – in the mornings, with 'Mrs Dale's Diary' in the afternoons – sit-com about Doctor Dale's household. Ugh.

Although 'Housewives Choice' could have its moments, with a few hot hits of the day. If you could put up with fruity-voiced Announcers, like Godfrey Winn, who spoke just like a woman and talked, awfully, gushing about "my mother's birthday". He was only equalled by Beverley Nichols (a man withal!), who went on, purringly, about cats.

Other tolerable 'Light' programmes included 'Henry Hall's Guest Night', in the evenings; occasionally 'The Brains Trust', where the English intelligentsia, like Julian Huxley or Professor Joad, often sounded like they knew everything... about everything...Very Impressive!

If you were ever around to hear The Light (or RE) at closing time you had The Shipping Forecast...which had a certain flat poetic appeal*, as the announcer reeled off a meterological litany for mariners: Dogger, Fastnet, (I always thought they said 'Parsnip') German Bight, Humber, Lundy, Finisterre, Rockall, Shannon, Cromarty, Irish Sea – each location getting its barometric tab: wind, rain, squall or gale.

"Gale-force" winds and gale warnings were best heard about in bed.

* * *

During the school day it was the Home Service we rushed home to hear.

Once a week, 12.25 precisely, you had 'Worker's Playtime' – a carry on from the war years: basic Music Hall – which provided "thirty minutes of mirth, laughter and live popular music", before the weather forecast at Five-To-One got you retuning to Radio Eireann.

'Workers Playtime' always included a couple of stand-up comics. Three such howls were Tommy Trinder, "Cheerful" Charlie Chester and Cardew "The Cad" Robinson. – You also got them, cartoon-style, in 'Radio Fun' (comic). WP often gave a spot to promising young talents, like Bob Monkhouse. (Also still in full flight, on TV.)

Another day, at 12.25, you had 'A Life Of Bliss', a situation comedy starring George Cole as a shy batchelor of The Old

---

* Not lost on Joyce. A "Gael warning" is given towards the end of Finnegans Wake, "in the free state on the air" (Shem the Jackdaw's reference to Radio Eireann), followed by a short fractured meterological guide for Joyceian tars: "Eyrlands Eyot, Meganesia, Habitant and the onebut thousand insels, Western and Osthern Approaches".
  Who said that The Wake never makes good nonsense?

School. He was to find fame and fortune as a 'Spiv' (con-man) in the St. Trinian films and again as a major television star. Another one still going, strong as ever.

Or you had 'Desert Island Discs', created in 1942 by the late Roy Plomley; still picking 'castaways' on the same wavelength (now Radio Four). With, I have no doubt, as much appeal for today's schoolboy (and adult), as it encourages celebrities to talk about themselves and select eight records to take on an imaginary island. A surefire 'human interest' device, borne out by an entry as the longest-running record programme in the Guinness Book of Records.*

I cannot resist mentioning, not least as a sign of the changing times in Ireland, that Radio Eireann now has an entry for the longest continuous broadcast – to wit: "an unedited reading of Ulysses by James Joyce (1882-1941) lasting 29hr 38min 47 sec on 16-17 Jul 1982". (How he would have treasured the 47 seconds!)

Another attraction of the Home Service was its function as a 'repeat' broadcaster of The Goons and other Sunday varieties; sometimes at the same weekday slot, 12.25; more often in the nightly schedules.

After school, if you were home in time: 'Childrens Hour', with 'Uncle Mac' in charge of the format. This was directed largely at 'the children of decent, refined people' and seldom included a working class voice – except to mock or tease. Uncle Mac went mainly for the Marklin Electric market; the kids who had maids in the scullery and libraries in the annexe. Whether or not we sensed snobbery, we never took much to 'Children's Hour'. (Nor the Radio Eireann equivalent.)

'Dick Barton, Special Agent' was another matter entirely. A nightly (6.45-7pm) fifteen minute serial, with tongue-biting cliff-hangers, that cleared the streets of child-life in my early

---

* BBC's 'The Archers', "an everyday story of country folk", which we used to make fun of in 1951, is there as the longest-running radio soap.

years. Dick was into a London and regional version of poly-ethnicity: Cockney 'Snowy' White was his right-hand man, fitfully assisted by Jock (the Scot), a coal-Daied Welsh choirman and a darlin' Stage 'Paddy'. ("Begorrahbejabers Dick.")

"Jock! Snowy! Forget me! I'm a goner. Get the girl! Sav – aagh!" Doh-dah-dah dah dah dah, doh-dah-dah dah dah dah... prestissimo blast of signature tune ('The Devil's Gallop'), making the hairs rise on you.

"IS DICK BARTON A GONER? IS THIS THE END? Or can his friends get to him, get the girl...and all get out...before the reactor explodes? Listen in tomorrow, for another exciting episode of – Dick Barton!!!"

We'd listen! And how. But...not half as well as we did later, when 'Journey Into Space', 30 minutes one night a week, cleared the streets of all earthly life. That went out on The Light, after The News and Radio Newsreel and the gossipy 'magazine' In Town Tonight.

The brainchild of Charles Chilton, earlier mastermind behind a long-running western serial, 'Riders of the Range', this truly gripping piece of radio recounted, over several unmissable episodes, a British rocket-flight to the moon. Realistically crewed by a balanced mix of men, the technical meritocracy was captained by a True Brit Rockfist Rogan type (with a three digit I.Q.): Jet Morgan. Producer Chilton was indispensably assisted by the BBC Radiophonic Workshop, which devised superb electronic music and created a spellbinding 'unearthly' atmosphere, to hold you totally in thrall.

Along with the aforementioned 'Dan Dare' ('Eagle' and radio serial – see also below), a local plethora of 'junior' chemistry sets (vaguely connected with Space Scientism) and our random acquisition of a book 'The Flying Saucers Have Landed' (by one, George Adamski – "he went inside a saucer!"), this set some of us up to become lifelong fans of

Science Fiction. – A passion further inflamed by Hollywood. As I will recount shortly, after a final word on other aural influences...from our own sturdy old 'Pilot' Wireless Receiver.

* * *

Still in a stellar domain:

"You're listening to Radio Luxembourg, Station of the Stars! Broadcasting live from the Grand Duchy, on two-oh-eight metres in the medium waveband and forty nine metres on the shortwave."

Schoolboy Heaven. Two-Oh-Eight was Great. The Greatest.

Radio Luxembourg was first beamed purposefully at the U.K. in the Thirties, by maverick English advertisers who defied the BBC monopoly (and international broadcasting regulations). It thus partly initiated independent commercial radio for English listeners, in conjunction with two short-lived French-based stations and minor input from our own Radio Athlone – later deprivatised and relocated from the central plain to Dublin, to become (c.1938) Radio Eireann.

To puritanical Sir John Reith at the BBC, RL was always the real bogey. (Unlike the law-abiding French and Irish the Luxembourgers persistently refused to play cricket, or back off on appeal, with regard to invading BBC air-space. They also bribed (pre-war) legalised English 'relay' companies – an early commercial broadcasting venture not unlike today's landlined Cable TV – to boost transmission and augment their penetration of the U.K.) For Reith, an equally committed Christian, this was not merely unfair competition; it was also the work of the Devil - for they had the complete gall to broadcast frivolity on The Sabbath (against hymns on the Beeb). Moreso after the War, when the occupying Nazis had installed a really powerful transmitter and made Lux a Voice of The Reich, so that it could now be picked up, on its own megawattage, as far to the west as Ireland.

A new generation of enterprising Englanders thanked the Nazi for leaving all this magnificent equipment intact – if only by bungling his attempt to dynamite the transmitter before he fled, Summer 1944. It enabled freed RL to saturate the British Isles and advertising revenue poured in from sponsors as far away as Liverpool. The tiny Duchy of Luxembourg became a major post-war force in U.K. Radio. (Although reception in parts of England was never perfect and easily distorted by atmospherics, we in Dublin seemed to be well-placed in that respect.)

Yet, for some peculiar reason we never 'copped on to it' until we were touching our teens. (I think it was never included, with RE and the BBC, in newspaper programme listings.) Then someone must have picked it up accidentally, the word spread fast and our radio nights were never the same again.

Most of the RE/BBC stuff was, well, stuffy – certainly compared to this ongoing carnival of informal badinage by identifiable announcers who spoke chummily on first name terms. Bob, Keith, Pete: these were friends. And, so unlike the first class degree types who fronted for RE, or the standard BBC-Oxbridge 'chinless wonder', these 'personalities' (and personable 'disc jockeys', or 'deejays' – new words to us then) were not complicated by excessive intelligence, with a projected mental age close to our own:

"This is your Deejay Bee Aigh!" – Barry Alldis was up and flying.

Lux was...A Party. Every evening from Seven to Eleven (or thereabouts), and well worth the risk of the leather next day, for neglected homework. The nearest thing to it, on the BBC, was 'Have A Go Joe', with over-hearty MC Wilfred Pickles "bringing the people to the people" and inviting old proles in cloth cap, cardigan or twin-set, to sing, reminisce and generally join himself and wife Mabel (always: "at the table") for "a little spot of homely fun" – including a singalong cum piano and a "general knowledge" quiz for small cash prizes.

135

That kind of backwoods bonhomie had small appeal for Irish Youth. – To the extent that rubber-faced Wilf's catchphrase (always delivered to the boom of a gong), "Give 'em the money Mabel!" was mimed derisively by my peers, who found his little spot of homely fun, at the expense of cackling geriatrics, just a bit too naff for comfort. Have A Go was no competition for 208, as far as anyone pre-menopausal mattered.

That of course began for us with the 'Eagle' (comic) Club, immediately followed by Dan Dare – 15 minutes of insomnia-inducing SciFi sponsored by 'Horlicks', "the bedtime drink that promotes deep, restful sleep". We knew what Dan, his astronautic chums and the deadly Mekon looked like from the 'Eagle' strip and could visualise accordingly.

The classless youth-fixated Luxembourg Party proceeded with a quiz show (maybe 'Take Your Pick', infectiously compered by ebullient Michael Miles), a 'free' competition (for some exotic trinket or other), a 'live spot' (Winifred Atwell's rag piano, or Pearl Carr and Teddy Johnson, dueting hits of the day)...another 'club' show ("Join the Ovaltineys by writing for badge and membership card.* Enclosing a wrapper from a jar of Ovaltine" – another soporific beddybys beverage)...and on to the rousing Ten O'Clock record shows, sponsored by such industry giants as Decca, EMI, Capitol Records...frenetically disc-jokeyed by such 'fruit and nut cases' as "jumping Jack Jackson" and primless Pete Murray.

"Time you were in bed now."

"Oh jayse Da" (or Ma), "just let us listen to a few more records."

"And have you dozin at your desk in the mornin?"

"Aw...please!!....I'll weed the garden for ye at the weekend?"

No tiny 'tranny' to hide under the bedclothes in those days; a later microminiaturisation that would enable a real trip to

---

* Always to a London address, where most of the ads and 'live' shows were in fact pre-recorded - 208 being managed from the U.K.

the moon. To bed then, your head filled with Luxtalk and jingles – "We're walking along, with a smi-hile and a song... we're penguins on par-ade!" (Penguin was a chocolate covered biscuit.) Or if they let you listen to the very end...the slushy slow signing off song: "At the end of the day, I hope and pray..."

Da da da da da dee...sleep tight, sweet dreams.

You fell asleep finally, to dream of droning Horace Batchelor, the Liverpool football pools guru. "My infra-draw method will enable you to beat the odds and win consistently." He sounded like a man who badly needed a good laxative and always finished his ponderous invitation to "write to me, Horace Batchelor", by slowly spelling out the name of the Merseyside suburb: Keynesham. "Spelt kay... eh..."

Of such compulsive trivia were fortunes made, on Radio Luxembourg, Station of the Stars.

They made stars too, often originating from the 'The Carroll Leavis Discovery Hour'. 'Carol' was a man. But never mind, some Irish RC boys were second-named Mary – gospel truth. (An error on his birth cert also gave us James Augusta Joyce, creator of Leopold Paula Bloom.)

Hughie Green's competing 'Opportunity Knocks' partly did the biz for three Dublin lads, The Harmonichords. More interesting for me as one of my friends had Dec Cluskey (one of them), for a classmate. They later exchanged harmonicas for guitars and became The Batchelors.

* * *

After commercial television and pirate* radio ships forever

* Uncannily 'previsioned' in a 1940 British Film, 'Band Wagon', starring Arthur Askey and Richard Murdoch and based on their radio show. The film poked fun at a Reithian BBC Boss and baited him with a pirate television station! (Run by Nazis who telecasted Adolf H.)

altered British broadcasting, in the late-Fifties and early-Sixties, many of the old familiar voices from 208 became resituated in England – often, piquantly enough, within the rapidly changing bowers of the BBC.

*   *   *

One afternoon in my early teens, home again from school on some pretext or other, I accidentally tuned in to a Fats Domino number. I had found AFN, the American Forces Network, broadcasting from Munich, Germany. The programme was 'Bouncing in Bavaria' and the DJ was a U.S. Army Sergeant.

This was a turn up for the books, not least because they played Fats and Bill Haley ('the new music' of Rock and Roll), which was virtually banned on RE and the BBC – but because they played the selections complete. (Luxembourg jocks often only played part of a record; invariably so on the big late-night shows, where commercial pressure made them pack as many new releases as they could into valuable air-time purchased by the record companies themselves.)

It got better (AFN). 10pm to midnight (11pm to 1am by their "central European time"), you got two solid hours of hot Rock and cool Jazz, on 'The Munich Night-Train'. No distracting plugs here for bangles, baubles and beads, by H. Samuel (Jewellers) – as during the Lux Top Ten – and you suddenly began to realise what a pain in the arse the commercials could be.

It was on the Night-Train that I first heard a new artist introduced by some rapturous G.I. as "a red-blooded American boy", belting out something that made my toes curl: Elvis Presley and his hound dawg.

We were also well into jazz by then and someone else stumbled on The Voice of America Jazz Hour, 11pm to midnight, which we caught when we could, relaxed parental invigilation permitting. Introduced by the sepulchral bass of Willis Conover – "Ti-me For Jazz" – that set the pulse racing with the opening bars of Ellington's 'Take the 'A' train'.

All this musical largesse from the States had its intended effect, as discreet propaganda, by fanning our Pro-American feelings. A bias only compounded, on the whole, by a branch of U.S. Entertainment that operated largely free of State Department jurisdiction – the brief and bitter reign of Senator McCarthy notwithstanding.

I mean Movies.

* * *

TELEVISION: A NOTE.

Statistics speak for themselves. There were 350,000 sets in the British Isles in 1950. Even after Richard Dimbleby's watershed commentary on The Coronation in 1952, which inaugurated the real Television Age, ownership peaked at two million sets. With maybe 1,000 in Dublin.

My Aunt Cathy knew someone who had a set – a thin-screened flickering thing - on which she once saw Muffin The Mule, Mister Pastry and irascible Gilbert Harding – the first UK Television Personality.

That was as close as I got to it, until the late-Fifties.

CHAPTER TEN

Dreams Made Reel

My most vivid memories of that even more massive extracurricular influence, Cinema, relate to those terrific (to us anyway) U.S. science fiction movies of the Fifties.

'War of the Worlds', 'When Worlds Collide', 'Them!', 'The Thing From Outer Space', 'Twenty Thousand Leagues Under The Sea', 'Invasion of the Body Snatchers', 'Forbidden Planet', 'This Island Earth', 'The Fly'...etc.

I revelled in this cinematic catalogue of fantasy and monstrosity and began to read, at the age of 11 or 12, some of the flourishing SciFi magazines – then producing some of the best writing ever in the genre. I will come back to that in the next chapter. For the moment: "the flicks"; or, as we more often said: "the pixyurs".

If comics and radio stimulated our imaginations and helped to shape both our 'world-view' and character*, the pictures had a truly electrifying impact. Earliest memories are of American gangster films and of my excitement at the wailing police car sirens, as cop chased robber in a way that hasn't changed much since. Only matched by the excitement of the charge bugle in westerns, with a fearless (many would now say 'genocidal') 7th Cavalry in hot pursuit of fleeing redskins.

---

* Even shaping our ambition, in that SciFi fired me, on a short-lived thrust, to become a rocket-scientist. I spent hours in a home-made back-garden spaceship, made out of soap-boxes and blankets, with cockpit equipment obligingly supplied by our latest lodger - an electrical engineer. I purloined a long domed bowl, usually plinth-set over our family statue of the Virgin Mary, as a nifty Space Helmet.

John Wayne, Randolph Scott, Joel McCrea, Audie Murphy, Jeff Chandler, Gary Cooper, Alan Ladd*...those were the boys then.

In Dublin the Western Hero was always, simply, "The Chap". Indians were always among the Baddies and Renegades – except when they reneged on their own kind, as keen-nosed Scouts who could smell another 'Injun', or Palomino Pony, half-a-mile away.**

The Mammy was a keen fan of romantic melodrama and often took me to squirm through some boring 'adult' weepy – other kids hissing whenever the kissing started. That <u>was</u> 'All About Eve' (1950).

At least she also took me to see 'Quo Vadis? (1951)' and we both loved Peter Ustinov, camping it up as grisly Nero. The Da took me to see Tony Curtis as Houdini (1953), probably just before I was considered old enough to picture-go alone, or with my pals – a sure guarantee that what you saw would be worth the ticket.

* * *

But my mother did take me to see that enchanting film 'Bicycle Thieves' in '47 or '48. I must have been able to read the subtitles and I little knew or cared that by it, Vittorio de Sica had first directed Italian Cinema onto the world stage.

Visiting an aunt in 1952, mater cleared the way for a good family gossip by packing me off to the local cinema (in Rathgar). 'Limelight' was playing and I instantly lost my heart to blooming Claire Bloom, even if she'd already lost hers to

---

* 'Shane' made him 'a living legend', just ahead of macabre gunslinger Jack Palance. – I believe that Jack Schaefer, who just dashed that epic story off, spent the rest of his life desperately, and unsuccessfully, trying to repeat it.

** 'Broken Arrow' (1950) and 'Across the Wide Missouri' (1951) – mountain man marries classy squaw – began to break that mould.

Charlie Chaplin. 'The Great Caruso' (1951) was another treat and may have encouraged me to join the school choir.

My father took me to see 'All Quiet on the Western Front' about that time. He blew his nose when the soldier got shot in the end – reaching over the top of his trench to try and catch a butterfly...He may have also taken me to 'The Red Badge of Courage' (1951), as he liked Audie Murphy as much as he liked "a good war picture".

If I ever saw the 1947 film of Wilde's 'An Ideal Husband' great lines like the following would have been well beyond me: "Morality is simply the attitude we adapt towards people who we personally dislike."

* * *

We were mainly dazzled by Hollywood, although British films like 'The Sound Barrier' (1951) 'The Dam Busters' (1955), 'Reach for the Sky' (1956), or 'The Bridge on the River Kwai' (1957) were equally compulsive. 'Kwai' was US-Columbia-funded, but we weren't into the root finances of film-making. Likewise, Henry Hathaway's Rommel 'The Desert Fox', 1951, passed for 'English' as far as we knew, with James Mason as the German General.

And who'd cavil about who made the 'Robin Hood' of 1951 (Disney), or the US 'Ivanhoe' of 1952? – 'Ivanhoe' was shot around Dublin and I remember that star Robert Taylor made himself unpopular by slagging off Ireland. We still went to see it, slavishly!

That was also the golden age of English Comedy, with Alastair Sim in drag as Headmistress of St. Trinians (1954 and '57). Or Alec Guinness displaying the virtuosity as "eight different characters!" egad, in 'Kind Hearts and Coronets' (1949) and again (less so – cribbing Sim) as a smooth rogue in 'The Ladykillers' (1955). A parade of classic humour that memorably included 'Genevieve' (1953) and 'Doctor in the

House' (1954) – James Robertson Justice the essence of upper class dominance as master surgeon Sir Lancelot Spratt.

If the British Secret Intelligence Services had set out to show that England was a land of of admirable and endearing people, they couldn't have done better than bankrolling their film industry at that time. For all that, maybe SIS still had a hand in it, long after Korda and others worked with them to help win the war.

Akin to that subject, we never regarded 'The Third Man' (1949) as an English film probably because Orson Welles was held in awe as a great American actor. For us the film was him, even if he only cameo'd into sight towards the finale. In general we had no interest in who produced a "grate pixyur", let alone in the director – except that the appearance of his name on the screen signalled the end of that whole long dreary roll of credits. I think the first time I ever thought of a cameraman as important was very much later, in 'Lawrence of Arabia'. Surely films were nothing at all without Stars? A point. But one that, too well taken by film-makers themselves, has bankrupted many.

A good score was more directly appreciated – the hit zither theme from 'The Third Man' being an excellent example of that. Music also "made" 'Genevieve', 'The Dam Busters' and 'Kwai' for you. It had a different, peripheral kind of value as an intrinsic element in the best British science fiction films since 'Things To Come': 'The Quatermass Experiment' (1955) and its 1956 sequel. Closer to horror than 'pure' science fiction, they recaptured the chilling frisson of vintage Frankenstein and Dracula, at a time when we were still of an age to Oh! (Hammer Horror came much later; I will leave that genre for the moment.)

The British were good at 'slice of life' police dramas. Even if the morality was often as black and white as the screen itself.*

* Technicolour remained a novelty until well into the Fifties.

'The Blue Lamp' (1950), for example, with Jack Warner (also Mister Huggett in the drab BBC radio sit-com, and the two films it spawned – 1948/1949) as steady London 'Bobby', George Dixon, smugly polarised good and evil. – Later spun off into a long-running BBC tv series, 'Dixon of Dock Green'.

Long before the hard realism of Sixties 'Z-Cars' began to show the viewer what real urban police work was like, reflecting a many-shaded ethical milieu where bobbies on moral bicycles became an anachronism, Dixon gave us a sentimental and whimsical slice of fanciful idealism by comparison. Yet we liked him, although we knew well that he was just too good to be true! ('The Lavender Hill Mob' deliciously sent up 'The Blue Lamp' later in the same year. – John Cleese duly pulled its ever spry director, Charles Crichton, out of retirement for 'A Fish Called Wanda'.)

(Inspector) 'Gideon of Scotland Yard' went to the other extreme, with serious crime being policed on the hard heels of Bulldog Drummond. Criminologist Edgar Lustgarten 'hosted' a series of short films on 'true crime' and only became a figure of fun for his trouble. He looked like a hanging judge, sounded like an undertaker, and took such funereal delight in seeing the miscreant caught, or topped, that we instinctively had him for a pompous sadistic prig. A fly to wanton boys, Edgar was also maligned for having "too much talk" in the bill.

Billy Wilder's 'Witness for the Prosecution' (1957) got the credit for being British, no doubt on account of the London setting and Charles Laughton; well-established in our minds as a British Type, after his 1935 'Mutiny on the Bounty' and 'Hobson's Choice' (1954). Marlene Dietrich gave a bad fright in 'Witness', as a deteutonified Cockney harlot baring her scarred face. (In a dowdy Euston Station Buffet where the bartender delivers a snooty line, straight from the clubs of Mayfair: "Care for another Sir?" – Even we knew that wasn't Euston talk.)

David Lean alone was noticed as a "janius of a director' –

long before 'Kwai' or 'Lawrence' – if only for that terrifying opening scene of storm and dread in 'Great Expectations' (1946), when the convict Magwitch accosts Pip in a desolate graveyard. More than a pin, or a pip, dropped at that; we were (dare I say it?) boweled over.

All the great Dickens stories were immensely popular as films, topped of course by 'Scrooge' and 'Oliver Twist' (Lean again) – which made you glad to be a CBS boy. Just as 'Brighton Rock'(1947) made you glad that Dublin gurriers had nothing on Graham Greene's chiv-carrying creation, Pinkie. 'Tom Brown's Schooldays' (UK 1951) at least hit out hard against bullying and had a plausibly happy ending...

...Not that Happy Endings were always expected, or relished. (I think that children in general can take more of 'hard reality' in this respect, than we usually give them credit for. – I once heard a boy dismiss 'Scrooge' as "a cop out. He'd never change, just like that.") Certainly the contrived resolution of many a B picture got the bird, as if we knew that Life doesn't usually take a tidy turn. Although we wouldn't have seen the 'happy ending' of 'Great Expectations' in that light - or cared that the novel itself was so 'nicely' rounded-off, against Dickens's own inclination for a darker denouement, at the behest of a fellow-scribe, Bulwer-Lytton.*

Much later (1959) the Boulting Brothers tried their hand at producing a more contemporary kind of 'social realism', in 'I'm All Right Jack' – all the truer for its humour.** They previously gave us a funny-authentic slice of army life in 'Private's Progress' (1955) and a snide glimpse into judicial

* Then again (life being complex!), we owe the plan of Joyce's 'Portrait' and the Nausicaa episode of 'Ulysses' to a positive influence from Bulwer-Lytton's play 'The Lady of Lyons'.

** Or satire, of a kind that impressed and duly inspired the makers of a BBC television sensation of the early Sixties, 'That Was The Week That Was' – a Saturday night programme where young (now Sir) David Frost first made his name...grossly debunking the British Establishment.

process in 'Brothers in Law' (1956). Indeed they produced/directed some of the best, including 'Brighton Rock' and 'Lucky Jim' (1957). Two more 'janiuses'.

A less favourable kind of Englishness, in our eyes, was evinced in 'The Chiltern Hundreds' (1949). Although the eccentric aristocrat, his twittish son and the family butler were all impeccably played (by A.E.Matthews, Ian Tomlinson and Cecil Parker, respectively), there was something about the whole lot of them you just didn't like. Perhaps it was the reek of privileged arrogance beneath the humour – as exemplified in a scene where uniformed soldier Tomlinson comes home to contest an election. His peer of a parent meets him off the train:

TOMLINSON. "I had a devil of a job to get leave. 'Had to see the colonel."

FATHER. (dismissive) "Old Jim! He used to be my fag at Eton."

There were many such films, still reflecting the kind of England that former colonial (not to say colonel-ridden) peoples, like the Irish, abhorred. In poking fun at their own ruling class, in a way to show the feet of clay, English film-makers undermined their mandarin social system, both at home and abroad. It was not enough to rely on great character actors (like Matthews) to obscure the reality.

People often believe what they see, rather than what is intended, and it only takes one weird aristocrat to destroy credibility generally.

However, the imperial age age was ending anyway and such films also reflected that.

* * *

The great team of Powell and Pressburger ('The Archers' films) showed how social change could be handled intelligently, to arouse sympathy for the fading Old Boy Brigade, in 'The Life and Death of Colonel Blimp' (1943). Made at the height of the war it met predictable official resistance, being nonetheless approved for release, with sound wisdom.

Filmgoers warmed to noble old Colonel Blimp and the story of his adjustment to a world where 'good old British values' didn't quite hold anymore. It helped the war effort as English people identified with an example of the best in their national character. In Ireland too, when we much later saw it, we saw "a decent man", not a stuck-up snob, and "Curnal Blimp" became an affectionate term for his type*. ('The Admirable Crichton' (1957) hinted that we all had a touch of the Peer!)

Apart from making the best fairy tale on film, 'The Thief of Baghdad' (1940), (which I sadly never saw in youth) and a bewitching fantasy 'The Red Shoes' (1948 – which I loved), 'The Archers' filled the Dublin Metropole for weeks with 'The Tales of Hoffmann' (1951).

They got just too 'radical' in the end and the English film industry largely ostracised them – truly scandalised after Powell directed his (compelling) Jack The Ripperish, 'Peeping Tom' (1960). He decamped in disgust to Hollywood and British films lost a giant.

'The Archers' inspired some of the best directors of the coming generation, including a boy who watched their work as the high of his young life: Steven Spielberg.

*　*　*

The 1948 film of Compton Mackenzie's comic novel 'Whiskey Galore!' was a predictable hit in Ireland, appealing to toper and minor alike. As comedy it was head and shoulders above Old Mother Riley and the Crazy-Gang. While George Formby, Arthur Askey, Ronald Shiner and Norman Wisdom,

---

* Much as that great bit-part player, bespectacled Richard Wattis, was loved as an endearing example of the nicer, bumbling-funny, BBC Man, British Diplomat, or the pompous and well-intentioned Upper Class Twit.

for all their custard-pie clowning, never stood a chance against Laurel and Hardy. The favourite English Comedian was Terry-Thomas, an absolute cad of a 'chap', who took bespatted Wodehousian humour way over the top. (Noel Coward was only known to us as the epitome of the Naval Officer – 'In Which We Serve' (1941).)

Richmal Crompton's scampish 'William' was "just like us", English or not; several films about him made the rounds as B Features. (Today's kids still warm to him on TV.)

Any film with Dublin actors (Noel Purcell/Eddie Byrne) was a must. However bad, it was like having kin on The Big Screen. – Of the US Ma'rines, O'Hara was 'Dublin' and O'Sullivan from my mother's parish.

('Let's be Famous', a 1939 film starring Jimmy O'Dea, said it all.)

But the great English matinee idols pulled well too: John Mills ('Scott of the Antarctic' and RN ad infinitum), Jack Hawkins, Richard Todd, Kenneth More, Dirk Bogarde, John Gregson...Anthony Steel – a Rockfist Rogan who also got the girls screaming, on looks alone.

Glynis ('Mad About Men') Johns and Diana Dors ("the English Marilyn Monroe") did as much for boys of a certain age, and their Dads. Jealous mammies also envied La Dors as co-star of heart-throb Frankie Vaughan. They had nothing to worry about, or envy, from Two Ton Tessie O'Shea. Ancient Margaret Rutherford for grandads, or gerontophiliacs...

Former flour magnate J Arthur Rank started into movie-making in the Thirties, competing with Associated British (Pathe) Films and motivated by powerful Christian principles. By the Fifties Rank dominated the industry, with many old independents, like 'The Archers', controlled by him.

An English De Mille, his films began with a lavish Old Testament touch – a well-oiled musclebound brute of a man*,

* *(Former) Bombardier Billy Wells... long since degonged, alas.*

striking a huge golden gong. In the key of a g-string that paganistically lured female filmgoers, into lascivious thoughts of a huge golden dong.

English 'shorts' were few, mostly tedious travelogues; although a Dick Bartonish serial, 'The Scorpion', caught on for awhile. Dick himself appeared in a few popular feature films. Pathe News was a regular diversion and the only visual news we then had. With the BBC's Radio Newsreel it set a pattern for later television newscasting.

* * *

Nevertheless, then as now, Hollywood set the standard in quantity of films released and for consistent watchability. Given the amount of cinemas in Dublin there was plenty of scope for that volume of output.

O'Connell Street alone had the Rotunda (later Ambassador), the Adelphi, Savoy, Carlton, Metropole, Capitol, with The Corinthian and Astor on the nearby quays. Several more scattered in the Central area off O'Connell. 'The Mare-o', in Mary Street, was avoided as a cheap haunt of gurriers, with a reputation for infestation by red fleas.

The only time I ventured there, with a battalion of pals, someone hissed: "Jaysus a red flea!" A moment of panic before we realised that the red 'thing' in his hand was a glowing cigarette-butt. Ho ho...

Across the Liffey on the south-side: The Royal, Regal and one on Stephen's Green. The Royal, like The Capitol, was notable for having a stage show instead of a "small pixyur" (B feature). – The main feature was "the big pixyur". The Royal also boasted a resident organist, Tommy Dando, who "came up through the floor like yer man, the phantom a the opera", blazing like a juke-box and with all the stops out. (You 'sang along' with him, from lyrics projected on the screen.)

'The Royalettes' – Dublin's version of The Radio City

Music Hall's long-legged Rockettes – were obscene if not heard, with the roars of randy youth drowning out the orchestra. Panto gave them a rest when film and show were supplanted by solid theatre.

Local cinemas also proliferated throughout the suburbs and we had four within walking distance, from The Cabra Grand to the Bohemian and State in Phibsboro, with another alleged flea-pit, The Broadway, in Manor Street. An incident there, when an ambulance was called, led to the most amazing piece of underground gossip I ever heard:

"It took a man and a woman away. They were stuck together! Es-Eh-Ex."

We soon enough knew what the back seats of a cinema were best for ourselves, reminding me of something which sounds like Ogden Nash off the leash:

The modern cinematic emporium, is not just a super sensorium.
It's a highly effectual, heterosexual, mutual masturbatorium.

All cinema seating was organised to cater for different levels of class/affluence – i.e., there were 'cheap' and 'dear' seats, strictly segregated in both Stalls and Gallery/ies. (Getting to The Gods in The Capitol was a climb for Edmund Hilary.) It was a rare treat to sit in comfort on a better seat. Until you began to "coort", when any back seat was as good as another, with your arm around "the moth".

(I cannot trace the strange etymology of moth, for girl, in Dublin. Nor that of 'austin'! 'Bird', a third, is a more universally known term.)

* * *

Very occasionally, we had a free film in our School Hall, in between School Plays or kids rehearsing the next Gilbert and Sullivan operetta. Usually an old western, enlivened by several projector break-downs, when pandemonium would break loose. That rarely occurred in your Local.

* * *

But back to American Movies and Movie Stars, with their unique glamour. Bogart and Cagney became household names in Ireland, as elsewhere.

WW2 movies and the De Mille-style Epic, duly competed hard with the stock gangster and western fodder. Even Duke Wayne changed his spots and bobbed up like a one-man army on Iwo Jima*. Victor Mature was the gladiatorial Rambo of the Roman Circus, with Kirk Douglas and Charlton Heston vying for Fifties Schwarzenegger.

'Quo Vadis?', 'The Robe', 'Fabiola' and 'Samson and Delilah' lavishly introduced us to the sword and sandals brigade. 'Demetrius and the Gladiators' (1954) still thrilled; but by 'The Ten Commandments' (1956) you were growing old enough to make fun of the American accents and generally see the funny side of Movie Religion. ('Ben Hur' (1959) and 'Spartacus' (1960) were just "a hoot".)

Hitchcock was in his element then, with 'Rear Window' (1954) packing 'The State Theatre' in Phibsboro and queues for 'Psycho' (1960).

The actual size of Errol Flynn's "lowry" was a constant source of schoolboy surmise and banter. When he died (1959), the story was that his corpse was already putrifying from the effects of sex, drink and drugs as they put it in the coffin. *Per ardua infra...*

That kind of rubbish may have been picked up from one of the lurid film magazines, which began to compete with comics at some point. No less than a film trailer, these magazines

* *'Epic' Wayne as ...Genghis Khan... in 'The Conquerer' (1956)... well, less said the better!*

knew how to pull by promising a great deal on the glossy cover. EXPOSE! SECRETS REVEALED. WHY DEBBIE DOESN'T LOVE EDDIE ANYMORE.

Gossip, 'romance', intrigue...appeal to envy of Wealth and Fame.

As for the Hollywood Studios, they could have have lifted the boast on the masthead of the (bestselling) English Sunday 'paper, 'News of the World', as their slogan: ALL HUMAN LIFE IS HERE. Not that it would have rang a bell in Dublin, where 'News of the World' was banned as pornographic. The Irish Censor having decided that their definition of life needed another adjective: low.

Hollywood, to be fair, gave us more like a variety of life – from low to middle; seldom high, or noble. But it had a solid core of pure magic amid the dross and I will run through a rough Hollywood Alphabet to provide an overall 'picture'. In this, I will concentrate for the moment mainly on some "pixyurs" that impressed us earlier on; the films of our late-teenage years will be mentioned in later context.

* * *

A was for Adventure, of the swashbuckling kind, including perhaps some films described as Historical Romances, a la Sabatini. – 'King Solomon's Mines', 'Ivanhoe', or the pirate and Dumas-musketeering films, with Errol Flynn or Louis Hayward. Not to forget such Disneyworks as 'Robin Hood', 'Treasure Island' and 'Kidnapped'. Or: "Me Tar-zan. You Jane." (This Boy/Cheetah/Simba (Lion). That Liana Vine. I swing. Awwwww!...)

Croc-fighting Johnny Weissmuller, lean Lex Barker...good old 'Jungle Jim', beloved of kids. (As was the Anglo-Indian, Sabu.) 'Gunga Din' and 'Beau Geste' – with 'Coop' as gritty Legionnaire – still ran.

B for Bible. It virtually became The Hollywood Bible in the Fifties. Many Old and New Testament Spectaculars, modestly foreshadowed by a truly 'seminal' movie called 'The Private Life of Adam and Eve'. (Older Dublin wags joked of a biblical western called 'Deuteronimo'.)

C: Comedy. Plenty of that, from the Marx Brothers, Laurel and Hardy, Abbott and Costello, 'Francis the Talking Mule', Martin and Lewis...to the "grate" 'shorts': The Three Stooges, Leo Gorcey and The Bowery Boys, Pete Smith 'Specialities'. We occasionally saw one of the old 'silents'; Harold Lloyd and cross-eyed Ben Turpin were favourites.

Bob Hope ('The Lemon Drop Kid' and the 'Road' movies) and Danny Kaye ('Knock on Wood' rather than 'Hans Christian Andersen') were two stalwart draws. Red Skelton was "okay". Clifton Webb (Mister Belvedere) was a rarely acquired taste, in the sphere of 'light' comedy. Ustinov was always a scream. Cartoons were as popular as they are with kids today – Bugs Bunny, Goofy, Sylvester and Mighty Mouse being major enliveners. Mickey Mouse and Donald Duck were considered a bit naive. But the Disney of 'Snow White', 'Alice in Wonderland', 'Dumbo' and 'Lady and the Tramp' was A1.

D for Detective. Classically headed by Bogie in 'The Maltese Falcon'; 'The Naked City' (1948), and taut movies based on the books of Ambler's U.S. disciple: Chandler. You also had Mickey Spillane's Mike Hammer (and numerous imitators) for unadulterated hard core private eyery. 'Dragnet' produced another Top Ten Theme. (An OTT skit on that by Stan Freberg also became a hit record.) No one, but no one, made fun of bullishly brusque Broderick Crawford.

E, for Epic, became synonymous with De Mille. Although Cecil Blount's wasn't the only studio to make with the Christian-eating lions and gladiators in tomato sauce. (Even 'Ben Hur' had that chariot race.)

F for films about families. 'The Swiss Family Robinson' and

'The Philadelphia Story'* got a lukewarm reception. Only Bob Hope's 'Seven Little Foys' hit the same spot in us as England's 'Life With The Lyons'. 'The Fighting O'Sullivan's' wiped out that brave brood, in war.

G for Gangster ('The Gangster', 1947, with John Ireland, no less!). ...Among a surfeit of same. Just as well. We couldn't get enough of them. James ("You durdy rat") Cagney, Edward G Robinson (Little Rico whispering filth to Bogie's Bacall in 'Key Largo'), Lee J(owls) Cobb, macho Bob Mitchum, suave George Raft..."Da boys" crept into our argot, inimitably gaelicised by some, into "da *buachailli*" – perhaps expressive of our awareness that gangsters with tommy-guns were kids, like ourselves.

Straddling Detective/Gangster: 'The Big Heat' (1953)...

H has to be Horror. Good old Frankenstein (and the Wolf Man). Doctor Jekyll – "you'd hide too, if ya saw him". Burke and Hare. Delicious Dracula, dreamed up by a Dublinman too...our first taste of vampiristic sex, sublimated into sophisticated violence. Boris Karloff and Peter Lorre became by-words for the macabre. I preferred Bela Lugosi and Lon Chaney Junior. The very name Bela conjured up for me everything that Ian Fleming later meant by his "deadly silent men from Central Europe". Horror answered a primeval need in you somehow...as science fiction later answered a need to stretch the imagination. 'House of Wax' became a well-marketed sensation, as the first film in 'lifelike' 3D. A pair of polaroid glasses, we were told, and you were in the film. – We had to rely on hearsay, as anyone under Sixteen wasn't admitted. By the time we were of age, Cinemascope had ousted 3D. Indeed by then Hollywood Horror had given way to Hammer U.K.

I for Ireland – John Wayne's Island, with bowler-hatted

---

* Remade as 'High Society' it became as little about recognisable family life as 'There's No Business Like Show Business'.

Barry Fitzgerald and a red-tempered colleen in every boreen: 'The Quiet Man'.

J for Jazz. We never saw, or missed not seeing, Jolson's 'The Jazz Singer'. Instead we had those biopics – Duchin, Miller, Goodman – and plenty of films that qualified, including of course 'High Society' and 'Pete Kelly's Blues'. Ella Fitzgerald was in that, the queen of jazz and looking so old and fat to us - she was barely 37 then! Louis was the King, no doubt of it; we flocked to see him In Person, singin in the ring of the South Circular Road Boxing Stadium, and blowin a mean horn. I remember he perspired profusely and used up a gross of big white hankies.

K for Kuties? We mercifully missed Shirley Temple, if 'The Good Ship Lollipop' was anything to go by. Mickey Rooney was passable.

L for Love. Ugh. Romance only ruined a good story. But a lot of boys got the smalltime hots for "Marilyn" or "Jane" (Russell).

M for Musicals. We goggled at Busby Berkeley's incredible choreography (magical memories of grand pianos stretching to infinity and Esther Williams-ish aquabatics) in otherwise forgettable films. Judy Garland was the kind of girl your mother wanted you to meet (someday), in 'Meet Me in St. Louis' (1944) and 'Easter Parade' (1948).

My first 'date', aged 12, we sat entranced through several showings of 'Seven Brides for Seven Brothers'. She was the daughter of a local soccer star and I was lucky not to get booted into touch when I got her home very late. Bless her beautiful hide...'Singin' in the Rain' – we all did just that, on the way home. The sheer Magic of it! And the spell cast by Oklahoma!, from the very first cornbelt moments – Oh what a bootiful mornin...(A far cry for Director Fred Zinnemann, from 'High Noon', WW2, or his later 'Day of the Jackal'.) 'White Christmas' and No Biz Like Showbiz were equally memorable. On a long hit list from the likes of Annie Get Your

Gun, Show Boat, The Greatest Show on Earth, Calamity Jane. Howard Keel for the girls; Mitzi Gaynor or Betty Hutton for boys.

Sinatra was slavishly followed, from On the Town to Guys and Dolls, etc. Bing alone was RC Approved, as Father O'Crosby. We put up with Dean Martin for the sake of Jerry Lewis.

N for Nature. Disney's marvellous 'The Living Desert' (1953), their first 'True Life Adventure', followed by 'The Vanishing Prairie', admirably began saving the Earth almost a decade before Rachel Carson's book 'Silent Spring' woke the world up to ecological issues.

O for Objectionable. The Censor made certain that kids never saw a real nightmare-stirrer, like Tod Browning's 'Freaks'; apart from that he let almost anything through for adults – with a notable total ban on 'The Wild One', to spare us a spate of imitative Brando Boys. Explicit sex was out of course, as was any flagrant irreligion.*

P – Prison movies. Some droll had it that 'I Was A Fugitive From A Chain Gang' was shown to the inmates of Mountjoy Gaol, to remind them how lucky they were. ('Riot in Cell Block 11' was screws only.) Any of the 'in da pen' movies of the time would have done as well; they certainly put us off prison.

Political movies were rare, although 'The Informer' (1935), directed by Celtophile John Ford, often re-ran and gave us the impression that the IRA were no more than incompetent gangsters in belted trench-coats...comedic *buachailli*.

Q for Quality. For us that simply meant Action, lots of it.

R for Religion. De Mille aside, I wrote to Warner Brothers, offering my services, when it became known that they were recruiting in Europe for 'The Miracle of Fatima'. A letter by

---

* *Reading Keith Waterhouse's autobiography reminded me that we – like he did, as a boy in Leeds – sometimes persuaded a patron "to take us in please, Mister", when the film was Adult Accompanied Only.*

return post, from Warner PR, politely informed me that...My friends were as impressed by the "parchment" notepaper as by the text itself. Of course we all went to see the film, parents included. Nice one, WB. 'The Song of Bernadette' (of Lourdes) was another such – equally extolled by priest, parent and teacher. 'Going My Way' and 'The Bells of St. Mary's' led to the beatification of Bing, P.P. 'Little Boy Lost' was hot papal PR.

S for Suspense. For that, nothing ever beat or bested the 20 minute totally silent burglary sequence in 'Rififi' (1955). A film that also brought director Jules Dassin back from McCarthyist isolation, as a (one-off) serious competitor to Hitchcock at his best. (Dassin later recreated O'Flaherty's 'Informer', as 'Uptight' (1968).) The very first US 'caper' movie, 'The Asphalt Jungle' (1950), was pretty tame by comparison. Another French film, Clouzot's 'The Wages of Fear' (1953), with its careening lorry-load of nitroglycerine, was tres taut suspense.

A PS for hot Saturday Morning Serials: Flash Gordon, Superman, Batman...you could get in to them for four pence in some cinemas, which became known as "the fourpenny rush" – those cheap seats being limited.

T in a similar key, for Thriller. Crossing with Detective in the mould of Hitchcock's 'Vertigo'; 'Casablanca' perhaps. And nothing was as chilling as Sidney Greenstreet's "Sir", in 'The Maltese Falcon'! On the borderland between thriller and horror came King Kong and Mighty Joe Young – a near tear-jerker about a misappropriated and misunderstood gorilla. I would also place 1950s Science Fiction in this category.

U for U.P.A., the cartoon 'factory' of the early Fifties. We knew it best for bumbling myope Mister Magoo – using the voice-over of Jim Backus; the actor later pointedly picked to play James Dean's bumbling bourgeois parent in 'Rebel Without A Cause'.

V for Violence. Rare by presentday standards – if you except a sniggering Richard Widmark shoving a wheel-chaired female cripple down a flight of stairs ('Kiss of Death', 1947), or a hood throwing scalding coffee in a woman's face ('The Big Heat', 1953). Fights were mostly Queensbury Rules; bullet wounds remarkably neat and sanitised.

Which in a way, brings us to W, for both War and Westerns. War was most memorably 'The Steel Helmet' (1951) and 'Stalag 17' (1953). ('Fixed Bayonets' ('51) had a fleeting bit player…young James Dean.)

By any measure, the western was the most popular form of film entertainment, well into the Fifties, certainly for the pre-teens.

Joyce was missing the beat when he once derisively referred to "deadwood dicks" – admittedly in the context of their stringing up "niggers". He hadn't sat through 'Shane', High Noon', 'The Flame and the Arrow', 'Winchester 73', 'Cochise', 'Union Pacific', and the rest.

Apart from picking up the basics of Good and Evil in terms of who drew the fastest, you could also get some useful info in a western: "It's impossible to hypnotise a man who's on guard, or who does not want to be hypnotised." Thus spake The Lone Ranger. To his own surprise.

Kemo Sabe and Tonto belonged to the 'innocent' tradition of clean cut heroes, before broody Alan Ladd arrived in elevated boots and needing a shave. We were weaned on the clean cut: Tom Mix. Tim Holt, The Cisco Kid (Cesar Romero), Lash La Rue, Tex Ritter, Buck Jones, Young Wayne, Gene, Roy and Hopalong Cassidy. – "'Je hear about the one-legged nun? Hopalong Chastity." Chaste they all were, even the prancing steeds. Even in formation, as The Texas Rangers.

Immaculate or trail-worn however, you could always depend totally on The Chap, to behave like a right-thinking sportsman. As you could depend on a Buffoon (Andy Devine, Smiley Burnette), or an Old-Timer (Gabby Hayes cornered that market), for a guffaw or two. "How-de-dee, Old Timer."

"Jehosaphat, Hopalong, I feels like a rattler in a rain-barrel."

Old Timers were all in Boot Hill by the advent of the New Wave: Ladd, Glenn Ford, Hank Fonda, ageing McCrea and Scott*; serious men on sombre business. Plastic-surgered Palance broke the mould of innocence, but it was Lee Van Cleef who really presaged the stygian-black, amoral spaghetti western (and lived to ride in it).

Slapstick westerns – the old silents, Abbot and Costello, Bob Hope's 'Paleface' – became whimsical memories...until 'Blazing Saddles'.

X marks the spot where Innocence ends, and Experience begins.

Y is for Youth and a new box office potential: The Teens.

Z, or Zee in the U.S., betokens the zero-ing of an Era.

* * *

The little Astor Cinema on Eden Quay specialised in foreign language films – French, Italian, Spanish, Swedish – some of them (apart from Jacques Tati as Hulot) coming beguilingly close to X-ratable eroticism. It was there that I had one vivid experience of cinema as High Art, watching Ingmar Bergman's 'Wild Strawberries' in 1957. Followed by similarly mind-jolting masterpieces from a defiant New Breed of Continental director.

Never forgetting Akira Kurosawa's 'Seven Samurai' (1954), which Hollywood reincarnated as 'The Magnificent Seven' in 1960.

Before Sergio Leone overturned all the tables and really scooped an enormous fistful of dollars, by super-commercialising Kurosawa (after Cervantes).

---

* *A jolting case of the frequent disparity between projected image and human reality – as a wealthy broker who often spent his time between takes consulting the 'Financial Times' or 'Wall Street Journal'.*

In a more curious cross-pollination of film 'cultures', Kurosawa's 'Yojimbo' (1961) which, with his 'Sanjuro' (1962), sparked the Leone/Eastwood alliance, was itself a homage to the old John Ford and Howard Hawks Westerns! 'Seven Samurai' owed as much to Ford, being scripted by Hashimoto...whose favourite film was 'Stagecoach'. He also scripted Kurosawa's 'Rashomon' (1950): Westernised as 'The Outrage' (1964).

FIN – the word that also ended many a film, in the Astor.

* * *

So, we say farewell then, to Roy, Bogie, Raft* and Chuck Heston. With a parting bow to Esther Williams, June ("Oh honestly!") Allyson, to Janes Wyman and Russell, and ultra-demure Deborah Kerr...Goodbye to Unca Donald, Bugs and the mighty mouse in Superman cloak and tights.

Bye bye to one mighty gunnelled raft of Screen Talent.

You all made your mark and left it too, in perpetuity.

What a pity we had to grow up and out of you. Perhaps.

* * *

A NOTE ON THEATRE AND OPERA

Apart from pantomime and the film-conjoined light stage shows at the Capitol and Royal, we never went to see live theatre, until a few of us took to it in the mid-teens. (More of that later.)

A couple of pals were regularly escorted by their parents to the operas at the Gaiety; we only felt sorry for them. I was into my Twenties before an opera buff finally converted me, to Verdi, Puccini, and the rest.

---

* *Incidentally: a joy to us as the man who pricelessly informed a girl on the Baghdad-Ankara-Istanbul Express: "I just blew in from Baku."*

CHAPTER ELEVEN

COCA-COLONISATION...

In 1956 another bomb struck Dublin. That was Rock and Roll and it catapulted us, in line with half the world, into The American Age.

We all trooped to queue outside The Carlton in O'Connell Street, where 'Rock Around The Clock' was showing with some awful B feature. In no time at all the local youth could quote reams of dialogue from the B, in that they often sat through the entire day in the cinema.

A manager in a tuxedo appearing regularly on stage with the fraught appeal: "For Jayse sake will those who have seen Bill Haley once please leave the house and let the people queuin' outside in the rain have a go."

No chance. The ones inside were well and truly hooked, by a totally new kind of musical experience. ("See you later alligator", they'd shout back at hand-wringing Manager, "in a while crocodile!")

My father called that "tin can music" and wondered where Glenn Miller and Bing Crosby were gone.

We couldn't care less. This was the kind of stuff that made the blood boil. (When Haley's Comets played the Theatre Royal a year or so later we had to stand on our seats to see them. With everyone else up and roaring their heads off, nobody heard a note.) Breaking up the cinema came later, when it became known that English 'Teds' were setting the example in cinemas across the U.K.*

* * *

Teds, or Teddy Boys, were a curious phenomenon of the early to mid-Fifties.** They dressed in what was called the Edwardian Fashion, in flashy drape-jackets with velvet collars, drainpipe trousers ("tight as a nun's cunt") and wedge-soled suede shoes. Silk shirts in electric primary colours and black shoe-lace ties completed the ensemble. The hair was always shaggily side-boarded, long and greased, coiffed out at the front – "the Tony Curtis look". It was parted neatly down the back in a 'D.A.' (duck's arse) and razored level above the neck. Although this apparel also owed a great deal to the overdressed elegance of the Western saloon-gambler, Dublin Teds were regarded simply as "animals", with an inflated reputation for viciousness; although many never left home without a bicycle-chain – a fearsome weapon in close combat.

Real violence of the modern kind was nonetheless exceptional and there wasn't a Ted in Dublin who didn't live in fear of Garda Sergeant Lugs Brannigan. Lugs (because of the big ears) constituted a one-man vigilante committee, on behalf of the D.M.P. He seldom wasted time in arresting an errant Ted, preferring to pummel him to pulp on the spot. – A true exponent of the short sharp shock school of remedial jurisprudence...

* * *

* *Perhaps as much provoked by 'The Blackboard Jungle' (1954), with Glenn Ford battling a school-full of juvenile delinquents – where 'Rock Around the Clock' made its first impact playing over the opening credits.*

** *Not only in Ireland and England, but, as part of an emergent international youth subculture, with their equivalents in France, West Germany, Sweden and Japan. Even Moscow had its 'Stilyagi' (style-boys), in the brief period of civil truce after the death of Stalin.*

Teds were already in place before Elvis The Pelvis gave them a manifest reason-to-be. If kiss-curled Bill Haley was a disruptive influence, to our elders and betters, curl-lipped Presley was a manifest menace.

"You have only to look at him" was their wisdom.

As I have previously indicated, most of the 'hard' rock 'n rollers were initially banned by Radio Eireann and the BBC. Radio Luxembourg remained for a long time the rockers godsend, unless you got to know about AFN. ('Calypso' was plugged by RE - a poor alternative.)

Nobody could ban the sale of rock and roll records however.

I duly acquired a small collection of shellac '78s', playing them on an old Garrard deck which needed the needle replacing after four or five 'plays'. Each record cost six-and-eightpence in the old coinage (30p today), or a good week's pocket money in our circle. Boxes of needles were fortunately cheap. Long playing records were well beyond our budget, as indeed were the dual needle record players they required. A household that had both became a hot venue for group listening.

Instead of comics we now swapped rock and roll records and you soon got your fill of Haley, Presley, Fats Domino, Chuck Berry, Buddy Holly, Jerry Lee Lewis, Little Richard, and other legends-to-be. AFN prompted my own first purchase: Bill Doggett's big hit, 'Honky Tonk'.

Juke boxes in ice cream parlours and chip ships did a (truly) roaring trade. A few entrepreneurial young men-about-Dublin got the bright idea of buying in bulk and charging for Record Hops. Our own favourite venue was The Carlton Hall in Marino.. We cycled there religiously on Tuesdays and Friday nights, to jive like the American teenagers in 'Rock Around the Clock'. Doing our best to look hip in dowdy sports 'coats' and charcoal grey flannels. Girls in tight skirts were "arsy tings". Or 'Reet Petite' – the record playing us in on our very first visit.

(A UK Christmas No.1... in 1986... as backing track to a video of... clay animated figures...)

* * *

We know now that there were Carlton Halls flourishing at that time, in every city, town and hamlet throughout the English-speaking world. A whole new youth culture was emerging, despite regular prognostications by beleaguered 'squares', to the effect that rock and roll (as the greatest inflammatory influence) would soon be dead.

(Some kids in Liverpool had their own ideas about that.)

For us, The Carlton was a trip without drugs – unless you included the music as one. Although the Dance itself was strictly run, to exclude 'undesirables', by a hard young man who made short work of unwanted trespassers – mainly Teds. Danny was after the better class of clientele, the kind who belonged to lawn tennis clubs and would go on to university. So, you were 'vetted' by him, or his mates, as you went in, and anything in drapes and drains was refused admission.

This paid its dividends and the Hall began to attract the intended type in volumes. Even gaining the approval of the local parish priest, who would 'pop in' occasionally, "just to see that the boys and girls are behaving". (In time, The Parochial Halls would throw their own Hops.)

The priest had very good reason to snoop as it happened, for none of us had the slightest doubt that rock 'n roll* got the girls going, no less than ourselves. While the smoochy numbers made for close-up dancing, known as "lurching" (dancing on a dime) and all that went with it. Many a Good Irish Catholic Girl found herself pinioned in a most peculiar manner, with her arms around his neck and his hands cupping her plump behind, while Connie Francis wept or Fats Domino

---

* We had no idea that the term is Blues argot for fucking.

low intoned 'The Valley of Tears'.

That often led to deep (French) kissing, but seldom far beyond. Girls who let you take them home, with a feel up in an alley on the way, were like gold. And almost as rare in those days, with the high price on virginity. A girl who really 'did' could end up alone on the cattle boat, disgraced; taking the bun in the oven to England for delivery.

Rock and Roll gave some nubile girls a very hard time.

* * *

The Carlton Hall management was astute enough not to ban 'respectable' kids from the poorer home, in that it was surrounded by many such abodes. A gang of the less respectable who inhabited this labyrinth of streets, was appropriately nicknamed The Puzzle. Their attempts to infiltrate dances added a touch of West Side Story to the scenario.

Indeed we all admired the Leader of The Puzzle, a charismatic Fonz of a youth who looked positively dapper, even dressed as a Ted. He also "jived like a dream" in the opinion of 'the women', always with his own stunning "bopper of a girl". Yet he had manners enough to rise for a Ladies Choice, when some lip-smacking racquet swinger moved in for a bit of rough trade.

So even the vigilant Danny relented to admit the lad and his boys initially, before he had to break up one fight too many. And Out. Charismo countered by starting a rival record hop, which succeeded in drawing custom from the Carlton, in a dingy hall and against all odds.

The showdown came when one of The Puzzle made the mistake of threatening Danny's kid sister. Hearing the news, Daniel abandoned his turntables and set off black-faced to beard the beasts in their rival den. As we heard it, he burst in like some lone avenger and set upon the Puzzler in question, beating him up while the others stood well back. He came back to the Carlton a Hero, incidentally killing the competition stone dead in the process. Such were the times...

My friends and I kept well clear of trouble, getting well out of the way at any prospect of "a rumble". Which reminds me of an incident which I'd certainly prefer to forget, as a right bloody humiliation.

* * *

Soon after the above fracas, Danny's 'kid' sister – the same age as myself at Fourteen – asked me up for a Ladies Choice and a brief relationship ensued. (I must have passed her brother's vetting test.)

It was a welcome boost to my confidence as my first 'line' had ended disastrously some months before, when I got 'dropped' by her. She was partly fed up with my shyness – I just couldn't pluck up the courage to kiss her – and finally disgusted by my failure to protect her.

With good reason there, I fear. For when put to it, it seemed that I couldn't pluck up the courage to fight either (a gutlessness I later contrived to excuse as...a poet's disdain for physical violence).

Our courting took the form of nightly walks in the Phoenix Park, in company with another young couple. We would perch, all four of us, on a park bench, when the boys were expected to kiss the girls.

At such times I would merely squirm uncomfortably, hearing the other two slurping away in the dark, while mine turned her face up to me in hope.

On this particular night the unimaginable happened – in those peaceful times. We were suddenly accosted by a group of youths, who as suddenly pulled my girl off the seat and began to molest her, in no uncertain manner. Still dumbfounded I had a glimpse of some oaf actually wrenching her knickers down, before my friend leapt to his feet and waded into the pack of them, fists flailing.

It was all over in seconds. The gang ran off shrieking with laughter, my friend was having a bloodied nose dabbed by his girl, and mine was pulling her pants up, crying her heart out. She didn't need to tell me that I had behaved like a coward. I knew it, just as I knew that my friend had behaved like a lion. As we took her home the others only made me feel worse by acting as if they hadn't expected me to make a move. As if to say, "you have no balls, but you can't be blamed for that". Given the way I felt afterwards, I was almost relieved when she told me that we were finished, the next time I met her. Poor me.

Well, here I was, later on, canoodling with a new prospect; one with a brother who'd knock the block off anyone who looked crooked at either of us. Not that it made up for past failures, to have no fears on that account. Indeed I suspect that his sister only liked me because I was so much the opposite of him, that my shy awkwardness was a novelty.

It didn't last long anyway, and I never kissed her either.

I was almost Sixteen when I kissed my first girl, in a laneway. She almost ate me up. Then I had the stupidity to blurt out that I'd never kissed anyone before...After a moment or two of staring at me, she suddenly ran off squealing with merriment.

However, as far as I was concerned the spell had been broken and I only felt grateful to her. At last, I was a Kisser. That paved the way to becoming a Feeler. Unfortunately, the final fence in the sex stakes, losing my cherry, would not prove quite as easy to field. I would be a long time yet before I became a Fucker, in that respect.

* * *

Apart from Rock and Roll, parkland and alleys, the back seat of the cinema was often the nearest we got to heavenly eroticism. Yet again, a lot of this was in the effort rather the attainment.

For my friends and I it was a long and arduous – albeit often electrifying - process, where watching the screen was the last thing on your mind. You began by kissing her until she began to 'weaken', ears cocked for the first sign of sigh or moan. Then you squeezed her well armoured dugs, doing your best to get a hand inside blouse, sweater, or bra. A feel of naked tit was real progress; to hit the nip was Valhalla.

Especially if it was hard like a hazel-nut and she began to pant-kiss.

Your hand on her knee if the weather was fair, slipping like a clammy clam up...and up...hoping her contrary vice of a hand wouldn't descend on yours: desist! If the weather was hot you got as far as the gusset and maybe inside. A hairy reception unless she opened the thighs a little, when you began to find out what it was all about, forefinger slipping and sliding into that mysterious bountiful slit.

At any one of the above points your cock would be bursting and straining for release, in every sense of the word. But it never occurred to me, or to most of the friends I exchanged notes with, to put her hand on him – even over the closed flies. It was as though we accepted that we should do all the work and expected the girl to remain essentially passive. If there were girls who spontaneously touched and wanked their 'fellas', we sought for them in vain. – Until, in my own case, I nearly passed out with passion, in a cinema in Holloway Road, when a black girl I was kissing unzipped me and began to knead the steaming knob.

That was my first taste of London Life, aged 17. (Detail later on.)

I did have a couple of close friends, in Dublin, who had what it takes to bring out the beast in a woman. But even they never got beyond sucking or being sucked, or mutual masturbation − although that was pretty far to my mind − to what the priests called 'consummation'.

As one of them habitually climbed a drainpipe, entered his girl's bedroom, undressed and crept naked into her bed (her sister pretending sleep next to them)… but without getting the lot, the force of female inhibition against premarital intercourse must have been prodigious.

A debonair ladykiller I often played snooker with (more of that game shortly) was a Fucker, 'cum' laude. "She'd do anything for me" he'd say of the latest moth (of many). "I shag the arse off her." He wasn't bullshitting, being generally regarded as "god's gift to scrubbers". He once told me how his girl apologised for "having the flags out" (periods) and "hoped I'd be happy with a tit-roll instead of the usual".

Of course he was and he gave her a "pearl necklace".

A couple of the older 'lads' fazed us with stories of their sexual exploits at Barrys Hotel. That was where the nurses danced and nurses were, by all accounts, pretty free and easy. Nurses were, they said, "grate for a gamarouche" (fellatio) and often carried illegal french letters "for the full treatment. − But you have to have a car for that." No problem: one of them often borrowed an old banger, for the bang.

The pushiest of that pair once failed to "get off" with a "young country girl" who worked in a shop on the Cabra Road.

"All I got out of her" he complained, "was her name. Edna O'Brien."

If he ever saw her again, it was probably on television.

I later had a bit of luck in Barrys myself. But for the years from 14 to 17 there was a lot more talk than action in matters of sex. Although, if I hadn't been so screwed up I had at least two golden opportunities to 'lay'…the annoying ghost of my own virginity.

It goes back to the girl who threw me over for cowardice. As a result of that unhappy experience I resolved, in the crazy way of callow youth, never to be dropped by another girl. I would drop them.

That was all very well, until you started to drop the girls who, if you'd only known, would have done 'anything' for you. I had, as I say, at least two such teenage admirers, and all I did was break their little hearts by behaving like an unfeeling young bastard.

I guess it served me right, desperate as I actually was for sex, to remain an idle prick in consequence. – No less than the philosopher Origen, who castrated himself in the name of self-conquest.

The really awful part of it was that my friends admired me for being "a Deaner". James Dean, a curse on you. We all slavishly idolised you then, as a rebel who could afford to treat girls like dirt (so unlike our gangling selves). – Rumours that you might have slept with Clifton Webb were mercifully far ahead; although I don't think we would have countenanced for a minute any suggestion that Jimmy Dean, of all people, was into brown-hatting.

You got us all moping about, grunting like yourself (after Brando), in the hope that someone would spot us for "real Deaners", and set our social stock soaring. Moodishness in this context became the very height of happiness. In the above sexological context, it also favoured onanism.

We were a right crowd of stupid wankers. Before Nature eventually got the better of Nurture and the real priorities re-emerged.

* * *

Yes, Dean was a cult – still is today – and his three movies set the seal on our early adolescent behaviour. Providing one extraordinary instance of the power of Cinema, in altering attitudes and determining social behaviour – at least in the impressionable Young.

170

By saying little or nothing, mesmeric Dean seemed to speak for us all. More than that he represented, as vaguely as we did ourselves, uniquely adolescent values; including distrust of the adult world and its cant. He was irresistible to females; a blessing we only shared, for the most part, in our wildest dreams.

Inspired perhaps by the High School kids of films like 'Rebel Without A Cause', many of us subscribed to the more sedate rebelliousness of the Crew Cut/Flat Top, as our non-Ted hairstyle.

A barber in Moore Street – yclept "The Moore Head" – made a fortune out of perfecting it, charging four times normal cutting rates for his special expertise. Emerging from The Head as shampooed and blow-dried hedgehogs, also gave us some idea of the high cost of Fashion.

Admittedly a crew cut wasn't, quite, Dean, but then neither were the drab conventional clothes we wore: ill-fitting jackets and baggy flannels, shirt and tie, 'sensible' socks and laced brogues, with the rough roll-necked sweater or blanket of an overcoat in cold weather. Hardly the outfit to go mumbling and Method Acting (or rockin) in...but there it was.

Fortunately, the afflicted seldom mock their fellows.

Only one of my pals had the personal force and style to turn up in class wearing a black leather jacket and jeans, there to slouch deep in his seat ignoring the lesson, and get clean away with it. He was closer to Brando than Dean, with his long greasy hair and studied scowl. He did look like he might erupt at any moment and teachers preferred to ignore him in turn.

I had started to write a bit of poetry about then and I remember being startled when he showed me some scribbled verse one night at a dance and declared himself a fellow-poet. The first line, "Don't laugh at me because I'm black" struck me so forcibly that I felt like Keats' friend Browne, when he first read 'A thing of beauty is a joy forever'.

Such are the halcyon moments of Youth...

Before I deal at length with our forays into literature I will briefly discuss two other diversions that competed with sex and rock for our pubertal time and energy: snooker and jazz.

Snooker is now a major international industry, largely by virtue of colour television. Long before Pot Black started the whole caravan rolling, on BBC tv, we were well into it in Fifties Dublin. In those days proficiency at snooker was "the sign of a misspent youth".

A snooker hall, The Cosy, opened locally when I was Twelve or Thirteen, no more than five minutes walk from my home. It became a nightly point of congregation for my own circle of friends and we all became passable players in time.

The novels of John Steinbeck were then going the rounds – a taste probably fostered by the film of his 'East of Eden'. We began to think of The Cosy, with its loafers and sad-sack characters, as our own Cannery Row. (We even had our own 'Doc' – a star player.) The place certainly had atmosphere, with icy cigarette smoke drifting through a morgue-like silence; broken only by the softly clicking balls, on those brightly lit rectangles of green baize.

Of the eight tables, Number One was reserved for the very best players. Of which we saw quite a few, including some who achieved the maximum break of 147. Born before their time insofar as professionally capitalising on their skill was concerned, their fame was cloistered but no less profound for all that.

Number One always had an avid audience, swelling to prize fight proportions for the finals of an annual Handicap. Two of our friends won that – Doc was one – during the two or three years that The Cosy dominated our evenings.

A few players preferred to hide their light under a bushel, and lure some unsuspecting greenhorn into playing them for cash. You soon learned to avoid them, as "sharks", but it was against 'the code' to warn off anyone else they targetted.

With Paul Newman in 'The Hustler' (1961), it became apparent that sharks existed wherever cue struck ball competitively.

(We ourselves seldom played American Pool or three ball billiards.)

I once got caught by a hustler – or very nearly caught. I knew he was good but he lured me into playing "the best of three" by offering me some points on the board, for half a crown a game. He easily won the first two frames, which should have been the end of it. Then, when I was fingering the five shillings to pay him off, he challenged: "Doubles or quits?"

Momentarily off my head perhaps, I took the bet. Then he made a mistake, by suggesting that we "make it quick", by setting up six reds instead of the normal fifteen. No doubt he was anxious to get out for a pint or two with the ill-gotten gains and wanted to finish me off in ten minutes instead of twenty.

He certainly wasn't counting on the extraordinary luck that would so often feature in my young life. I must also have been feeling lucky to take the bet in the first place. As it transpired, I potted three or four reds, with colours, after his opening break. Then I 'weaned' (freaked) a nice bit of safety, tight against a cushion.

While he was working out how to take a shot that would open the game again, or put me in trouble, one of my friends arrived to stand next to me at the table. A superb player, he was in fact the second of the two aforementioned, who won a Handicap Tournament.

"What are you doing, playing with him?" he hissed in my ear.

Staring back at him, picking up the warning vibes, I suddenly remembered that I didn't have ten shillings – more like six.

When, after my next shot, I confided same to my friend he

turned kind of grey. "He'll do you" he snapped, "if you can't pay."

I looked down on the muscular figure lining up for a shot.

'Do' me, he certainly could. And I couldn't blame Stan Laurel for this. I also remembered something else – that this was the one who had a bloody fight, back of the Cabra Grand, with that Casanova I mentioned earlier. How could I have landed myself in it? But I had.

Playing on now, for dear life, I somehow survived to a black ball game. Then I left the black 'on', for a relatively easy pot. I glanced at my friend, sitting by the wall – he made running movements with his hands.

Years later, I felt for Dennis Taylor, who left the black on for Steve Davis in the final frame of a marathon U.K. Final.

The same Providence must have been working for both of us. For just as Davis missed his pot, enabling Taylor to win, so did my shark. (He mis-cued.) In a daze, cold as stone, I got down and sank the black. I don't know which of the three of us – myself, friend, or shark – sighed loudest.

Looking from me to the cup holder, I think the hustler read the whole story. For he began to grin at me, in a most evil fashion, before grasping my hand and pumping it. Nice shot, he was saying, nice. When he suggested that "we split the docket" (the tariff on table-time) I nodded readily. That wouldn't cost much more than a shilling apiece.

"Jayse Divvy you're blessed" my friend muttered as the other strode away. To add, a moment later: "Get that!"

I followed his eyes to where sharkie was disappearing through the exit, waving back at the owner of the hall.

"Get what?"

"He's telling Percy" (the owner) " to put it on the slate! He must be flat broke. Which means he had you taped as a right mug."

A couple of years later I got to drinking and playing cards with said shark. When I confided the truth he only guffawed.

"Winnin is what matters at such times" he said with a shrug. "You won. And I'll tell you somethin. I hadn't enough on me to pay the docket."

"You fly old bollocks" said I, as if I didn't know.

Storm on a cue-tip perhaps, but only with hindsight...

* * *

About that time, I was playing snooker one night when a neighbour found me, to tell me that I'd better get home fast as my father had collapsed. I'm afraid I only felt annoyed, at having to quit the game, so little was my filial feeling then.

It proved serious enough: a stroke. (I can only hope that my own kids will be a little more emotionally responsive if I ever have one.) He was hospitalised and recovered, apparently unimpaired, until a second massive attack killed him fifteen years later, in 1971. By then at least I knew him well enough to mourn and miss that sad, life-battered man.

* * *

After the snooker hall, when we weren't dancing (drinking comes later), we would often hike off, three or four of us, for a music session in someone's parlour.

In between listening to rock or jazz, on radio or player, we had the kind of animated discussions that many readers will remember from their own teens - with new sensations of self-discovery and mental forward movement. Littered with gossip about parents, teachers, friends, girl-friends, dirty jokes; more earnest debate about news and current affairs...the arts... philosophy, religion and the meaning of life in general.

But we seldom chattered while a serious jazz solo was playing.

I have already outlined our first experience of that music, through radio and films, indicating that we had many avid fans in our locality. I was deeply impressed one day, at about the age of Nine or Ten, when I came upon the older brother of a friend I was visiting, laid out on their settee and listening very seriously to some soulful jazz sexophony. He signalled us kids to get lost: Do Not Disturb Me.

So jazz could do that for you I thought – make a monk of you. My best friend for many years, who became an absolute addict of modern jazz (including The Monk Himself – Thelonius), later recounted a similar instance, when he found the "intellectual" teenage sister of another friend identically supine, digging some way out stuff.

"All she did" he told me, "was give me an airy wave and say: 'Lennie Tristano, the polytechnician'".

It figured, in that we regarded modern jazz as a fairly cerebral preserve.

That may sound very jejeune, but it did seem to us that Jazz and I.Q. roughly related, in that the brightest youths we knew favoured the music from Charlie Parker and Lester Young onwards, while the duller buff remained locked into the era from New Orleans to Armstrong and the Dorseys. Dizzie Gillespie was okay, as a bridge between the two styles.

I'm not sure how we reconciled our elitist attitude to jazz with our love of rock and roll – which many Trad fans we knew derided in turn (with some justification) as an inferior form of rhythm 'n' blues. (They would point to 'Big' Joe Turner, as a sad example of formidable Blues poacher turned lucre-lovin Rock gamekeeper.) – Less so when I remember that we read Norman Mailer's essay 'The White Negro' about that time and were struck by his remark that "jazz is the music of orgasm". I guess, in our basic musical ignorance, we got that lumbar kick from rock and roll – which stirred our feelings in a way that traditional jazz/blues simply did not.* (Big Joe

---

* There were some odd hybrid-hits like Earl Bostik's 'Flamingo' and Ellington's 'Night Train' which entered mid-Fifties rock charts.

Turner aside.) Modern jazz, Jekyll and Hyde fashion, became our Classical Music...

Anyone remember that one-hit-wonder, Red Prysock's 'Paquino Walk'?

All a very far cry indeed from the real spirit of jazz (as Mailer would have heard it) - that original form born in the steaming plantations, combining European hymn and folk-song with 'speaking' African drum...to produce the Negro Spiritual, the Work Song and The Blues...together providing the blend of salvationism, fatalism and, most of all, raw animality, that makes for exuberantly 'orgasmic' Jazz.

In the beginning was the African Drum. Our Trad buffs were right. Without that, no Rock (or modern jazz), or indeed no popular music industry. An incidental observation? Perhaps. But worth reminding ourselves that we would live in a very dull world, musically, if Negroes had never existed.

However...confirmed in our absurd musical snobbery we seldom bothered now with the likes of Louis or Bob Crosby, reserving ourselves mainly for the new West Coast Jazz – particularly the Mulligan, Brubeck and Modern Jazz quartets. 'Bird' Parker and Miles Davis became equally talismanic, with a host of other players – Art Blakey, Bob Brookmeyer, Coletrane, Johnny Dodds, Gil Evans, Stan Getz, Coleman 'The Hawk' Hawkins, Johnny Hodges, Lee Konitz, Shelley Manne, Monk, Oscar Peterson, Bud Powell, Andre Previn, Max Roach, Shorty Rogers, Sonny Rollins, Bud Shank, Zoot Sims, Sonny Stitt, Ben Webster – gradually amassed among our collective collections.

Initially much of our listening was done on brittle (and breakable: "watch it!!") 78s, many recorded on the legendary Vogue Label, with up to four minutes of music to a side. – A temporal constraint which some artists, notably Mulligan and Brubeck*, often used positively, to hone and sharpen their

His 'Take Five' was so popsie it became a '60s Top Ten Hit.

succinct performances. Aimed at College audiences, theirs was also a new kind of populist Campus Jazz.

The advance to more pliable extended and long-playing records (EPs and LPs) began after someone got a set of LPs from a cousin in Canada and pestered his folks for a suitable Deck. We played one of the LPs – the Oscar Peterson trio – until the minuscule grooves were visibly worn.

The same happened to 'Milestones' and Previn's 'My Fair Lady' LP.

There was also a wealth of jazz EPs at that time, giving the boys a bit more scope to improvise – up to 10 minutes playtime per side - on the Fontana and Esquire Labels. – Labels had a lure/allure of their own!

Kenton was an earlier revelation, with those Afro-Cuban rhythms. Woody Herman and his various 'herds' were definitely in, with Basie and Ellington. Frank Sinatra's work with Billy May was only matched for us by his unique 'Only The Lonely' album. Johnny Mathis was simply terrific, jazz or not. And we certainly weren't 'above' listening to the Blind Lemon Jeffersons, Bessie Smiths, or Mahalia Jacksons.

Pragmatism remains the prerogative of any snob.

Moving slightly ahead to mention the film 'Jazz on a Summer's Day' (c.1958), some of my happiest memories are of summer days, lying around a record player with my friends, windows wide open to the sun, listening to Mulligan's burping baritone, Chet Baker* trumpeting, in full glorious flight, or a stratospheric solo break by Paul Desmond, Brubeck or Milt Jackson...

* * *

Through a BBC jazz programme compered by Steve Race we

* He later lost all of his teeth in a mouth-mangling brawl and had to learn how to play, anew. I remember being horrified to see him, shortly before he died, ravaged and just...blown out.

became aware of the modern jazz movement in England – specifically in London.

Ronnie Scott's Club in Soho would become the first place to head for when we started to fly the coop. (Just as Birdland, in New York, would compel two of our group who duly got that far.) Settled in London I would see and hear many of my teenage icons, playing in Scott's.

My last year in Dublin (1959), we were starting to visit our own jazz club, on Stephen's Green, where the Ian Hendry Quartet became the main attraction. Hendry looked like Brubeck and (in our view) tickled his ivories almost as well.

Insofar as we could judge, in that only two of our number played the piano or read music. One of these developed a party stopping line in heavy-handed boogie woogie, being otherwise slow to try and imitate the Hendrys or Brubecks. Our second pianist liked to dabble, Shearing-style, over a 'standard' or two – Gershwin etc. – but was more at ease with drawing room etudes, by Chopin or Debussy...

"You play the pussy dee-vinely" we'd moue at him, leery-ambiguously.

CHAPTER TWELVE

Oh, the sound of simian mirth!
Mind, issued from the monkey's womb,
Is still umbilical to earth,
Earth its home and earth its tomb.
                                    – Aldous Huxley

The four lines leapt out at me and I collared a friend, co-scouring the shelves of Phibsboro Library, to share my excitement. It was, we agreed, "fantastic stuff". We were soon devouring Aldous whole. In tandem with a growing library of our own, of literature old and new.

*   *   *

The most sublime memories of those great years, between 13 and 18, relate to my literary awakening and the discovery of words as a powerful force in the world. I remember Dublin as my Athens during that period.

I may just have been in the right place at the right time, but I have seldom met an Irishman who wasn't interested in some form of literature – which largely explains the disproportionate amount of it that has consistently issued from that tiny underpopulated island.

In my own case I was more than usually fortunate to have among my pals several youths who positively loved good books and read voraciously.

So, when I wasn't rocking and rolling, or trying to "get the feel" in some cinematic emporium, I found myself discussing a range of authors and philosophers – from, say, Homer or Plato, to Huxley, D.H. Lawrence, or the "Deanish" Orwell of 'Down and Out in Paris and London'.

Hard into our anti-clerical phase, we revelled in Rabelais and the Joyce of 'The Portrait'. A covert copy of 'Ulysses' was prized and savoured, both for its radicalism and Molly Bloom's "horny" soliloquy.

"Where did you get it?" we asked the proud owner.

"The moth bought it for me birthday" (his sixteenth). "From under the counter in the communist bookshop across from the Abbey Theatre."

"Jayse she has balls for a moth, to go in there and buy it."

Although we found many echoes of ourselves in Lawrence's 'Sons and Lovers', it was inevitably Joyce who most perfectly echoed our ongoing estrangement from Irish Catholicism. The more revolting and tasteless he became in that respect the better we liked it. I recall a particularly crude passage where an altar boy lifts a priest's cassock and inserts a carrot in his "bare hairy arse", which we found *tres piquant*.

By this time many of us had finally severed the Catholic umbilical and stopped going to church. This apostasy was predictably the most shattering aspect of our overall rebellousness, for those elders and betters who duly discovered it. If it provoked domestic "ructions", it also baffled them. For no one of their own generation had even 'strayed' in thought, let alone given up on 'their duty'.

What was the world coming to?

* * *

As far as we were concerned it was coming to a liberating point where anything on the RC Index of forbidden books was required reading. We weren't particularly in search of high-minded literature, only in books that broadened the mind, for better or worse, with all that entails in terms of imaginatively stimulating fresh thinking.

The main effect was bound to be iconoclastic, in that most imaginative literature or reformative philosophy stops short with questioning or attacking held religious/moral/social convention; we have yet to produce an influential body of writing which provides a positive, viable, alternative to the more destructive beliefs and ideas that still dominate our western culture and civilisation.

Although we did not know it then, we were in fact living through a watershed era in that respect; as the kind of positive literature and philosophy we need, to create new values and generally revitalise our moribund society, first began to glimmer into life during the Fifties. (I will duly expand on that.)

* * *

We were in search of laughter and sex as much as enlightenment and in that respect nothing was sacred – not even the Greek Greats, who we often made light fun of as avocational brownies. A copy of Apuleius's 'bawdy' Classic, 'The Golden Ass' (title alone ripe for ribaldry), made the rounds, providing a slant on Life in Ancient Rome that was far from the untranslatable Latin of Vergil or Livy - our school textbooks.

One of our number had an uncanny knack of defusing with humour, if we became just too pompous in our discussions. He once broke up some heavy Freudian talk on the Oedipus Complex with the quip:

"I'd a puss" (mouth) "like a monkey".

In the same Dublinish spirit we made fun of fruity fiction. Among the books to be read with one hand, Alberto Moravia's 'The Woman of Rome' was an early 'classic'. A passage where a woman emerges from a bedroom after a bang, "her hands dripping with sticky sex", was legend. 'Without Shame', a flagrantly pornographic novel by one, 'Hilary Bellamy', which had somehow found its way from Paris to Dublin, became a source of great hilarity, as well as "the bedside book for wankers".

Even the horrible 'rape' by 'Popeye' in William Faulkner's 'Sanctuary' became a joke: "He oiled his Olive with a corn cob." 'Lolita' was written to amuse and we had many a dirty belly-laugh over Humbert Humbert; nevertheless we mostly appreciated it for Nabokov's consummate linguistic felicity. Voltaire's 'Candide' was another howl, mainly for the 'philosophical' seduction of "Cunnilingegunde" (his Cunegunde) by light-fingered Doctor Pangloss.

A slim 'clinical' volume on homosexuality, in surrept circulation, proved too difficult to understand to be readily burlesqued.

If Hemingway moved us, in 'For Whom The Bell Tolls', his 'Little Rabbit' of a *senorita* also tickled the *cojones* – the word becoming another source of merriment in itself...

All this may indict us as reflecting the kind of mentality which led Shaw to flee Dublin in disgust. Mocking young men characterised, as he wrote, "by a certain flippant futile derision and belittlement that confuses the noble and serious with the base and ludicrous". That from his 'Immaturity' Preface, in the context of praising Joyce's 'Ulysses', as describing "with a fidelity so ruthless that the book is hardly bearable, the life that Dublin offers to its young men, or, if you prefer to put it the other way, that its young men offer to Dublin."

In defending us, I would contrarily indict Shaw for narrow puritanism in that respect; or failing (for once) to grasp that young men, everywhere, are naturally sex-obsessed and inclined to find echoes of their own condition in everyone else – saint or sinner – and to make fun of them accordingly.

In coming to new terms with life, through the influence of poetry, philosophy, literature, etc., we often, in youth, begin, literally, at the bottom, and work up to the 'high-minded'.

For our own part I think we always knew when to draw the line between the "noble and serious" and "the base and the ludicrous".

There was also much reverence, where warranted, for superior creative accomplishment.

* * *

However, to establish some kind of coherent chronology here, I will refer back to my earlier discovery of another kind of literature, which did not depend on humour, sex, or violence to achieve some truly creative/imagination-stirring effects. That discovery began for me at an old Liffeyside monastery mill on the low road to Lucan.

It was a spot we often cycled to for a bathe in Summer.

There were trees to climb and a cascading weir to test your puny prowess as a poor swimmer. In fact I nearly drowned in the current on one scary occasion, before I somehow made it back to the bank and managed.

One such afternoon, sunning myself after a dip, I fell into conversation with another boy of my own age – we were about Thirteen then – who soon intrigued me by professing total atheism. Bertrand Russell was the only man, he proclaimed, who knew anything worth knowing. And the sum of his knowledge was not at all theistic.

I had no trouble with that, as I was fast losing interest in the god of our fathers myself. But it was nice to know that there were already other, more knowledgeable, agnostics out there. However, my real interest was aroused when I discovered that my new friend was a positive maniac about science fiction.

Our lodger, the electrical engineer, had really got me going on that subject, by giving me a battered copy of 'Astounding Stories' a short time before. I had, as they say, lapped it up and been wondering where to get more of the same when I met my atheistical friend at The Mill. To my delight, he got

'Astounding' regularly and was soon offering his hoard for my own delectation.

After then giving me a short lecture on the "incomparable" cover art of Kelly Freas, he really delighted me by saying that 'Galaxy' had even better covers and, in his astute opinion, better stories, and that his collection of Galaxies was also at my disposal.

So began a durable comradeship, which incidentally opened my eyes to some of the most (astoundingly!) creative fiction of our time. Some people – idiots all! – might have called it cheap trash. For such people, we had no doubt, were fortified in their ignorance by never having read a page of it, or having the brains to appreciate it if they had.

Heinlein, Asimov, Bradbury, etc etc...these were literary giants.

SF was the literary equivalent of modern jazz and had a curiously similar appeal as a cerebral and sophisticated art form. It thus came as no surprise to my that me new pal was also a modernist and I soon introduced him to my best friend – who had earlier impressed me by understanding everything in that 'Astounding' and was equally into modern jazz.

Before long, our new recruit's front parlour became a regular nightly listening haunt for our close circle of 'intellectuals'.

I think he first put us all on to the Voice of America Jazz Hour.

* * *

We were our own elite until the results of the Intermediate Certificate, a couple of years later, confirmed our 'superior' status to the local community in general. My friend of the Mill, a dedicated 'swot', was an A boy and, in line with everyone in his class, attained honours in seven subjects, out of seven. Of the rest of the 'Deaners', most of whom made a virtue out of not studying 'seriously', two of us got five honours – I was one – and the others managed three or four.

In fact I only got two of my honours by a few marks, but that made no difference apparently and I was duly astounded by the way my stock began to soar, socially, both at school and in our home neighbourhood. It was an unexpected taste of 'success', with boys who had got little or no honours actually knocking on our front door, to congratulate me on my scholarship. Even my (proud) parents were awed.

What I really needed, I got from no one: a caveat to the effect that five honours, two of them poor, was a mediocre attainment on the broad scale, for someone who fancied himself as exceptionally clever. I needed to be warned that having a potentially first-rate mind meant little or nothing if you failed to apply it to the work in hand.

If there had been such a Devil's Advocate, to ram home the truth that my 'success' was second rate and brace me accordingly, I just may have risen to the challenge of persevering to really perform in my Leaving Cert – the one that really mattered – instead of ducking out of school completely at the first bit of bother.

But it would have taken a good and clever counsellor to set me right at that time. Instead I remained as I was, incorrigibly big headed and arrogant without true warrant, to follow my own crooked road. My friends admired me unreservedly and that was all I wanted – let the future take care of itself. By then, also, I was setting my mind on a literary career and taking the example of many great writers, in turning my back on conventional education and all it stood for, career-wise.

In all this, I am not saying that the studious course would have proved the best for me, in the event, or that a university degree would have eased my path in later life. One simply cannot tell and I have no regrets on that score alone. What I am saying is this: that whether I subsequently went for it or not I would have benefited then from being told, convincingly, that I wasn't, as I imagined, some kind of natural achiever. In this context, fortuitously passing exams – only a few tests of memory after all – can create a ridiculous sense of self-importance which is, in life, more of a liability than an asset.

It is, finally, something that no Romantic "I'll just dash off a masterpiece" young poet wants to hear – that there is absolutely no real success in art or life, without consistent grinding hard work!

* * *

Young Dylan Thomas dramatised himself as "the Rimbaud of Cwmdonkin Drive" (his birthplace in Swansea). I also briefly cast myself in the wild mould of Rimbaud (with overtones of James Dean), after that other magic name entered our expanding pantheon of Genius. Briefly, because my mind was sparking and questing in so many new directions.

Our friend of the Mill got me into hard philosophy, plying me with volumes on utilitarianism and empiricism which, he claimed, would prepare me for that guru supreme, Bertrand Russell. He also encouraged me to improve my "general knowledge" by reading 'Time' magazine and the two 'quality' Sunday 'papers – 'Observer' and 'Sunday Times'.

Against this and for light relief we listened to 'The Goons', read 'Mad' magazine and competed to tell sick jokes after Mort Sahl – prompted by a feature on him in 'Time'.

Including the book reviews, 'Time' provided a rich source of data on new developments in literature, the arts, technology and the social sciences in general. We began for example to search for and read Galbraith ('The Affluent Society' in particular), Riesman's 'The Lonely Crowd' and Packard's 'The Hidden Persuaders'. All of these influential and bestselling books in their day and extremely useful commentaries on the dehumanising effects of modern economic, corporate and advertising practices.

I was highly receptive to all this, and occasionally intrigued by news of my friend's hyper-IQ'd classmates. – One of whose parents had given him 'The Catcher in the Rye' as a birthday gift, which we all read avidly in turn. ("Mothers are all slightly insane", the Catcher confirmed!)

Our parents seldom even read a book.

With one quite incredible exception – the father of my oldest and closest pal. His 'old man' worked on the railways, in some capacity which meant he was away travelling about the country for days on end. During his long train journeys and stays in hostelries this plump short unassuming man read copiously and variously.

He read translations of Greek and Roman Literature, he read the medieval and renaissance poets, he read the Elizabethans and Romantics; books on philosophy, art and science; the Huxleys, Eliot, Pound, Joyce, Yeats, St. John Gogarty, Shaw, Synge, O'Casey, D.H. Lawrence, Hemingway, Steinbeck, O'Neill, Scott Fitzgerald...virtually anything that smacked of quality or durability.

Here was the source of the Penguin (upmarket fiction) and Pelican (Classical Literature) paperbacks that duly found their way down to us. And indeed the many other hard and soft cover volumes that went to swell our library of new knowledge. – He even supplied us with some of John Lehmann's excellent 'New Writing' anthologies. His sudden death from a heart attack, in 1958 or 1959, shattered our little *cenacle* and totally devastated his elder son, my friend, who simply adored him.

*   *   *

About that time my own poetry was being passed around and some began to take me for granted as the next Joyce. (We read or knew relatively little of Shaw.) The rebel who had surprised me with a sample of his own verse was now deep into Wilde and reading aloud to us from 'De Profundis'. It was strange to hear someone who looked more like a Brando leather-boy than Aubrey Beardsley proclaiming that he was "an aesthete".

Then, sometime in 1958, our beleathered aesthete announced that he was reading "an incredible book" by a new English writer, which he'd pass on to us in due course. That was 'The Outsider', by Colin Wilson, which, with John Osborne's play 'Look Back in Anger', had launched the English Angry Young Men Movement in 1956.

We in Dublin knew nothing about that when 'The Outsider' and its sequel, 'Religion and the Rebel', first came to our attention. Indeed, had we known about the rapturous reception of the first book in England and America, or the contrary castigation of its sequel (and the author himself) in late-1957, we would have relished the entire scenario as but a typical instance of Genius At Bay.

As it was we immediately recognised 'The Outsider' as a key book of our time – those of us who did take to it. For some did not and it subsequently split our little group into pro and anti Wilsonites.

My friend of the Mill did not like it at all, not least for a few disparaging references to logical positivists (like Bertrand Russell.) But everyone had to admit that it was an undeniable *tour de force* of its kind – on readability and apparently effortless erudition alone.

It must be said that the sharp opening chapter had a certain salacious appeal, with its (then shocking) account of a sexually insatiable 'Outsider' in search of relief.* This, the French hero of a novel by Henri Barbusse, was also uncannily like us in his frustrations and desires. – Watching womens dresses blow up in the wind and wishing that he could have

---

* Publisher Victor Gollancz, who knew his public, cannily scrapped an Intro by Wilson and opened on the sexual theme as a sure-fire 'hook'.

the lot of them. We knew just how he felt.

Wilson describes how he visits a prostitute, slaver slaver, but still feels frustrated. He tries voyeurism, boring a hole in the wall of his rented room and watching a couple making love next door. Still no real relief. Later at a dinner party, the hero (or anti-hero) listens to someone recounting the rape of a child and finds echoes of his own 'abject' condition in the expressions of the other diners, as they pretend to be detached while their faces betray lusts worse than his own...

We had certainly never read anything to match this.

Wilson's own intention, to demonstrate his Outsider's 'existential' need for real love, closeness, meaningful communication with another, etc...was rather lost on us, as indeed it was lost on many people who bought the book and began to read it with similiar *frisson*, hoping for a lot more of the same.

They would have became disappointed by chapter two, when this apparently promising exercise in arcane erotica buttoned up its flies and began to gravely philosophise.

The Man Outside ('ordinary conventional society') had, in the event, a lot more on his mind than Sex. Which rather limited his continued appeal for the average, sexually immature, bourgeois Insider – or indeed your average teenager – who often thought of nothing else. Initial sexual titillation aside, it seemed to me, as a book in general, Prodigious. I was awed by the easy freshness and daring of the writing.

For instance it struck me as delightfully relaxed in a philosophical work to mention jazz-singing and Wodehouse's "young men in spats" in virtually the same breath as Professor Whitehead (whoever he was) and T.S. Eliot (who I knew of but hadn't then read).

Although much of 'The Outsider' was then above my head and I had difficulty in following it rationally, I intuitively grasped what Wilson was about. The book's quest for integral human identity, its passionate attempt to understand life and the meaning of human existence, rolled off the pages and engulfed me like some keen ambrosial spiritual vapour.

By the time I read 'Religion and the Rebel' Wilson also had me convinced that becoming a writer was the only worthwhile ambition.

* * *

About that time one of our number went to London for a jazz concert and brought back a paperback called 'Protest'. Subtitled 'The Beat Generation and The Angry Young Men', this provided a compilation of extracts from their writings; including, the first chapter of 'The Outsider'.

This filled an important gap in our reading, as we knew even less about Beatniks than we did about Angry Young Men.* Although we did get to see Osborne's 'Look Back in Anger' in the little Guinness Theatre in '58 or '59. And we saw 'A Taste of Honey' in, I think, the tinier Pike Theatre, soon after – a play by Angry Young Woman Shelagh Delany.

'Protest' included material by Osborne, Amis, Braine, Wain and J.P. Donleavy – we hadn't yet managed to get hold of his (banned) 'The Ginger Man', that classically picaresque account of Forties Dublin, with Brendan Behan cast as bejaysus-belligerant Barney Berry, which (barely) fictionalised the bawdy Life of Gainor Crist - an actual rogue.

But it was the Beats who really jangled our sensibilities.

An extract from 'On The Road', where Kerouac opens with a passage about a Beatnik answering his doorbell stark naked, seemed to us the very last word in Deanerism. The raw jazz-

---

* *We can't have been reading 'Time' too carefully as it carried many features about both camps in the mid-Fifties. We had read a Time-piece on the Russian poets Yevtushenko and Vosnesensky, who apparently represented something like a (Post-Stalin) Beat Movement there. - With such massive popular appeal for Stilyagi and others that they packed Stadia for recitations of their New Poetry.*

prose of that novel barely prepared us for Ginsberg's poem 'Howl'. – "I saw the best minds of my generation destroyed by madness, starving hysterical naked/dragging themselves through the negro streets at dawn looking for an angry fix." Jaysus...What an Opener! Who were these "angelheaded hipsters" he went on about?

For Kerouac they were part of a new American Blessed Trinity, of "Poet, Hoodlum and Junkie" and, we found, in Norman Mailer's essay 'The White Negro', that they were, as hipsters, bordering on sexual psychopathology; at the very least sexually restless and insatiable – shades of the Barbusse 'Outsider'.

From Mailer we also learned that the title of James Dean's second film had been judiciously abbreviated by Hollywood, as the screenplay was apparently based on a book called 'Rebel Without A Cause – The Hypnoanalysis of a Criminal Psychopath'.

No wonder we liked it, incorrigible youths that we were.

Certainly 'Protest', with further extracts from Clellon Holmes's 'Go', a 'Sunday Dinner in Brooklyn' (by Anatole Broyard) that described our own 'generation gap' with our parents perfectly, and an eye-opener, 'My First Days on Junk', by 'William Lee' (Burroughs)...all combined to radically re-factor our perspectives on modern life.

We added 'Hipster' to 'Outsider', in the new vocabulary of social protest.

* * *

We would have been even more delighted to know that this disparate combination of new writers had created a real social storm for awhile.

For despite their differences in style and cultural temper, both the Angry Young Men and the Beats were united in their hostility to power-politics, big business, and the drudgery of urban-industrial life. Their work in general reflected a liberal humanity which opposed cant, hypocrisy, prejudice, repression and injustice in all their forms.

Unfortunately, although their hearts were in the right place, these disaffiliates had, finally, nothing more to offer than revulsion for the rat-race. Politically naive and impractical for the most part, they failed to appreciate that their protest had a hollow ring, coming from the beneficiaries of the very system they attacked. They were equally discredited for arrant self-indulgence and an 'irresponsible' lifestyle based too much on sex, drugs and rock and roll (or jazz).

All in all, it wasn't the right time to start a social revolution. However and although many of the crazier new spirits would finally shrivel in the paranoid atmosphere of the Cold War, their melody lingered on...to become a flower power refrain in the Sixties.

* * *

That said, let me briefly indicate some of the more decisive influences for sociocultural reform that began to emerge in the Fifties, evidenced here by a relatively focussed intellectual ferment and personified by some rather less vulnerable harbingers of change.

It is noteworthy, for example, that such sturdy-minded social commentators as Galbraith, Riesman, Packard and Whyte, working as respected figures within the established system, never incurred anything like the opprobrium levelled at the Angries or Beats.

Yet, they were saying much the same thing about western capitalist society: that it is economically unjust/distorted and favours a powerful minority, at the expense of an enslaved majority; that it is intrinsically corrupt in many basic respects; that it encourages mercantile trickery, lies, deceit and a general devaluation of people.

What might be called their 'humanistic psychology' became mirrored in turn by a new psychological movement in the United States at the same time – under that heading and also known as Third Force Psychology. Maslow for one was developing a form of industrial psychology which put people first and would have accordingly excited any (egalitarian) Beatnik. (His book on this became a bestseller in Japan.)

The Psychology of Sex simultaneously became far less Freudian (or theoretical) and convulsively pragmatic, after the publication of the two Kinsey Reports (1948 and 1953) brought sex, literally, to life. Given the emotive charge of his material, on the hitherto cloistered sex lives of ordinary men and women, Kinsey (an apparently impeccable, crew-cutted Academic)* was universally castigated. But he had 'changed the world', in matters of sex and the common perception of it, forever.

There was also, in the Fifties, a revolution taking place in theological thinking, reflected by changing attitudes to God, Church Worship and many other fundamentals of religious practice. *Pere* Teilhard De Chardin was an undoubted influence here, and not only on Roman Catholic Thought.

Radical theologians like Berdyaev, Niebuhr and Tillich were also ecumenically effective. While the Zen Buddhism advocated by many Beatniks led in turn to a more general tolerance of Oriental religions.

Philosophy also became less concentrated on Pure Logic and Language Analysis in the Fifties and began to move back towards its original human concerns, with the post-war movement to Existentialism.

It only remains to say that this increasing re-evaluation of hidebound thinking in our time, began to gather decisive momentum in the Sixties.

Partly through the work of such maverick 'academics' as

* *Later research, on him, revealed a truly voyeuristic streak!*

Chomsky, Marcuse, Eysenck and Skinner. If their radicalism often inspired bloody student riots as well as peaceful protest movements, it also helped in putting an end to that abominable war in Vietnam.

* * *

I have to rest there, with the above brief outline of some Fifties intellectual developments that have since gradually permeated the mainstream of Western Culture.

Religion, philosophy, psychology, politics, economics, education, the social sciences, business and 'everyday life' in general...in almost every area we are, literally, changing the way we think, as a longterm result of inexorable reformative forces – first clearly discernible in the Fifties.

CHAPTER THIRTEEN

A TASTE OF MONEY

1959. End of my last completed term at school. I was seventeen and in London for the Summer with three other classmates.

Having assured our parents and teachers that we had summer work lined up in Forte's London cafeterias, we got off lessons a couple of weeks before the official holidays in June, to travel. As far as I was concerned that was perfectly true – that jobs were pre-arranged for us – at the time, our organiser having pledged that all was "set up".

We were sitting in the train on our way to the Mail Boat Pier in Dun Laoire, when this ebullient young man casually informed us that the jobs were not "axshually certain". – All he had was the address of the Forte staff-recruiting office in the West End.

"No need to stare at me like that" he said. "You'se'd never have agreed to come if I'd told yese the truth." We couldn't fault that.

"Cheer up" he went on, "there's plenty of casual work over there."

Such was the atmosphere, on a bright May day, sitting there with more money in our pockets than we usually had in a month of Sundays, that the whole thing suddenly seemed a glorious joke. Besides, the optimism of our leader was truly infectious and we were all young, fit and, we presumed, infinitely resourceful.

"London" he picked up, "just think of it. Cliff, Tommy

Steele, Billy Fury, the two eyes coffee bar!" And he strummed an imaginary guitar; he wanted to be a rock 'n roll singer and knew all the ins and outs of it.

So did his close friend, all greased hair and studied sneer; a dead ringer for Elvis apart from the acne. The third youth, a good friend of my own, was more interested in English girls. Just as well for me that nothing would have stopped him getting near one of them by now, for I had persuaded him to join the expedition in the first place. Myself, I was just thrilled to be getting away.

My parents had 'given in to', rather than welcomed, my plan to travel – I had started to get my own way in most things by then – to make with the fares and a few pounds on top. Much nose blowing and sniffling as I marched off with my suitcase, promising to write...Although I was marked to return for school in late August, I think that they both feared I might never return. (I almost didn't, and when I did it was for my own sake rather than theirs.)

Cunt that I was, I didn't write home to them for six long weeks.

Even more absolute cunt, I thought on the train of my current girl-friend, expecting to see me at a record hop that same Sunday night.

I simply hadn't bothered to tell her that I was going away. Just like James Dean wouldn't have done...She was a bloody gorgeous girl too.

I never saw her again.

*   *   *

Meanwhile, on the boat-train, our leader was ribbing me, in front of the others, about two "scrubbers" we tried to pick up in Portmarnock awhile back. I could only join in the laughter when he told them that the one I was trying to make backed off, "because, she said, he has small eyes!"

197

It was quite true. She did and I had (have).

There was much mutual badinage of that kind, although I noticed that my quieter friend and our Presley lookalike were showing the first signs of mutual dislike – a hostility which would build up and finally flare into a London fist-fight.

But personalities fell aside with the novelty of our first sea voyage, and we all stood together as one on the upper deck, watching the Irish coastline recede and vanish. We were truly on our way.

Holyhead at midnight. The strange voices of Welsh porters as we boarded a train whose carriages seemed to stretch back to infinity. Our leader returned from a recce flushed and excited – look what I got!

A Harrison Marks girly magazine, with naked bum and tit galore, bought openly and easily from the station news kiosk. Here was Pagan England at last, sex on open display and the further promise of limitless legally sold french letters to smuggle home, in due course. (There was then a brisk black market trade in "frenchies" on the Dublin streets.)

I can't remember if any of us had a wank to Harrison Marks in the train 'jakes' (toilet); if so it was the last one we'd have for some time – several incredibly continent weeks in my own case – as we duly found out what it was like to come back from work so knackered that we could barely keep our eyes open, let alone think about sex.

(When I passed through Holyhead a year later I was more set on the bar than sex mags, having already supped my way across the Irish Sea.)

* * *

But this was the first crossing and it was great just to be in Holyhead.

Llandudno, the cathedral night arches of Menai Bridge, Chester, Crewe, Rugby...then you were blasting at eighty miles an hour through the grey brown mists of dawn, by night-shrouded grimpen English fields in a Turneresque landscape... coasting slower into the North-West suburbs of Greater London, through Watford, Wembley and the marshalling yards of Willesden Junction...slowing, clanking processionally over the shifting switching entry points to Euston.

London – "the very name tolls a knell in the solemn belfry of the rural mind" (I wrote later). Even though you were tired, stiff and subdued in the platform bustle, your legs buckling with the weight of your suitcase, you were...elated.

Ireland, Dublin, parents, school, jazz sessions and mock-urbane chatter; all seemed already long ago and far away.

Here was Reality. And it felt good.

We washed in the Gents and trudged through the platform barrier, avoiding an evangelical purveyor of Catholic pamphlets.

"How to avoid the pox" someone joked wearily.

Then we were negotiating Hardwicke's magnificent century-old Doric Arch in search of breakfast, found nearby in a cheap workmens' 'caff'. Afterwards, the amazing hurtling Tube train, to Piccadily Circus, where we presented ourselves for employment by Forte.

Our leader was instantly vindicated. We were welcomed with open arms, as alleged students of University College Dublin (and thus income tax exempt – our boy knew all the little tricks). I worried a little about adding a year to my age on their forms...but if that was what it took...

Luckily we had deposited our luggage in the Euston lockers, for Forte's put us to work immediately. Myself and Elvis were sent round the corner to dish-wash in the Circus Branch, while the others went as counter-hands to Regent Street. We would work from 4pm to midnight, six days a week and receive the princely (it was!) sum of £6, per week.

At that age, dish-washing is, fortunately, an adventure and I mucked in quite cheerfully, grateful for a half-hour break and a meal on the house.

We all regrouped as prearranged by the statue of Eros, after our first shifts. Wandering into Soho we found Eros everywhere.

This was shortly before a law was passed, curbing soliciting by prostitutes in public, and buxom berouged females in bum-hugging skirts, open-slash blouses and black fish-net stockings abounded.

"Fancy a nice time, Dearie?" one actually asked us, from a doorway.

"Not tonight Josephine" quipped our leader, quickening his pace.

We couldn't believe the bustle of the streets, at a time when Dublin would be dead and snoring. Flashing neon – BOOKS BOOKS BOOKS ("durty books") and GIRLS GIRLS GIRLS (dirty girls), hamburger stands and glitzy thronged Gaggia-Espresso coffee bars.

Our rockers led on to the famous '2 Is', where Tommy Steele, Cliff Richard and a small stable of current English icons had made their debut. It was packed. Music blaring from a Sieberg juke box while the sounds of a live skiffle group competed from the cellar.

London girls seemed dazzling, even if they stumbled about in weird pointy-toed high-heeled shoes – the currently fashionable 'winkle-pickers'. Their neat tight-skirted suits, bouffant hairstyles and perfect little pale faces, contrasted oddly with the carefully dishevelled appearance of several male escorts, who mooched about, hair in disarray, in scruffy lumberjack shirts and jeans. A few boys, more in the fashion, sported neat ultra-short Italian jackets (bum-freezers) and sharply cut, razor-creased tweeds, their sixteen inch 'bottoms' resting on black-glossed chrome-buckled male winkle-pickers. They wore white or blue shirts and expensive-looking slim-jim ties. Long or short their sleek hair was a tonsorial triumph.

To us, this was Look/Gape, Don't Touch (or speak)

territory; we felt like ragged yokels. But we spent an hour or so exploring the inner depths of the '2 Is' and had our first taste of foaming espresso coffee. Our leader and Elvis were in seventh heaven, but this was not really my scene – an indifference shared by number four.

We caught the last tube back to Euston, where we dossed down for the night on huge ornamental marble catafalques – which then lined the old entrance hall. We did that three nights running, having no clear idea how to go about getting suitable lodgings - or, more probably, little inclination, as there was so much else to see and do.

Then, by chance, I found us a place.

* * *

In doing so I incidentally found my own *metier*.

On the third night, making my own way up to Euston on foot, I stopped off at a dingy dark cellar coffee bar called 'The Nucleus', in Monmouth Street. Drinking a coffee I was suddenly accosted by a broad deep growling Dublin accent:

"You don't look like a bohemian. This place is for bohemians only."

I focussed on a face and figure that would have delighted Lombroso – that discredited phrenological classifier of criminal types.

This was Ned – built like a brick shit-house, with matching bullet-head. Something like a smile flickered, cariously, across the stubbled visage and I sensed that he meant no immediate harm. Instead he slumped into a seat opposite me, shaking my coffee cup by merely resting a massive fist on the scarred formica table-top.

"Ye're a towny, isn't ye?" he growled. "I heard the brogue when ye paid at the counter. Dublin?" I nodded.

He tapped his hooter. "Nothin escapes Ned."

"You're from Dublin?" – a pretty rhetorical gambit.

"Broombridge. – Ye wouldn't have the price of a cup an' a bun?"

"Sure." I found some change for him.

"Ye're a star. I'll give it back to ye when me fancy woman arrives."

He himself was back with a mug of tea and a cheese roll before I had time to digest that he had a 'fancy woman', treating me now like an old friend and plying me with questions about Dublin. Ned had been a very long time away and had no intention of returning before "I make me pile. When I do" he went on, "I'll be drivin a Rolls Royce." He laughed, like a running drain. "That'll show dem all! Feck dem."

I warmed to a fellow-Romantic, by now totally at ease with him. To the extent that I was soon confiding our homeless plight and asking if he had any ideas...He had:

"Yere troubles are over. Tell your mates that all four of yese can bunk with Ned." Happily he did not mean in Ned's bed, but in his "gaff" (rooming-house) in Highbury which specialised in lodging Irish navvies.

We would move in there the following day. Ned was a real find.

While he was giving me the address and directions I noticed that a youngish woman had come into the fast-crowding basement eaterie.

At least it looked like a woman, with some disturbingly androgynous components – for example I overheard 'her' talking to someone in a husky male voice.

She was very tall and slim, indeed breastless, and she moved with a slow unnatural sinuousness, in sweater and clinging black slacks, and in a way that gave me the creeps. Her swept-back shoulder-length hair was jet-black, fine and sleek – a wig withal, as I duly discovered.

This was Angel, Ned's fancy woman. He jumped up, animated. "Darlin!"

"Hi, Sweety Pie." Husky as hell, but her eyes lit up for him alright.

She called me Sweety Pie too, after he had given her a bear hug and introduced us. Angel called everyone Sweety Pie.

"Even her clients" Ned told me later, when we were alone. "She's on the game."

"She is?"

"Didn't ye guess?"

I hadn't. Partly because I couldn't imagine anyone, except Ned, being turned on by that strange being, or that nauseously cosmeticised face, literally morassed in heavy mascara.

"She wears make-up to cover her bristles" Ned further confided, before divulging with something like pride: "Angel is a hermaphrodite." Spoken so perfectly that he had obviously learned the word by heart.

That she had "a hearta gold" I couldn't dispute. That she was generous I couldn't doubt, as she slipped him a ten shilling note before excusing herself, moments after her arrival, with a long-lashed wink to Ned, "to keep an urgent appointment".

"She loves me" he said simply. "Because I understand her."

(Good as his word, he paid me back for the refreshments now.)

He certainly knew what she most wanted in life, and why she had to whore to get the money for it: "Angel's savin up to go to Copenhagen for an operation which will change her sex permanently." He tapped his crotch. "She's still male there."

I just had to ask how 'she' thus functioned, as a Pro.

"Blow jobs. She's an expert at them. I get the specials."

Ned was the only bohemian navvy I would ever meet.

* * *

Back at Euston I gave my friends a rundown on all this new experience; they couldn't wait to meet Ned, or see Angel, not least to find the house in Highbury and sleep again in a proper bed.

Early the following morning we were on the tube to Arsenal and carrying our cases up Highbury Hill to the house of our dreams – I mean the house where we could hope to dream without steam and whistles. For it was otherwise a decrepit old mansion, set in scraggy surrounds.

A frowsily dressed Irish woman welcomed us cagily enough.

"Ned sent ye? How is he? Did he give ye any rent for me? He did not? Tell him I said he's a durty blackguard. Now, how many of ye are there? Four. I have four beds and ye'll each have yer own lockers. But don't leave anything in the lockers, unless you want to get rid of it. We have one or two theeves here. I'll want rent in advance. One week from each of ye. Twenty-five shillins apiece. Have ye got it?"

When she got it, and the assurance that we were all working in "permanent jobs", she mellowed into a motherly matron.

A couple of weeks later she disappeared and we had to move on. We had thought that she owned the place until Ned then put us wise:

"She managed it. And she's run off with several months rents."

He chortled. "I'm off the hook now. I owed her a bomb!"

Meanwhile, we were being shown into a vast dormitory room with twin rows of low iron bedsteads, arranged in the military manner. Each bed had a tall locker by its head; none of them locked.

Our leader was not fazed and told us the first job would be to go back out and buy padlocks for the latches, to secure our luggage. That did the business, for the short period we stayed on Highbury Hill.

In fact we proved to be the only occupants of that room. Until Ned himself rolled in a few nights later, long after midnight, well-oiled, to scare the daylights out of our leader by mischieviously lifting and overturning his bed, with him fast asleep in it.

Apparently Drink brought out the frustrated weight-lifter in Ned.

There were about twenty* other residents, spread among the many rooms of that massive old house. All of them were bona fide Irish navvies ('Paddies' to the trade) who we seldom encountered.

They were gone to the site by 6am and seldom home before pub closing time. The front door was then locked but they all – as we did – gained access by shinning up a drainpipe to a landing window, which was permanently open.

There was a 'television room' in the basement, which we only looked into once, getting a brief taste of English commercial tv. (I had only once seen a few minutes of BBC tv in Dublin. That was the pop programme 'Six-Five Special', viewed at the house of an acquaintance whose family boasted the only set in our neighbourhood.)

The drainpipe arrangement proved disastrous for our leader. A week or so later he lost his balance on the climb and tumbled back on the hard ground below, breaking his ankle. To his absolute chagrin, he ended up with a plastered foot, being summarily shipped back to Dublin.

Then there were Three...

* * *

We had one other contact in London. My workmate, Elvis, had an older brother training in catering at the old Berkeley Hotel, by Green Park.

We had actually met up with him briefly on the morning of our second day, when he took us to Ward's 'Irish House', a famous pub in Piccadilly Circus. I was persuaded to drink a

---

* We guessed that 'theeving' manageress had got away with a tidy sum.

heavily lemonaded beer 'shandy' (an interesting variation on that familiar term for wanking), which was my very first taste of anything alcoholic. He was working as a chef waiter and mentioned the possibility of getting a couple of us 'in' as commis waiters. The pay would be better than Forte and there were tips...

Soon after our leader's mishap "the chief", as Elvis played on his brother's title, contacted us to say there were commis jobs for three. My friend in Regent Street, who was making a fair few bob on tips himself, as a personable counter-hand, and hoping to 'get off' with a "delectable" manageress, declined. (Telling me on the side that he didn't want to work with Elvis anyway.) I leapt at the opportunity, without the slightest reservation – I was getting on famously with Elvis.

We informed our manager at Forte, who asked us to complete another week there, otherwise wishing us luck. We were doing so well on the dishes and making so many friends among the chefs and waiters, that we were more than happy to oblige. They were a great bunch of exotic Greeks and Ities to us, even the little chef who got fired during our first few days, after being caught trying to smuggle out a couple of cooked chickens. (Apparently he was unlucky to be tumbled; we soon found out that food-stealing was a regular practice among the staff.)

For a few days we contented ourselves with the routine, which included further Soho explorations after midnight. To the extent that we missed the last tube a couple of nights later and relied on Ned's directions to a night bus, which only took us to Euston. By the time we finally walked to Highbury it must have been close to daybreak.

Then, noticing a crate of full milk bottles outside a dairy near the house, we did some stealing of our own. A bobby, on a bicycle, rounded the corner to catch us red-handed, quenching our thirst with stolen milk.

Allo Allo Allo then, what have we got here? Theeves.

He proved a right Dixon of Dock Green in the event.

Taking our names, ascertaining who and what we were, before chiding softly. "This is no way for students to behave. What would your parents think?"

"We're very very sorry, Officer. It will never happen again." Lick lick.

"I should hope not. Now be off with you, before I change my mind."

He had given us a bad fright. It didn't happen again.

* * *

I had introduced the others to Ned, on the night we moved into Highbury.

They were very wary of him, although they respected his bulk and acted friendly enough. Our leader had him for "an old lag".

Ned subsequently told me that he had done some time "for Her Majesty".

They seemed to me rather lost in 'The Nucleus', unable to mix with its weird denizens and sitting apart like three odd men out. Shaking their heads at me, while, in my element, I delved into jazz and beat poetry with a handy, hairy, bohemian. (He told me about a coffee bar in Frith Street that had modern jazz on the juke. I was there the next night.)

By the time Angel appeared, more the painted doll than ever, and began to execute (I do mean 'kill') a 'provocative' sinewy dance routine, straight from Ancient Egypt, the others were frantically signalling me to belt up and come on, out.

The following night they were back at the '2 Is', while I was elsewhere on my todd, finding the place that had 'Django' and 'My Funny Valentine' on the box. Later again I found my way to Ronnie Scott's Club and was about to turn away, put off by the admission price, when Scott himself came out for a breath of air. He had me in an instant. "Did you want to go in?" Did

I! "We're closing shortly." I still nodded. He turned to the doorman. "Let the gentleman in."

That's Jazz. That was London to me, nothing but good.

* * *

About the time we finished at Forte our landlady did her runner. It soon became apparent that the house was set for total anarchy. We had to find ourselves somewhere else, fast.

Someone informed me that newsagents shops had outside boards carrying cards with accommodation vacancies. I found time to do some looking, startled to see that many of these lettings cards had NO COLOURED and/or NO IRISH blocked above the script.

I was a White Negro.

I homed on a room above an Indian Restaurant in Holloway Road. Mister Ali, the Pakistani restauranteur, had "a ver' niz room". Nice enough for me: clean, bright, with three single beds, overlooking thundering Holloway Road itself. Same rent as Highbury. I took it.

The other two were delighted and we moved in the same day. Clearing the way and settling two of us, for our new job in the hotel.

All we needed before starting was to buy a pair of black wasp-waisted waiter's trousers from a caterer's tailor in Soho; fresh white button down tunics would be supplied every day in-house.

The Berkeley was heaven (after dish-washing anyway). We would work the luncheon shift – 11am to 3pm – and return for the dinner shift (6pm to 10/10.30). That meant we could spend the afternoons sunning ourselves in Green Park – a glorious summer it was too, in '59.

Here we would get £8 per week and a couple of pounds from the 'tronc' (of tips) every two weeks. We would also get two full meals (including some delicious desserts that the sated clientele hadn't touched). To cap it: three full days off a fortnight – what could be better?

Only the changing-room, with its dilapidated lockers and sticky-sweet smell of stale sweat, reminded you of Forte.

There were several magnificent restaurants and we alternated between the Grill Room and Buttery. This was sumptious stuff for a boy fresh off the boat, even if your lowliest rank meant that you never got near a bejewelled diner. (It never remotely occurred to me that I would be eating in such places, on the receiving end, a decade or so later.)

Commis helped lay the tables and generally did the fetching and carrying – of enormous heavy silver trays (laden with smaller covered salvers of food), from the catacombed kitchens upstairs to the dining-room.

(Wesker's great stage play, 'The Kitchen', catches the below-stairs freneticism of such places perfectly.)

You tottered up the primeval stone steps, between weeping plaster walls, to enter the elegant eating chamber and lay your burden down at your 'station' – one of many customised side-boards set back against the side-walls. Each station had two commis assigned, as well as a tidy hierarchy of waitorial grades who were each deputed to handle various stages of the actual table service.

The Station Waiter was, I think, the Supremo on this ranking. He supervised the dishing out and actually spoke to the gourmets. There were also some free-floating senior waiters who specialised in various functions.

I remember the ancient Wine Waiter as a particular card.

"I would suggest Twenty Six, Sir. The pink Moet is superb, Modom."

After which you would bump into him, on his way back to the cellars, red-nosed and tottering in his waiter's weeds, muttering to himself. "Fucking cunts" was his favourite mutter. Or "fucking cunt", if he had just passed the svelte French Restaurant Manager, gliding open-armed between the tables, like George Sanders in Noel Coward, effusively welcoming an old familiar:

"Mad-Ame is looking glorious! Cannes was up to expectations?"

Most of the senior waiters were English. My own station waiter was a tiny gnarled worldwise Cockney who had learned to speak like a toff. (Except behind the scenes, where everyone was a "bleeder".)

The middle rank waiters were mostly Greek, with a few dark handsome Latins – one of whom liked to fondle commis bums, playfully, with a saturnine Colgate smile.

There was one moon-faced and pockmarked young Turkish commi who got unmercifully ribbed by the Greeks.

"Pushtera" they jeered at him, until he sniggered back, not at all offended: "Pushtera you!" I gathered it meant something like bugger.

Us commis were a mixed lot, including two incredibly handsome young men who commanded enormous respect from everyone. They were Hungarian and had fought the Russians during the ill-fated Uprising of 1956. In their offhand way they would tell you, if you seemed okay, that they had "killed many Russians", or destroyed many tanks, with Molotov cocktails and the like. We got to know them well, even to playing snooker together in a hall opposite the Windmill Theatre. They both spoke excellent English compared to most of the other foreigners.

My real find here was a brilliant young Jewish boy from North London, who was a genuine university student, of higher mathematics. He was also a great Reader and we became fairly chummy until he quit commis-ing for a pre-term holiday with his betrothed. (I owe him for the verse about the modern cinematic emporium.) He later spent a year on an Israeli Kibbutz and we corresponded occasionally for a time.

Conversations with him were the nearest I got to those of

my Dublin circle, until I befriended another 'smart Jewish boy' during a later stay.

As Nietzsche himself insisted – despite all the ill-founded rumours of his Anti-Semitism – there is no one to match an intelligent Yiddisher for truly subtle, creative thinking. My own experience, culminating with my discovery of psychologist supreme, Abraham Maslow, and philosopher supreme, Edmund Husserl, bears that out.

'

* * *

It would have taken an inspired psychologist to get to the twisted root of Ned's philosophy. He was certainly not a stupid man, if you define intelligence as the ability to adapt in adversity, and survive somehow, against all the odds. For, from what he told me, the dice of life had been loaded against Ned from the off. He grew up in real poverty and saw little but hatred, violence and drunkenness from the cradle. He had barely learned to read and write.

He was also intelligent enough to envy us our relative youth, our innocence, our middle-class upbringing and education. He admitted as much, in so many words. That he was deeply embittered and capable of viciousness we had no doubt; but we never saw the nasty side and, to the contrary, he became (drunken 'de-bunking' aside – an act of envy in itself) curiously, awkwardly, self-conscious in our company. A sad kind of man. I guess he felt life owed him that Roller, at the very least...

As things stood, Brawn was his only passport. Yet, like some other 'heavies' I have met, he had a certain awe of Brain (or education) in others – as if sensing that that is the personal attribute which finally matters, in the struggle for self-betterment. – Even so the savage man I once met who saw no way back at all, from what he had become...and done... Indeed I had to look very hard for humanity, let alone brains, in the monster who nailed an antagonist's tongue to the floor boards of a remote deserted warehouse...and left him a sharp knife.

Perhaps, no less than Ned, he was not born so, but bred.

* * *

I saw less and less of Ned after our move to Holloway ("only a stone's throw from Pentonville" he joked, "me old gaff".) When I did drop by the 'Nuke' occasionally, he was seldom about.

On a later visit there I approached a ragged old man with the beard of a Methuselah. I had often noticed him before, hunched over a cup of lemon tea and poring (intriguingly) over a table-full of papers and charts.

This was Ernest Page, Astrologer.

I never made much of Ernest, who truly inhabited a zodiac of his own. He made a precarious living reading horoscopes for tourists. But as I never saw him eat a morsel, I presumed that he needed no more than the price of lemon tea. He'd let you buy him one, but he never wanted your money.

I told him, glib as ever, that I was "a writer".

"Ahh...I have known several." (Ernest had the lovely locution of a Don.) "I am going shortly to Soho Square. If you like I will show you a cafe there which is frequented by artists and writers."

Strolling down Shaftesbury Avenue with Ernest was like being with Moses when he parted the Red Sea, as oncoming pedestrians moved to right or left, warily skirting this lumbering tatterdemalion from the stars.

We parted company at the 'cafe' (a snack bar). However, if Page was a Sage he'd missed a beat on this one; the place was a haunt of whore, pimp and costermonger. It didn't even have a juke box.

...On the way down the Avenue, we may even have passed

212

the most famous busker of the day. That was the alleged 'Earl of Mustard', who dressed as an oldtime buccaneer, complete with three-cornered headgear, wheeled a big pram and tap-danced for queuing theatregoers...

* * *

For a time, apart from commuting, I stayed out of Soho altogether, having found a new kind of excitement closer to our new base – as close as next door in fact.

One of the tenants in our new 'pad' was a dapper Jamaican. We first met Tony in a communal kitchenette which we used to wash our shirts and underwear. They soon dried strung up on a makeshift clothes-line, in temperatures that never seemed to drop below the Eighties. Tony shared a room upstairs from our own with a slim dark-haired English girl, who obviously adored him.

"You must come to my club" he invited me. "You will like it there."

Some understatement. The Amaso Club, one dimly-lit ground floor room entered by a narrow alleyway adjacent to our digs, became the place, as far as I was concerned. Tony introduced me round on the first visit and I was afterwards welcome to go there as I wished, or to bring my room-mates. That we were usually the only white faces in the place, apart from English girl-friends of the main West Indian clientele, never seemed to bother anyone. Irish were apparently AOK.

How I blessed Tony – I'd never even have found it without him, as the big display window out front was blacked over and the Club sign hidden beneath the arch of the alley. Inside you had a small bar and a few drinks tables and chairs, leaving plenty of standing, or (close) dancing, room in the centre. A highly convivial confine, all in all. Or a piece of Jamaica transferred to the temperate zone.

I just loved these boisterously friendly West Indians and we talked a great deal of glorious nonsense together. Oiled, inevitably, by alcohol, as I began to imbibe my first glasses of fizzy apple cider.

But it was the music on the juke that made me a real addict of the place. Almost from the moment I entered to hear an incredible silky voice – more Mathis than Johnny himself – rising high and falling deep, to a unique rocking beat, lusciously backed by sizzling strings:

"High-er than the high-est mountain and deeper than the deepest sea..."

The velvet voice of Brook Benton, singing 'Endlessly'.

He was certainly played endlessly in the Amaso – an American who breathed the very soul of the Caribbean (and incidentally produced a string of hit records in the States). Brook always managed to sound like the light-hearted gentleman he was – I saw him interviewed on tv in the Eighties, shortly before his death – whatever the song. Indeed his style was as individual as any of the great original Rockers; more akin to the Danny Williams of 'Moon River', than to Mathis or Nat King Cole.

Another Amaso favourite was the Reggae Rock of Prince Buster – the West Indian 'Elbis' – who later got cut to pieces, financially and physically, by the gangsters who run the Jamaican pop music 'scene'. (I just spun his 'Judge Dread', vividly bringing back nights in the Amaso.)

The juke also featured some good hard rock and raw rhythm 'n blues.

* * *

In the Amaso I got talking to a beautiful second-generation Jamaican girl, under the watchful eye of her immigrant father. (Many West Indian parents are almost Irish in their protective chaperoning of daughters.) Like me she was an only child. However, if I was partly spoiled, she was thoroughly so, with the well-to-do Father wrapped round the proverbial digit. We shared a passion for early Elvis – "I have every one of his records" she said proudly. After a bit of covert whispering she agreed to come to the cinema – but only on the following Sunday. Hot as a tom-cat on a griddle, I resolved to take the day off.

She turned up trumps, standing outside the local cinema when I arrived – looking like a Ted in my new drape jacket, snazzy summer shirt, black drainpipes and...matching winkle-picker shoes. Whatever she thought of scrawny me, she was an absolute dish, in white blouse, tight red skirt and cute elevated shoes. After you, My Dear, after you.

I was too shy to suggest the back row of the stalls and we ended up somewhere in the middle of the half-empty auditorium, sitting in front of a couple of kids who made rude noises when the lights went down, and I put my arm around her. She didn't seem to mind, snuggled right into me.

The kids hissed. I looked back at them warningly and they mercifully shut up. Praise be the Ted rig-out.

Then I went stone deaf anyway, as I was blind to the action on the screen. For I had no sooner turned my face to hers than she was kissing me full on the lips, darting her tongue (as they say) into my mouth. That literally went on for the entire duration of the film, with enough further refinements to teach me what real passion was all about. Anywhere else I'd have lost my cherry, with my mind.

As it was I had her half-naked before long. Blouse open, bra down, over two heaving brown titties, nipples hard as bullets. The kids behind us were quiet as mice. I unzipped her skirt and plunged my hand down her poor excuse for proper panties, feeling feeling feeling, probing between the parted thighs. That was when she went for my lowry and squeezed even more life into him, before unzipping my fly and holding him tight through the cotton Jockeys. She giggled softly at the moist result. If moist is the word, I was absolutely sodden with

215

the great gush of it and feeling like I'd been hit by a bus.

By the time the lights came on I looked like the wreck of the Hesperus. I couldn't believe how cool, calm and collected she looked, or how quickly she re-arranged the blouse and skirt: spruce as a moose.

Then we decided we'd had enough of the cinema – milked dry no doubt. I was well-satisfied anyway. From her dazzling smile, she was happy too.

It didn't bother me when she insisted that we left the cinema separately, in case we were seen by anyone she knew. Not because she didn't want to be seen with me, she explained, but to save me being knifed by her compatriots. Apparently they drew the line sharply, in both senses, at white men going out with black girls.

Only afterwards it occurred to me to wonder why then, she had arranged to meet me in the first place. We might have been seen together in the cinema? Another possibility didn't occur to me: that I hadn't proved as good with her as I imagined I was.

That, in effect, I was being given the push.

It just might have been the case, borne out by our next casual meeting in the Amaso. She was with the pater and seemed friendly enough. I slipped her a piece of paper on which I had scribbled:

'Once I found it in a Negro Girl
That inward grace
Surmounting puberty
Unspoiled her face.'

She glanced at it. And giggled. Soon after her father took her away.

She never returned to the Club and I never saw her again.

Was that, maybe, my first rejection slip? Or just a bad slip? Equally likely... we were merely using one another, as 'novelties'. I would have thus satisfied her curiosity about White-y, As Lover – apparently doing little for racial integration on that score in the process. For I was a poor 'lover' in the sense of knowing how to really romance a girl, with sweet talk and all the other little tricks of a polished seducer. I hardly spoke to her in kind, or knew how to.

Or it may just have been the winkle-picker shoes.

She in turn confirmed everything prurient I had heard about Horny Black Girls (the old Rastus and Lulu jokes etc.), although I never thought of her as a whore, or 'dirty'. Whatever it was I don't think either of us took our encounter all that seriously, or moved beyond sex to even think of love.

Far from being heart-broken, I soon put the whole thing down to (a marvellous) experience and moved on to whatever new adventure. If only I knew it I would be waiting a long time yet for another taste of such forthright female sexuality. That was no fault of Tony who, as the days and weeks wore on, tried to persuade me to move into a flat with him in Finsbury Park and stay on permanently in London.

"We have a nice English girl for you" he tempted ("we" included his current girl-friend). "She will be good for you. I know!"

As she was an old friend of his own "woman" and still resident in the Midlands, I could only take his word for that. Or that she was "coming to London in September". I may well have missed a glorious opportunity, to meet the girl of my dreams, but I declined.

Persistent as ever – he was a right little pimp at times – he offered to "help" me find a woman now, if that was the problem. No, my friend, it wasn't. The real problem was that I was getting homesick.

* * *

Before all that however, life had been far from dull, even after the cinema. For one thing, we were increasingly discovering the early benisons of alcohol – in the initial form of mostly mild intoxication.

I think it was after a scour of the market bookstalls one Saturday morning, that myself and my closest buddy – still coining the tips at Forte – dropped into a pub for a cooler downer. A couple of bottles of cider later and we were feeling very expansive indeed.

Thus the Rake beginneth his retrogressive progress...

The pal admitted that he hadn't as yet managed to pull the young manageress. "But she fancies me" he insisted. "I'm certain of it. Anyway" he went on, "I had a bit of luck during the week." I ohhed. "I went into one of them cartoon cinemas for awhile." He grinned. "You'll never believe this!" Try me. "The oul wan sitting next to me only felt me up." He was joking? No, he wasn't – even more: "Afterwards she took me out for tea and cakes. She's about forty, but very well-preserved."

"Jaysus" I said. "Did you have a come – in the picture-house?"

He smirked. "That'd be tellin. Anyway, I have a date with her. But tell us - how are you gettin on, sex-wise?"

"Nothing much" said I, "but you never know." (This was before the Amazing Grace episode would put me well up in his league.)

It was soon after, on a night when the three of us sampled a pint of light ale with our ciders, that our gigolo and Elvis fell out badly. Over little or nothing, just enough to excuse the open hostility, as one took a wild swing at the other, getting a punch in the gut back...before a couple of responsible citizens separated them. To, I imagine, their own relief as much as mine: it had gone far enough.

Oddly enough that seemed to clear the air between them and I spent the following morning telling them, in the name

218

of the Redeemer, to stop apologising to one another. But I was no less pleased – two sworn enemies sharing the same small room with me would have been unbearable. I guess they knew that too.

* * *

About a month into our stay I wrote a delirious letter to one of the Dublin *cenacle*, telling him what a ball we were having. A letter back warned that my parents had been on the point of dementia, waiting to hear from me. He'd passed on that I was okay, but could I please drop them a line, pronto. (I had sent them no more than a postcard, on the day we arrived.) Anyway, I did the decent thing now and received a letter back, by return post, from one greatly relieved "loving Mammy". At least that was the only time, during a string of later trips, that I kept them waiting for my letter.

About then the others complained that they had not received their own regular letters from home. Tony tipped us the wink and we ended up going high upstairs, to where a multitude of Pakistanis roomed. We often met one of them on the stairs, going in or out, and nodded Hello for a dusky smile. Now, in a vast attic room that seemed to be one great bed (of beds), we found the missing letters, lying open for all the world to see, on a chair. Elvis apoplectically rounded on the nearest individual, who only spread his hands: I know nothing. Two or three others only looked sheepish, with a few more asleep, or feigning it well, under their bedclothes. Suddenly at a bit of a loss, we made much of warning them never to touch our mail again. And they didn't.

"Someone hoped to find money" Tony explained later, with a merry laugh.

"Bloody cheek, Tony. But how many of them are there? It's like the black hole of Calcutta up there, with bodies."

He shrugged. "Who knows? They work shifts in kitchens or

factories and take turns in the beds." He winked. "Good business for Mister Ali."

Come to think of it, I never found out what Tony did, to live.

So I had no trouble safely receiving another letter soon after, from my old friend of the Mill. He was so intrigued by my tales from The Smoke that he intended to come across himself, for a few weeks. Could we get him a job in the Berkeley? We could and we did. He was with us in no time, with Ali delighted to squeeze a fourth bed into our room, which was now worth a nice round five pounds a week to him.

Unfortunately, he began by hating the room – "you've asked me to come and live in a bee-hive" – and positively detested the hotel work.

Nonetheless, our Cockney boss took a shine to him and he managed to make a brittle go of it for awhile.

He did enjoy our extracurricular activities. I 'showed' him Soho – the Nuke (Ned appalled him), the modern jazz coffee bar, we even had a session at Scott's – and introduced him round at the Amaso. He too began to drink and we got legless together one night on cider, lager and sherry.

But it was still a great relief to him when his mother rang the Berkeley one day and said he had passed muster for a (pre-applied) clerical post in the Irish civil service. Could he return home right away?...To celebrate his deliverance we had one last glorious binge.

I suspect it was his departure that started me thinking of Home.

Early mornings we often went to the open-air swimming pool at Highbury Corner, which possibly also aroused a yen for the sea-baths at Blackrock – with the sea itself on tap if you wanted a real cold plunge.

All-in-all I was realising that a bit of Dublin Summer, while it lasted, might not be a bad idea. I decided to give my notice at the Berkeley.

On my final Saturday, Ned turned up at the Pool, with a neat-looking, quiet-spoken Englishman of about his own age – late 20s – who he surprised us by introducing as "me best friend".

On closer acquaintance, Simon, who sported a Van Dyck beard, turned out to have a streak a wild as Ned's.

"He can handle himself in a mill"* said Ned. *Dublinese: fight.

Simon compelled us by telling us about his latest girl-friend. "She loves Sixty-Nine." He sighed. "I have lock-jaw from licking the man in the boat last night." It took us awhile to ascertain that "the man" was his term for her clitoris. We found it very funny. (Although we only knew roughly that a clitoris was "a sensitive spot".)

We spent awhile watching Ned preening about the place, doing a bad imitation of Charles Atlas, in baggy black woollen swimming togs, before we parted company with them.

That was the last I saw of Ned.

"Never forget" he'd once advised me, "that a wall is a natural weapon."

Chapter Fourteen

THE BLONDE IN THE BLACK DRESS

That is Dublin slang for the long black pint of draught Guinness, with its thin flat peroxide head settled in creamy smoothness.

You saw it regularly advertised on British TV awhile back, with 'Blade Runner' star Rutger Hauer smoothly proclaiming it is "Pure Genius".

* * *

By the time I returned to Dublin in August 1959, all of my old friends and indeed most of the teenagers I knew, were starting to quaff the stuff.

We now met as often in 'The Homestead', a pub by the snooker den, as in the Hall itself. A second choice was Hanlon's, a pub by the cattle market on the other side of our home streets, where we sometimes drank with my father. He had no objection to my new pastime, providing he wasn't expected to do too much of the buying.

I had returned from England with only a few pounds to show for it all and soon relapsed into dependence on parental largesse. As we were all in a similar position, the usual economic restrictions on drinking came into play and it became mainly a Saturday night affair. A post-prandial (half-pint) "bottle of stout" was more the rule during the week, before you moved on for a game of snooker, or a cheap seat in the Cabra Grand.

At that time we were more than happy to get "mankey" once a week, on Saturday night, and meet up for a "hair of the dog" on Sundays, lunchtime, before "leaving it alone" for the most part on weekdays.

I later became quite adept at cadging a few drinks, even through the week. To the extent that my friend of the Mill dubbed me "Freddy Freeloader". – That was mainly during the brief period after I had left school and was effectively 'unemployed'.

Personally, I never thought of myself as a bum and regarded my entertainment value in company as well worth paying for. Which reminds me of a very interesting little story...

* * *

One of my wealthier friends certainly savoured me and subsidised many such drinking bouts just for the fun of being with 'Divvy'. (This was in fact the chap whose priest-uncle slept with his mother and who once made a habit of joining a girl-friend in bed.)

He was an incredibly handsome boy – who looked Twenty when he was only Fourteen – and we'd begun by excluding him from our elite close circle as no more than a 'mickey dazzler' who'd had "everything given to him on a plate": looks, 'boyish' charm, talent, money, etc etc. (All but real brains – or so we liked to think then, in our spiteful envy.)

On the face of it, we were justifiably jealous as hell!

Item: his family were rich and snooty enough to educate him at St. Paul's. (That pissed us off although we got on well with another local who went to Blackrock College, calling him "Rocky". And we had time for a quiet Protestant boy who attended Belvedere.) Item: he could have given Cary Grant lessons in style and Tony O'Reilly rugby-lessons. Item: at parties he pulled every female in the place, to crowd round the piano while he belted out current pops and 'boogied' superbly. Item: he was everything socially slick, smooth and sportsy, that we detested.

He also loved jazz and did everything to win our friendship on that count – longing to be admitted to our little record sessions.

He told me later that the afternoon he first called to the session house and was turned away from the door, it shattered him for days afterward.

I remembered the instance – we had crowed among ourselves at being able to reject him. Conceited little inverted snobs that we were.

Anyway, he persevered in trying to cultivate my best friend, who startled me by saying one day, "Saint Paul's is an okay bloke." This pal was an infallible judge of character, apart from having an ability to elicit confidences from others that would put any priest or psycho-analyst to shame. ("He had a way of drawing people out", as Byron wrote of Childe Harold, "without their knowing what he was about".)

And boy had he extracted some from our ostensibly stuck-up snob. ...About the clerical uncle having the mother...about the domestic hell he endured at home, with his (law-de-daw) parents often fighting-drunk, in a way that made my own seem like true lovers.

His earliest memory was watching his warring parents literally trying to pull his howling baby sister apart, as they fought for possession of her. I began to see what my friend meant – this was a boy whose bland appearance belied an awful lot. All the money he wanted, without any real love or family feeling, was the least of it. Then I heard about the plucky 'Deanerism' of invading his girl's bedroom, to kiss and canoodle in the nude...He was...quite a 'bloke'!

Endorsing that for me later, the man himself described a particular night when his beloved's father had suddenly entered the room.

224

"I was under that bed like shit off a shovel and lying there, trembling, me cock practically in me mouth, listening to him saying he'd heard a noise and asking the girls were they both alright...And Jaysus Divvy, I was prayin he wouldn't see my shirt, still on a chair!"

That was pretty meaty stuff, to a shy little wanker like myself.

...And all-in-all a sharp lesson in not summarily judging others by appearances. There is always more to people than we see.

Oh yes, by the way, he did have brains too! More than most of us probably. As well as a tremendous sense of fun which revelled in dirty jokes and poking heresiarchical holes in the Roman Catholic Tradition, like the rest of us.

So by the time I left school he was a popular part of our pack and one of the warmest, most supportive and generous of all my friends. Particularly in those empty days after I "abandoned my education" (as my father insisted) and was trying to justify my idle existence by writing poetry and short stories; when he would roll up to our house on a Lambretta scooter and whip us both away to Town, for a glorious night of drinking and dancing, at his expense.

Having by then started a job in the Bank of Ireland he was generally 'loaded' and I owed him a great deal for brightening my life accordingly. I remember most, that we laughed together a lot.

Drinking pints (and the odd 'small one' of whiskey) we would make glorious plans for the future, inevitably involving my writing "the grate Irish novel" and possibly doing a libretto for his planned (Irish) answer to West Side Story. Doesn't it all seem so simple in those great days of youth, before life begins to turn a screw or two!?

We often ended up at a dance in The Swiss Chalet Ballroom. His generosity of nature extended to never abandoning me later, when as usually happened, he picked up a pretty girl and I was left Joe Solo. It just never even occurred to him to go after his oats and leave me to walk home alone. Greater friendship hath no man for another!...

When I got a job over the subsequent Christmas period I was able to pay back some of the hospitality. Then he became embroiled in another fierce love-affair and we drifted apart for awhile. By then I was also doing "a strong line", with a girl I very nearly married.

To get to that, I must recap a little on other activities.

*   *   *

By the time I returned to begin my final, 'Sixth Year', at school I was a confirmed Saturday Night Drinker and regularly joined 'the guys' in a pub called 'The Hut' in Phibsboro.

They had installed a tv and our nights began with watching 'The Valiant Years', a series of 30 minute programmes based on Churchill's war memoirs. – Given the supposed antagonism of the Irish for the English, it is interesting to note that we all relished the series and identified completely with the British, standing up so doggedly to the Nazis. I guess we sensed that all this stuff about the Blitz, the RAF, El Alamein and so on, transcended mere propaganda and was based on the historical facts of a struggle that saved Ireland, as much as England, from being terminally jack-booted.

I do remember that all pub talk ceased and you could hear a silent fart, when the credits began to roll and the anthem theme music – the March from Tchaikovsky's Sixth – drowned the surrounding sounds of glassware.

Then on to talking, drinking, more talking and drinking, until we had each 'sunk' six to eight pints and staggered out at closing time to make for a nearby dance at Charleville Lawn Tennis Club.

Unlike the Carlton Hall the clientele were mainly people we knew – if sometimes only to see – or well-spoken scions of the best families in Drumcondra. We were well-known – not least to the dinner-jacketed 'bouncers' – and always got in, no trouble. The small wooden hall would be full to the rafters by the time we descended. Hot and humid as a Turkish wrestler's jock-strap, with a white-shirted Quintet on a small stage working through 'Red Sails in the Sunset' for the umpteenth time, the brylcreemed alto-sax proving that he could split a reed with the best.

Many of us were "doing a line" at the time and "the women" would already be waiting at the dance, having paid their own way in, like the good Irish girls they were (expected to be). Not only did they accept and tolerate our swaying condition, but most of them were positively pleased to see us. I suppose that they knew that a few drinks was as much a male necessity as powder and puff was to them. They were certainly very good-humoured about it.

Even when their 'man' occasionally disappeared into the Gents, to have a swig from a Baby Power (small bottle of whiskey) which one of his friends would be 'carrying'. ("Are ye carryin? Grate! See ye in the jakes in a minit.") So we topped up.

And sometimes threw up. That never happened to me as I possessed the incipient alcoholic's high tolerance for the poison. (If drink makes you sick or gives you a ferocious hangover, count yourself lucky; you are unlikely to develop a serious drinking problem.)

I often found myself supporting a friend who'd had "one over the eight", watching him pewk his guts out against the (exterior!) slats of the dance hall wall.

On one such occasion I felt honoured to find myself doing the honours for a young undergraduate who, older than our circle, moved in far more rarified circles of his own and rarely gave us 'kids' more than the time of day. He dressed and looked – even to the square-rim spectacles – like "a real intellectual" and impressed us enormously by always having his head buried in a book, even walking down the street.

"D'ye know who he was readin the other day? Immanuel fuckin Kant."

That was absolutely true and now, here he was, holding my hand for dear life and blubbering like a baby – not to say mewling and pewking. Recovering, he thanked me for my "solicitude" and reeled off in a homeward direction. Next time I saw him in 'The Hut' he bought me a pint and we got to talking about books.

At some point I asked him had he read 'The Outsider'. He had. "It is a compilation of utter rubbish!"

With that he turned his back on me and, furious beyond words, I am extremely ashamed to admit, I spat at him.

"He just spat on you" someone drew his attention to it.

He swung round on me. "Did you!? Spit!?"

"I did not" I am even more ashamed to say I replied, "I was only fumin." He turned his back on me again, uttering, no doubt, some Neo-Kantian epithet. All over in seconds, with no credit to me, at all. Obviously my hero-worship for CW did nothing to kill the coward in me.

* * *

However, extracting my tail from between my legs and tucking it well up out of harm's way, I am ready to dance again.

Fat chance! I had only to make a move towards some unescorted wench and she was making a bee-line for the Ladies, to get well clear of my leery beery intent. Or if I got to her before she saw the danger, to startle her with a slurred "'Like ta dance?" in her shell-like, I likely got a straight No. Only if she was wilting (and desperate) did I 'get' a dance.

The unwelcome (to me) exception might be a Ladies Choice. While my less obnoxiously scuttered friends were being selected by their 'steadies', or, if unattached, like me, by fairly reasonable looking LTC ladies, the rest of us left to pair among ourselves...you'd suddenly sense something. Or notice that your fellow-dregs were vanishing towards the Gents. Or, maybe, you'd get a hysterical hiss in your ear:

"Jaysus, will ye look what's comin for us. She's all yours Divvy."

Whoosh! The Warner was gone. So were you, if you were quick enough to spot an Eternal Wallflower coming at you, her (final) Choice, carting fifteen stone of determined femininity, avaricious eyes blazing lustfully in a face "like the back of a bus", reaching out for you, for your essential manhood, waiting to clasp it to her forty-eight inch bosom and crush it to pulp. Blub-lips forming the Invitation: "Dance?"

If she got you, and often she did get you, with your reactions at a low ebb, you'd make the best of it...letting yourself be drawn bodily onto the floor, pulled into a bear-hug and trying to fox-trot, each of you legless from different afflications...until you squinted out from under an enormous boob, to see one of your pals watching you, pointing, rolling his own drink-red eyes, convulsed at the sight of it. Afterwards jibing at you about Moby Dick and Captain Ahab...with a few tasteless double-entendres about harpoons.

This was long before the days of politically correct euphemisms for obesity and the like, remember. And it may sound like a criminal libel on girls who were as often as nice to know as they were overweight; but there it was and that's how we were.

In fact, for once to my credit, I later went out with a disfigured girl who no one wanted to date, because I liked her and she was intelligent, and I know that my attentions there – to kissing her passionately - did her a power of good.

Later again, I regularly dated a lovely lively girl with a leg shrivelled by polio, and tickled her pink by mentioning that James Dean himself once fell for a one-legged 'chick'. – Or so was the legend.

"He even used to tickle her stump" I said, which really

broke her up.

"Ah gwan, you're only going out with me because you're imitating him." (She was a very bright lass.) "I am not" I'd reply, "I'm not that much of a fan. And I'll tell you something else – " eyeing her leg-brace.

"What?"

"I'm not a scrap-metal merchant lookin for cheap aluminium either. Now hop into my lap and give us a birdy." (kiss)

She had such a marvellous sense of humour that I was even able to quote her some lines from Ginsberg:

> Now cripple girl comes limping down the walk
> Loping fuck gestures of her hips askew
> ...Someone will dig that pelvic energy for sure.

* * *

Back again to the Dance, I eventually joined the ranks of those doing a line, as follows:

The general arrangement was males gathered on one side of the (inactive) Floor, with females clustering against the opposite wall and paired couples interspersed. During the intermissions we, the unattached, did our best to spot some likely-looking 'bird' and sallied forth to Put The Question as the next set began.

Obviously we struck oil sometimes, drunk or not, as life is never totally just. At the same time it must be said, given my own poor prowess with the feet, I seldom caught the same fish twice.

But Dutch Courage prevails.

On this particular night I beadied on a pair of girls who seemed as susceptible and fancy-free as any. I girded the proverbial and entered No-Man's-Land. They didn't move away. Then, I was popping the Q to the one I most fancied and...dancing. Or trying to.

"You're drunk" she said, as a pure statement of fact.

"Not exactly."

"Inexactly then." There was something different about this one. "You needn't be ashamed" she added.

"I'm not ashamed."

"You look it."

"Then I must be drunk."

"I heard you had plenty of blarney."

"Oh. From who?" I was suddenly very much at ease with her.

"Someone I know who knows you."

It turned out that she did know one of my friends, making it even easier to talk to her. How we danced I don't know, but it suddenly didn't seem to matter. This girl was talking literature to me, saying: "I hear you write poetry. Tell us about it."

I must have told her something she wanted to hear, or maybe she'd just taken to me, as she made no bid for freedom after the set. Instead we continued the conversation and her girl-friend joined us.

I liked her too and was never so drunk, or foolish, not to know when I was making a hit of some sort. By the time we danced again I was murmuring: "You're the first intelligent girl I've ever met."

"And you're more grown up than you seem."

Well, it could hardly go wrong after that, and it didn't. I spent the rest of the dance on the floor with her or sitting between sets with both of them. Her friend wasn't getting many dances it seemed. "Because" she confided, "I won't dance with just anyone." Fair enough. I amused them by saying that they let far too many drunks in...

I was feeling pretty chuffed with myself, sensing that I had found a girl in a million. She had a nice full figure, as opposed to the voluptuous, and dressed soberly in a flared skirt and plain white blouse. I thought at first that her face was plain, until I later saw her made-up. (She tended to disdain cosmetics or 'sexy' clothes, putting me in mind – as I inevitably told her! – of Julie Harris in 'East of Eden'.) Kim Novak she was not.

Lorna relied on personality, character and intelligence, rather than 'looks', to make her effect, although she could titivate to present devastatingly on occasion. – At a later dance – "to make you proud of me darling" – she wore the lot: 'chantilly lace and a pretty face', cascading shoulder-length tresses, sky-high heels and a tight buttocky skirt that had every male drooling (and girl glaring). It was a nice novelty for me to have the prettiest girl in the place clinging to me, kissing me adoringly, loving me. Or to have a real dago I knew making a play for her. She gave him a dance.

"He asked me out" she said afterwards.

"What did you tell him?"

"I told him I was your girl."

Oh the pampered vanity of it. Luscious Lorna was All Mine. Well, almost all: "Stop it! Stop it! You're driving me crazy, Gay." Pant pant. "But I love you…I want you…"

That, needless to say, much later, when I wrestled for full possession of her on the big sofa in her home lounge. We had many a hot session there, wrapped round one another with ears cocked for the sound of returning parents. No ears on the writhing snake however, who would have been quite happy to risk everything for one peep in a sea-food store.

As it was, they'd arrive home to find her sitting serenely with me, bra and knickers back under wraps, and nothing on show but brighter eyes than usual. Her father would smile cordially at me, and I'd smile back like a seraph, while John Thomas sulked, wept and frizzled below.

If I said that I loved her in moments of urgent electric lust, I probably meant it at such times – as most randy young men do. In fact, although I was far too self-centred then to love anyone but me, I came pretty close to the bona fide feeling with her. She adored me. But the seeds of our ultimate parting were sown when she began to try and change me – into something more marriageable (and manageable) than a pagan sot.

For Lorna was in her soul an abstemious Catholic girl. The wonder of it was that she cleaved to me at all, or for so long, before she concluded that I was beyond redemption. Possibly I was sober enough often enough to give her hope on that score. While her confessor may have reassured on religious matters by saying I was "going through a stage", or the like, and would eventually "grow out of it". He lost his bet alas and it all ended a year or so later when she lured me into an empty church and urged me to pray. I remember feeling betrayed!

Meanwhile, beginning with my walking her and her friend home from the dance, we had many months of rapturous bliss together – to the point that she came to visit me (back) in London the following Summer, as something very close to an official fiancee.

Apart from her own incurable Catholicism she was one of the nicest, brightest girls I ever met, with a sharp artistic intelligence and a corresponding love of things creative and imaginative. We had a lot of the kind of fun I'd only previously experienced with male cronies; a shared sense of humour that is the best cement for any real relationship and almost, not quite, won over worldly gravitas in keeping us together.

In the event however, no sensible woman will stay with a man simply because he makes her laugh. I needed another nutter there.

But a girl who was hep enough to read 'Mad' magazine and share your rapture at 'Black Orpheus' in The Astor (cinema) was a fair few steps in the right crooked direction. And it was an advance to discuss the book reviews in 'Time' or the Sundays, in between passionate kisses and having a go at the zipper of her skirt. We became an envied 'item' (as they say in jetland) to friend and foe alike and my friends had no doubt that I had excelled myself: "She's bloody lovely, Divvy."

* * *

Now all this was very good for me – and, I hope, her – even if I still didn't get what I really needed: regular sexual intercourse.

"You only want one thing" she'd laugh, conscious also of the *cliché*.

Laugh – if she only knew! how much I needed it. – Or if I only had the real skill to 'take' it, on many occasions when a bit of natural male aggressiveness would have won. The selfish ape in me is speaking here, for I am otherwise aware that sexual satisfaction isn't everything and may incubate whole sets of new problems.

But tell that to any teenage boy in heat.

With any girl I always only wanted One Thing. Females expect that and are as often willing to submit, for they also want 'it', especially if they like you too.

But seduction itself, even with the dice loaded in your favour, is ever an art. Doubly so if you are after a Catholic Virgin, where all the wiles and patience of Casanova must come into play, or be played out in a set ritualistic fashion. Patience is the key-word here, powered by brute perseverance, and, psychopathic hipster than I was, I was never much cop at either. The alternative was calculated rape – totally beyond my mild-mannered nature.

I only know, with handsight, that there were times when I came close enough to Casanova, in the soft words, sweet music, chocolates and orchids line, to have deflowered her easily...but I could never recognise the infallible 'signs' enough to act on them, or literally press home the advantage; partly because of my own Catholic upbringing, in sexual fear and guilt, and of course, last but not least, my congenital lack of

234

machismatic self-confidence.

But enough, I hear you yawn, enough of this crassness.

Crass it may be. But tell that, again, to the lusty lad!

On a more serious note, I suspect that she 'wanted' me just as much as I wanted her and that the full consummation of our joint need would have radically changed everything, for better or worse, in terms of our future lives – together or apart. I don't know about her, but a few 'shags' then would have changed my ideas...but who is to say how!

All our past lives are pickled with such Ifs and Buts, and there is finally no dividend in too much speculation or surmise. "I yam what I yam" says Popeye The Sailor Boy, with near impeccable wisdom.

*   *   *

Now seeing Lorna on a regular basis, there was still a lot going on in my life otherwise. With respect that is, to my overall development.

Or arrested development, some may add, if I say that doing a line, for any of us, was no barrier to regular masturbation. Rather, given the half-cocked wrestling on sofas, did it provide 'new' material, for more voluptuous erotic fantasising.

So wanking was still a hot topic among us and the source of endless ribaldry. I became celebrated as the proponent of a form of non-manual masturbation, dubbed "the telekinetic wank".

Look, no hands! Vindicating The Power of Thought. You simply "tought of an arsy ting...with her knickers down, bendin over...the soft white cheeks beckenin ye" (anal echoes of Molly Bloom's "smellow yellow furrow") and concentrated "like a monk", until the veins stood out on your forehead... and...glub glub glub. Eureka. ("Yew reek a sex.")

Oh the sounds of simian mirth.

Leavened by brute blasphemy. For one of my peers

welcomed me back from London with 'news' of a long playing record album he was compiling.

"I've taken the 'standards'" he said, "Gershwin, Cole Porter and so on, and retitled them for an el-pee based on the Passion and Death of Jesus H. Christ. Take 'My Funny Valentine' – that becomes 'My Funny Jesus Christ'." And so it went on: 'Tea for Twelve', 'That's Why Our Lady is a Tramp', 'The Crucifixion's Over', 'Moonlight in Gethsemane'.

The kind of thing that might have got us all crucified if it ever became public. (Years before 'Life of Brian' could capitalise on such stuff.) There were many boisterous nights spent in various front parlours, talking telekinesis or concocting and perpetrating other such infantile mischiefs. (For example we experimented with a Grundig tape deck by recording our farts and belches.)

I often became so loud and rowdy that a resident mother, her patience taxed beyond the limit, would burst in and plead with me to keep my voice down. I was indisputably "bad company" for many a mother's son. (My own mother had given up on me, but I was ever her pride 'n joy for all that, as the only vital element she had in life.)

* * *

With all the flippancy however, our ears still cocked for the cultural.

"We met an oulfella in the Homestead last night" someone told me apropos. "You must meet him Divvy. We think he's a bit of a genius. He quotes Goat" (Goethe). I met him soon after.

His name was Larry and he drank nothing but gin and angastura bitters. He must have been Sixty but looked Ninety, with a face terribly ravaged, pitted and corpse-gray, by heaven knew what awful experiences. Reminding me of Gorky's description of the life-worn Dostoyevsky of 50.

Or Yeats's lines: "I am worn out with dreams/A weather-worn, marble triton/Among the streams". I sussed him instantly as a sage of sorts.

A quiet-spoken old prole of a Dublinman, with slate-grey eyes that looked through you, into another, better dimension, Larry spoke of poetry and philosophy in the coarse argot of Cabra West or The Coombe.

He quoted Goethe all right, often in German, and further astounded you by snippets of Greek and arcane references to great authors of the past. "I have a personal philosophy" he duly confided, as he raised the glass we bought him and we clustered around him with foaming flutes of stout. "It is this. That Life is a great pull and push between two opposing forces. A dichotomous pattern, Lads. Di-chotomy is the word."

Silent and still as the Sphinx for awhile, lost in his mirror of gin, he came to and focussed on us, with the softest tiredest smile I'd ever seen. "As the poet said: that's all we know and all you need to know."

We met him a few times and never understood him or what he was really 'about'. Although my 'Childe Harold' friend duly found out that, like Socrates, Larry had a shrew of a wife. We never doubted that he himself was some kind of Socrates, even if looking up dichotomy in the dictionary proved highly inconclusive.

Then one night soon after we asked a barman if Larry had been in...

"The old man who drinks gin? He just died. Of a heart attack."

"Jaysus...That's terrible..."

If he had a great philosophy, he'd taken it to the grave.

I still feel that his death was a tragedy, in that we'd missed out on a chance to get to know someone of rare gifts.

I recall his one piece of good advice to me: "If you think you have something to say, as a writer, as you seem to think you

237

have, keep at it. Never let other people put you down and never, ever, give up. Die first."

I often wondered if he himself had 'something to say', or had said it, or died before he could.

Chapter Fifteen

THE MAN WITH THE GOLDEN ARM

I would include card-playing under the broad category of our cultural pursuits, mainly because of its psychological value in determining key traits of personality and character. And is Life itself not all about winning, losing, bluffing, and keeping (or losing) your nerve?

I had taken to playing poker, five card stud and pontoon (or Twenty-One) as early as Eleven or Twelve, when I first joined a regular 'school' run by the boy who had cheered me on during that pivotal bout of fisticuffs.

He was a great Sinatra fan (long before 'The Man with the Golden Arm' made him the patron saint of card sharks) and four or five of us would play on his kitchen table, backed by the sound of The Voice from a radiogram in the lounge. We played for pennies then. As Frank sang of 'the same old story...a fight for love and glory'.

"Jayse" the fan would sigh, "isn't his diction superb!"

Into our teens more 'serious' card schools proliferated throughout the neighbourhood and became a regular part of all our lives. At times they competed hard with all the other pursuits and sometimes even kept us 'at home', in someone's house, playing through Saturday night.

There would be plenty of booze about and I played particularly well after a few - whether because drunken fearlessness pleased Lady Luck or because I was a sharp player anyway, I can't tell.

I do know that my winnings often subsidised my lunchtime

drinking on Sunday and a trip to the pictures in Town, with enough left for the pub on Sunday night. There was the further indemnity, that if I didn't win, someone I knew well would...and accordingly "make with the bevvies" on Sunday.

There was nothing like going up against a good hand with a better one and knowing it – an easy enough 'trick' in itself if you 'watch the cards' and follow the play closely. Particularly with a jack-pot pool of shillings, florins and half-crowns on the table and the poor eejit opposite you raising the stakes on a Full House, while you held a virtually unbeatable Straight Flush.

"See ye and raise ye a shillin" he might say.

"See ye...and raise ye half-a-crown." Sit back and watch his face...

I was never a great bluffer, drunk or sober, which no doubt says something for or against my own basic character. But I envied those who were, which doubtless says something else, about my basic meta-bollocks.

I will skip hastily on to one use of the winnings, for Art.

* * *

Cinema again, but this time reviewed far less expansively.

Sunday afternoon Cinema, in the latter half of the Fifties, became for me as (culturally) important as Sunday lunchtime Radio had once been, a few years earlier.

And where better to begin, in the gradation from innocent entertainment to hard-lived experience, than with the aforesaid 'Man with the Golden Arm' (1956). The first film, or 'movie', to really defy the old Hollywood Production Code – the Hays Office Rules on 'morality' which had circumscribed film-making and defined what was 'fit to see', since 1930.*

* *Although some film historians regard Preminger's 1953 'sex farce', 'The Moon is Blue', as the (im)morality watershed, in that he refused to obey the Code by excluding such forbidden words as 'virgin', 'pregnant', 'mistress', and 'seduction' from the script.*

Here was an uncompromising, and uncompromisingly realistic film, about back-street drug addiction in metropolitan America, based on a novel by Simone De Beauvoir's hipster lover, Nelson Algren.

A film more darkly echoed by 'A Hatful of Rain' (1957), with evil Crypto-Freudian pusher Anthony Franciosa maternally cajoling a sweating fixer: "Every junky needs his mo-ther..." That had a definite undertone of Sex, compared to Kim Novak lying on writhing Frank Sinatra in the aforesaid Man with a Perforated Libido – trying to calm him as he goes cold turkey. 'End as a Man' (1957), with venomous cadet Ben Gazzara, starkly portrayed bullying in a U.S. Military Academy.

We also saw 'On the Waterfront' (1954) about '57 or '58 and understood why Dean idolised Brando. ("I coulda been a contender" the missed fighter famously whines to bad brother Steiger.)

Based on Budd Schulberg's idea for a novel it incidentally led on to our reading his real masterpiece of Hollywood Life: 'What Makes Sammy Run' (1941) - which we thought much better than that other 'shit hits big' tale 'The Great Gatsby', by Schulberg's own idol, F Scott Fitzgerald.

(I much later read Nathanael West's 'The Day of the Locust' (1939) – arguably the 'Great Hollywood Novel').

Then indefatigable Kazan directed another Schulberg story, 'A Face in the Crowd' (1957), attacking the cult of personality on US Television.

But even after 'A Streetcar Named Desire' (1952), which came to us in the Mid-Fifties, we continued to rate Dean above Brando. That other great film-adaptation of a Tennessee Williams play, 'Cat on a Hot Tin Roof' (1958) was memorable for 'East of Eden' Support, Burl Ives, transformed into an Orson Wellsian 'Big Daddy'.

I think the film of William's 'The Rose Tattoo' was banned in Ireland; certainly the play caused a notorious scandal and was taken off at the Pike Theatre as obscene.

I suppose Brando was just too versatile for our liking and not enough of a hard-dyed Wild One - which Dublin knew enough about, despite the strict ban, to send sales of leather jackets soaring. (We never saw his first film 'The Men', in which he played a paraplegic...)

It was hard enough to take to him as a Mexican bandit, Mark Antony, or Napoleon ("for jayse sake!") and you could forget 'The Teahouse of the August Moon'. Or likewise, his 'experiments' in 'Guys and Dolls' and 'Sayonara'. (We wouldn't have lasted long as professional film critics.)

Nonetheless, you couldn't take your eyes off him in 'The Young Lions'. Or fail to admire the incredible shift of character, between the Nazi Officer there, and the masochistic loner who got bull-whipped by Karl Malden in 'One Eyed Jacks' (1960). - The story was that Brando insisted on taking an actual thrashing, as a dedicated Method Actor. (Presumably, as co-director, he also insisted that Take One was a Print.)

Sadist Malden certainly seemed to enjoy every minute of it.

By the time his uneven acting in 'Giant' puzzled us, James Dean was canonised beyond any fear of detraction. But it did look like his tragic pile-up in the Porsche had stopped a move in the Brando line. - For we knew that he was to play a boxer, Rocky Graziano, in 'Somebody Up There Likes Me', before Paul Newman stepped into the posthumous shoes... having earlier lost out to Dean for the lead in 'East of Eden'.

We did begin to focus on Newman as a very compelling actor, on the strength of 'The Long Hot Summer' (1958). Most of us were still in Dublin for 'The Hustler' (1961), which rather crowned him.

Montgomery Clift – badly traumatised by a disfiguring car crash in 1957 – had been a great hero of my own since I saw him in Howard Hawks western, 'Red River' (1948), at 9 or 10.

We all felt for him as the sensitive Jewish draftee, slagged off for reading a "filthy book" ('Ulysses'), by a dumb C.O. in 'The Young Lions'.

Five years earlier his performance in 'From Here to Eternity' (1953) almost won him an Oscar. While his on-set coaching of Sinatra helped to revive that performer's moribund career, winning him a Best Supporting Actor Award, as Clift's 'good guy' buddy.

By the time Clift played Freud, in a 1963 biopic, he was a chronic toper (largely because of the auto-trauma) who badly needed therapy himself. He never got it and died prematurely in 1966...at 46.

Through him, more than his disciples Brando and Dean, we first got to hear about Method Acting - in which Rod Steiger, another "grate actor", excelled. (Even miscast as dud yokel Jud, in Oklahoma!)

A book on its Founder, Stanislavsky, duly made the rounds.

Of the older school our real hero was Spencer Tracy – a bit of a Method man too. His one-armed bar fight in 'Bad Day at Black Rock' (1955) became the talk of Dublin; going to Blackrock Baths was never the same afterwards. He memorably reincarnated for us as grizzled fisherman in 'The Old Man and the Sea' (1958), at a time when Hemingway was being avidly read.

His performance in 'Inherit the Wind' was a highpoint of 1960. While of course the film itself was grist to our own 'heresy', fanned a flame of Darwinism and, when I looked that up in the library, led me personally on to discover another great future influence: Sir Julian Huxley. In itself a good example of the mind-stirring potential of certain films – or why Status Quo often favours censorship!

* * *

Censorship itself became increasingly applied in the Fifties, as Hollywood attempted to hit back at the new threat of Television, both by technical innovation and more lascivious scripting.

With regard to the former, Technicolour now became common – as opposed to the expensive luxury it was deemed previously – and audiences were tempted by more 'life-like' wide-screen panoramics: CinemaScope, Cinerama, 3-D, etc.

In the latter instance the Irish Censor became increasingly busy with the scissors and many a good scene (or film) was "cut ta ribbons" accordingly. Although when we saw the much-hyped 'Baby Doll' (1956) – a stillborn collaboration between Kazan and T. Williams – we were hard put to guess where the cuts were. Carroll Baker. in the baby doll nighty, seemed to us on the asexual level of an air-brushed 'Playboy' centrefold.

Indeed I think that that, Hugh Hefner's 1953 brainchild – 'a sex magazine for sophisticates' (!) – was considered harmless enough for limited sale in Ireland. Incidentally, the first of the novels that would further define 'sophisticated sex' (as sado-masochistic) for 60s filmgoers also appeared in 1953: 'Casino Royale'. (The Bond-Age.)

The 1957 film of Grace Metalious's bestselling novel, 'Peyton Place', was also promoted as seamy-sexy, but heaven alone knew why. We had never seen such a bunch of sexless creeps in our lives. Our ignorant loathing transferred to the unfortunate authoress, when we later heard that she was "a ravin alkie'. She wrote shite. Serve her right.

What a nasty little crew of intolerants we could be at times.*

The 'sexy' Continental films, usually shown at The Astor, came under particularly severe scrutiny. But you couldn't minimise the impact of Brigitte Bardot in a bikini, short of banning 'And God Created Woman' (1956) altogether – with her so nearly in it at times! (We saw her interviewed on TV,

---

* The real story of 'Peyton Place' is a tragic soap opera in itself. It is that of a humble American housewife who wrote an expose of small town life which sold 10 million copies (1956-1966), making her 'rich and famous'...and so plagued by notoriety that she was driven to drink herself to death, at 42. Little we knew of that kind of strain...

where she simpered that she had "a leetle pet mankey. He-go pee-pee everywhere!" A Simian sousing the muff of delectable BB.)

Compared to Bardot, Monroe seemed more like a convent girl.

From a fairly liberal-progressive convent nonetheless, where they taught you to sing that diamonds are a girl's best friend. Many a boy wanted to be the millionaire who married Marilyn.

Paired with sultry Jane Russell in 'Gentlemen Prefer Blondes' she became a popular pin-up in Dublin, as everywhere. (Based on a play by Anita Loos GPB had a B-Side, sagely shirked by movie moguls: 'But Gentlemen Marry Brunettes'.)

On the subject of Sirens, Gina Lollobrigida was another hot glamour puss who you'd like to see with her dress blowing up, over that famous air-shaft of Monroe's.*

Personally, I found Sophia Loren very sexy, in a sweaty earthy kind of way, after seeing her in 'Two Women' (1961). The Astor ran that fairly uncut – even the savage rape scene.

If I could just about warm to her 'light comedy' with Rock Hudson the same year, in 'Come September', I was only numbed by her duetting 'Doctor I'm in Trouble' with Peter Sellers – whose own light comic mimickry of an expatriate Indian physician made the song a smash hit; possibly too, doing something for better race relations, in an England then flooding with immigrants from that former Possession.

'Sweet Smell of Success' (1957), with powerful Burt Lancaster as a star columnist shredding snake-in-the-grass 'Sidney' – Tony Curtis – was a study in men corrupted by Mailer's "bitch goddess" (success). "Match me Sidney!" was Lancaster's epiphany, as, exuding wealth and power, he held his cigarette out for ignition, to quivering gofor Tony. (Burly Burt

---

* F.N. Oddly enough, we never felt the same about Elizabeth Taylor.

had been top-rated in Dublin for years, not least for that Hays-baiting beach-scene with Deborah Kerr in 'From Here to Eternity'.) If Gregory Peck as 'The Man in the Grey Flannel Suit' (1956) brought David Riesman's "other-directed" executive zombie to life for us, Burt and Tony heavily double-dotted the O of Stateside soul-lessness.

Another kind of raw insight, into the very bowels of that air-conditioned nightmare across the Pond, was provided by the aforementioned 'The Blackboard Jungle' (1955), with taciturn crew-cutted Glenn Ford doggedly out to educate a High School classroom of retarded slum kids – dopes or rogues to a man – down to young Sidney Poitier.

Again as aforesaid, the opening music – 'Rock Around the Clock' – prepared the world for Bill Haley. By the time it came to us, late in the decade (well-cut but unbowed), Bill had come and gone and Elvis was in US Army fatigues.

The film was attacked by our elders as "a very bad example for Irish Scholars" – as if we'd dream of carrying flick-knives and baiting the "Teach". In fact we knew it for what it was: a plea to clean up the society that provoked such delinquency. Before, as has since happened, the situation became irretrievable and schools across the States turned into increasingly lawless and violent armed camps.

The simple horror of 'Odette', being tortured by Gestapo thugs in double-breasted suits, seemed almost clean-cut by comparison; certainly far more explicable, in traditional terms of Good versus Evil. So much so that we could thoughtlessly joke about piano wire and "Ve haf ze vays.." (of making you talk).

We saw that in the Phibsboro Bohemian, shortly before they put on a bowdlerised version of 'The Brothers Karamazov', with Yul Brynner mixing up his Dostoyevsky and his Gogol and coming across as the brigand Cossack, Taras Bulba* – sans Fyodor's tormented truth-seeking.

* *Duly picked as natural lead for a 1962 film of the story.*

"Never mind" someone sighed, "we know the story now. No need to plough through that grate tome of a book..." (I only read it in the Sixties.)

Yul was no less anesthetic in 'Anastasia', but he did come into his own in 'The King And I' – which we found passable as a musical. (He maybe facilitated Kojak, having made baldness 'box office'.) We are back to 'West Side Story' for a real musical, as far as we were concerned.

Although the score of 'My Fair Lady' made such a profound general impact that I am surprised to discover (in checking) that it wasn't filmed until 1964. The songs were ever on the radio and the LP was in wide circulation; as well, of course, as Previn's superb jazz album.

'High Society' (1956) competed hard with rock 'n roll; Louis, Bing and Frank insisting "Jazz is King, Jazz is Best"...

'Gigi' was "for the moths".

Back to 'epics', King Vidor's 'War and Peace' (1955) did push me into reading that book, which I found totally enchanting. I felt a kick of kinship for mild-mannered Pierre Bezukov, of whom the gossiping salon ladies remarked: "*Il est charmant, Il ne pas de sexe.*" (He is charming, he has no sex.) He was too much the poet to give a girl the real hots...just like me. They only liked we spiritual supermen because they felt safe with the Clark Kent in us...alas!

Of the 'spectaculars', Kirk Douglas showed you what some girls really wanted, playing the original Ulysses in 1954: sword-hilts. – Or helmeted heroes in chariots, like 'Chuck' Heston in 'Ben Hur' (1959). Or Victor ('Samson'/'Demetrius the Gladiator') Mature, full stop.

Kirk as Van Gogh ('Lust for Life', 1956) was a different man, with the Homeric and Viking personas shredded in favour of real artistry. He had become little more than "an errant husband" to my girl-friend, in 'Spartacus' (1960).

'Gunfight at the OK Corral' (1957) gave you Kirk as Doc Holliday (reprising a 1946 role by Victor Mature!) competing with Burt Lancaster as Wyatt Earp (reprising 'Hank' Fonda) for Man's Man. We all forget our own cultural pretensions when it comes to a good Western!

'Psycho' (1960) deserves a line to itself, as unrivalled.

Returning to High Art, 'Doctor Zhivago' (1956) got us reading that long-forgotten literary sensation – and partly because of the ongoing furore over Commie-lashing author Boris Pasternak.

Poitier and Curtis as 'The Defiant Ones' (1958) provided equally serious fare. As, in 1961, did Gable's and Monroe's joint swansong, 'The Misfits'.

* * *

More classical Art came to us, very impressively, with Olivier doing something like a Method job in 'Richard III' (1955). And he showed a versatility to match Brando's, reincarnated as seedy comedian Archie Rice in the 1960 film of Osborne's 'The Entertainer'.

'Look Back in Anger' (1959) really hit us (after seeing a passable production in the Guinness Theatre), powered by Burton as Jimmy Porter.

'A Taste of Honey' impressed me in 1961 – the play at The Pike having been ruined for me by a friend who knew the leading man socially, and couldn't stop tittering every time the poor chap opened his mouth.

The British New Wave simultaneously brought more and more of 'real life' to the screen with 'Room at the Top' (1959) and 'Saturday Night and Sunday Morning' (1960). 'This Sporting Life' would notably extend that trend in 1963, incidentally doing for Richard Harris what 'Lawrence of Arabia' had done for Peter O'Toole a year before: star-making.

* * *

All that being but the tip of an iceberg of Films that fixed themselves somewhere in our collective consciousness.

It would take another full chapter to review even the most memorable – certainly including 'Some Like It Hot', 'A Farewell to Arms', 'The Naked and the Dead', 'We're No Angels', 'Marty', 'Desire Under the Elms'...'Around the World in Eighty Days'...etc etc etc!

There is no doubt in my mind however that many of these newer products of a dis-established Hollywood – moving further and further away from the old studio system and its carefully filleted 'family entertainments' – now provided us with the mind-broadening experience hitherto only found by reading or travel. We were being given glimpses of the real world out there, as a problematical place of varied, often difficult, people and the overall effect was bound to be leavening. Yes, it was a far cry from 'Seven Brides' to the streetwise buzz of 'West Side Story' (1961).

Much as my own trip to London opened my eyes to Life and gave me an appetite for more experience, as one good way of moving forward towards self-knowledge, the best films obliquely endorsed this need to know.

Although many of my friends no doubt took 'a good film' far more lightly, as they took Art in general far less seriously, those like myself who hungered and thirsted for Meaning, got a lot for our ticket. We also got the self-developmental buzz of participating, albeit by proxy, in a changing *Zeitgeist*: proclaiming new ideas, values, freedoms.

This was notably true of those foreign films we saw in the Astor, where the European New Wave in particular rammed home the existential value of individualistic (or eccentric!) behaviour, as a healthy protest against the restrictive, numbing, conventional urban environment we all inhabited, and were otherwise obliged to endure.

There was also a new kind of, purely visual, experience, or catharsis, to be obtained from certain key scenes, which often had the surreal appeal of great poetry. Bergman was rich in that kind of thing – very much so in 'Wild Strawberries'.

Other great screen 'memories' would include Satyajit Ray's loin-clothed Indian boy in a vast waving field of long grass ('Pather Panchali', 1954), framed against the distant rush of a speeding steam train on a high embankment, exuding unearthly puffs of snow-white smoke.

...A few terrified German youths, drafted under age to defend their home village, with mere pop-guns, in the closing stages of the last war...pissing themselves with fear in their slit-trenches, while a dread distant rumbling grows louder and louder, and louder, until, ahead of them, a gargantuan American tank looms into view and halts...long gun barrel slowly swivelling to point its snout straight at their defenceless position. That was in Wajda's 'The Bridge' and he evoked similiarly gut-wrenching visual tensions in those other two (anti-war) masterpieces: 'Ashes and Diamonds' and 'Kanal'.

...Certain dark shots in Fellini's 'La Strada' (1954), with Anthony Quinn dominating the action like some gross creature from Hades. ...The unforgettable sequence in 'Black Orpheus' (1958), where Marcel Camus has his mythical figure speeding underground to Hades, in a modern streamlined ambulance – sirens shrieking like audible Hell-Fire.

...The Bergsonian Resnais bringing Proust's warped time to screen life in 'Hiroshima mon Amour' (1959). Taking Art through the Roof!

* * *

For harder fare in the same direction you had to go to the theatre, and I still remember the thrill of first watching 'Ghosts' and 'When We Dead Awaken' in the Gate Theatre. No wonder Shaw and Joyce took to Ibsen! – both coincidentally launching their careers with critiques of the Scandinavian Giant; Joyce even learning Norwegian to fathom him better. I also saw 'A Doll's House' around that time and began to look up his other plays in the library.

Broadening the horizons accordingly, a few of us became avid theatre-goers for awhile. Busaras – the National bus terminus by the Liffey – had a tiny basement theatre, The Eblana. There, one Sunday afternoon we saw 'The Voices of Shem', based on the 'heroine' (both Goethe's Eternal Female and the ubiquitous Liffey Herself) Anna Livia Plurabelle, from 'Finnegans Wake', with Norman Rodway making an early acting mark. Brendan Behan attended and when we saw him with his wife in a pub afterwards, greeted us like old friends.

"How'd ye like the play lads? Wasn't Shem yer man?"

"Yes" we laughed, "but we could barely follow a word of it."

Brendan was stark staring sober that day; less so the next time I met him, casually, in Dolly Fawcett's shebeen*, on one of my night town jaunts. Drunk or sober, Behan was beloved by Dublin and well-remembered by Dubliners, when they later turned out in their thousands after his premature passing, for his funeral.

Another fond memory is Micheal Mac Liammoir in his element, playing Oscar Wilde, in a one-man show that was to take the world by storm – and almost rescue that indestructible impresario from a state perpetually verging on bankruptcy.

It is a nice comment on Dublin tolerance that "Meehaul" – well-known for his homosexual liaison with co-entrepreneur Hilton Edwards – could boldly stride the streets in drag and still be greeted like Royalty.

(The pair were also famous as the talent spotters who first gave a very young Orson Welles his first break, on their Dublin stage.)

* * *

* Drinking club/brothel.

251

Which brings me nearly to the end of my own beginnings, in Dublin.

I would spend the Summer of 1960 working in London. After which Ireland would become no more than a convenient temporary refuge, as I spent longer and longer periods away, culminating with my permanent domicile in London about four years later.

* * *

It occurs to me, completing this penultimate chapter, that throughout this volume, I have barely referred to those broader topics that come under the headings of News or Current Affairs.

An omission reflecting the fact that we really weren't all that interested in the affairs of the adult world, like many children and teenagers. – Sport being almost the only exception.

For my own part, I have had enough to do concentrating on the things that did interest us, without making another 'War and Peace' of it all. 'Things' like the Korean War or the French flight from Indo-China were bound to make some impression – war usually does.

Or sex crime: the notorious Christie murder case of 1953 was widely reported and avidly followed in Ireland. – Urchin whispers: "He shagged dead wimmin! Den he buried them all over his effin house."

As far as politics, economics and the broader ramifications of social life mattered, we picked up snippets in the newspapers, or on the radio, but generally ignored them as boring.

Into our teens, even the atomic bomb was seldom considered and the first time I recall taking a real interest in anything apropos was 1956, when the Hungarian Revolution caught our attention and somehow seized the imagination – after the manner of David and Goliath.

I remember a Sunday stroll to the Phoenix Park with a friend, when we animatedly discussed the affair, with a strange sense of Portent. We recalled the sick Communist humiliation and imprisonment of Hungarian Prelate Cardinal Mindszenty* a few years earlier (1948), which still confirmed for us, that however 'bad' our own Church might be, Soviet Communism was a great deal worse.

But that apart – and it is little enough – I cannot recall a peer discussion about anything much beyond our own little preoccupations which, needless to say, were never boring or trivial!

Sputnik, 1957, was impossible not to notice, or applaud – if only as science fiction fans; the 'dog in space' and Yuri Gagarin similarly wowed.

For some reason we came to regard U.N. Secretary General Dag Hammerskjold as "a bit of a Deaner" – possibly because we read a little semi-philosophical volume he did, called 'Jottings'. As politicians go he <u>was</u> a bit of a genius and we mourned his (mysterious and suspicious) death in a Congo air-crash, in 1961.

* * *

Meanwhile, in the Autumn of '59, all I was worried about was how to keep my parents off my back. They were now convinced that I had quit school for good and my uncertain future must have been a perpetual torment.

Some of the *cenacle*, a year or so older than myself, were now legally left school, the Leaving Certificate in their pockets, and into work or on the verge of doing so. My friend of the Mill had put The Berkeley well behind him and was now making the best of it as a humble (albeit well-paid) clerk – even after taking seven honours in his Leaving.

*Freed by the revolutionaries.

Such was the highly qualified competition for cushy jobs, in Fifties Dublin, that he would have to do a degree, part-time, if he hoped to really 'get on'. He planned to read economics at Trinity, and at least sustain the subversive image by defying the Church in doing so – a strict ban against RCs attending Trinity being still in force then.

Another worthy was doing a Course to become a Marine Radio Officer. Largely funding himself he would spend the Summer of Sixty with me in London, "to garner", as he put it, "some badly needed shekels". Our Brando poet had gone off to Wales and was working down a coal mine – a vague romantic obeisance to George Orwell. He sent us some hilarious accounts of a full-fledged affair he was having with a Welsh "rare bit." Telling us that she liked to kneel on all-fours, "wanting me to do it like the dogs do." By way of downbeat contrast, I had Lorna to wrestle with and a few daydreams of literary success.

So, while my parents were snapping and bickering at each other more than ever – I began to dread either of them getting drunk, for the really awful flare-ups – the spectacle of me, pencilling out a first novel on the dining-room table, hardly contributed to domestic stability.

All (all!) I wanted was to be left alone. But:

"When are you going to get a job?" my weary father would ask, again. "We can't go on supporting you."

I'd sigh or mumble. They just didn't understand...a 'riter'.

Prodded into it, I went for a job interview, to be considered as a temporary clerk over the busy Christmas Period, by the motor taxation department of Dublin Corporation. Although the interview went smoothly enough, I came away without much hope of being accepted.

Then my Uncle Paddy, at the behest of one desperate sister, my mother, pulled a few strings to get me an interview at Todd Burns, the big department store. I made my way through the dark dreary place, with its counter-hands like risen corpses, to

254

be 'summed up' in a dingy cubby-hole of an office, by a sharp-faced Manager. On the name of my uncle he took me on, to start the following Monday...at £2 a week.

I came away totally shattered, feeling shades of the prison house begin to close, with Saroyan's line "you go to work and die" ringing in my brain...and went home to write some very bitter poetry. In one poem I was a genius "with a casket of precious stones", doomed to serve Mammon. A sin against the Muses that took no account of the luck of the Irish. For on the Friday morning, a letter from the Corporation...I could start there, in a fortnight...at £6-10-0 a week!

I was delirious. The parents were delirious. I sat right down and wrote a Dear John to Todd Burns, regretting that, etc, etc. I think that all three of us got well and truly squiffy that night, with never an angry word. I was again respectable and "a good son".

Happy for them, I also had a very good feeling about the Corp; so well-borne out in the event, that it will help to enliven my final chapter.

I also liked the idea of a 'temporary' job which, I thought, would not compromise my overall intention to devote myself to writing.

I completed a short novel in London the following Summer and personally delivered the illegibly pencilled manuscript to the firm of Hutchinson. An incredulous young man reluctantly accepted this dog's dinner of a book. After a decent interval they posted it back to my London address, with the usual brief rejection slip.

I'd be a long time yet at the drawing-board, given my own slip-shod approach to writing. But I'd keep at it...dogged perhaps, as Dublin itself.

CHAPTER SIXTEEN

THE KILDARE STREET CLUB

Even a rejected novel did me some good, in Dublin.

Another neighbourhood 'intellectual', who did not like me at all, called to our flat in London the following summer, when I was finishing it; he liked and admired my flatmate a lot.

Told of my scribbling he was curious enough to peruse the partly-completed story. Afterwards he put it down and stared at me.

"I've always thought you were an irritating clown" he said. "I cannot believe that you have written this. It is highly literate."

He preceded us home and by the time I returned had put the word around generally, that I was a literary genius. More free drink.

* * *

But back to Dublin Corporation, the previous Christmas, where I met a man who impressed me as a real literary genius. He drank, a lot.

Reporting to the Motor Tax Department in Kildare Street, a stone's throw away from the fabled Club, on a Monday morning, I was put to routine form-filing, to break me in.

Everyone was terribly polite to me, in a typical middle-class manner, down to (or up to) the more senior staffers. I did detect just a little trace of snobbery here and there, or the patronage accorded a Temporary Clerk.

Never mind that, the work itself was like idleness and there was plenty of time to get to know the other temps – quite a few of us, with the turn of the year registrations massively imminent. Soon we would be writing out tax discs interminably; for the moment: chatter.

As the week progressed I began to savour my temporary status. It wasn't Franz Kafka or Metropolis by any means, but too much of this would kill me. There was for example a mounting sensation of immersion in some warm eventless womb of amniotic fluid, with hardly the need to breathe, let alone think.

The polite yawning pace of work here defied description. No one hurried, for anyone or anything. I understood now what people meant by "a cushy job". They meant one where lifting a finger drew a round of applause and completing a modest quota of tax discs on time, brought the house down. Suspended animation and mental pedestrianism were the buzz words here, where all de nice folk hung out…

Happily Diversion with a big D wasn't far away.

Intimations of its arrival came through a few snatches of conversation I overheard from the established staff. Apparently a man was coming among us soon, returning to rejoin their ranks after a long absence – due to "a serious accident on a motor-cycle" – who was variously described as "grate fun", "a character", "a menace", "a blackguard" and, best of all, with venom: "a danger to man, woman and beast".

My ears began to prickle.

By the time he arrived the following Monday I was more than ready for him, in any one of the above categories as may be. What I saw was a short slight elf of a man, neatly attired in dark suit and tie, limping the while and supporting himself with a stout walking-stick. He sported the full jet-black beard of a freshly minted prophet, and peered at you with two of the brightest, most piercing eyes I had ever seen. I guessed his age to be late-twenties or early thirties.

As soon as he opened his mouth I sussed a kindred spirit, of a considerably advanced type. Gerry was very polite, with a strange mocking edge to it. I heard him say Good Morning to several people in turn, in each case modulating his voice to 'fit', as it were, the recipient.

Thus he managed, by that single greeting, to convey either respect or derision, sometimes mixing the two deliciously, with the result – as was very apparent to me – no one knew quite what to make of him, or how to take him. There was something regal about the attitude.

I lost no time in making myself known to him. I sensed that I didn't impress, at all. But that never bothered me – then or later – whenever I felt that a person might have something new to impart. So I laid siege and persevered, finally hitting a nerve when I confided that I wanted to write.

"Indeed?..."

Well...as it happened...he did a bit of writing himself.

Had I read Joyce?

I'd read enough to persuade him that I wasn't as wet as I looked – "not quite the dreary Christian Brothers cast-off you seem". Gerry was a rabid 'Ulysses' man and could quote whole passages at the drop of a hat.

Joyce's use of "agenbite of inwit", for remorse of conscience, tickled him particularly, as "a lovely example of his way with words".

(It is. But, as I discovered later, the expression was in fact purloined by that inveterate literary omnivore, from Olde English.)

By Tuesday I was okay enough to be lured out for "elevenses" – a pint or two in the nearest pub. Replying to my caution that we might be over-stepping a mark he only laughed derisively.

"Do you think they'll miss us?"

Soon enough, I couldn't have cared less. Here was a true poet, and with a high sense of humour that rivalled Joyce's own. I sat back on my seat in 'The Lincoln Inn', enraptured by a raconteur who also rivalled Brendan Behan on heat.

It didn't surprise me to learn that he often drank with the Behans and knew Gainor Crist (The Ginger Man) well. He knew it's author too:

"Donleavy used to jot down Gainor's little gems...But then Joyce himself was no better, out to the lavatory every so often to make notes on the company..." A dry chuckle. "I suppose Wilde had a point when he said that the supreme vice is shallowness and that everything that is realised is right. Pity he only learned that for himself after the event..."

(He might have added there that Joyce was wrong when he wrote:

"The man of genius makes no mistakes. His errors are volitional and lead to the portals of discovery". ...They led poor Wilde to the portals of gaol.)

Gerry himself often recited poetry "to pay for liquid sustenance" in a little pub off Grafton Street, where I once found him surrounded by admiring pint-buyers.

He was happily wed "to a lovely girl" and had several children.

"You start off" he'd say, "with no children and ten theories on how to bring one up. You end up with ten children and no theories."

A militant pacifist he would not brook even toy guns at home.

I got a smile when I reminded him that Orwell, who also detested tin soldiers, felt obliged to remark that tin pacifists are no substitute.

He had a story about Behan turning up for a drink at The Bailey, just after city pubs closed for "the holy hour" at two o'clock. "'Dye know what time it is?', the irate country barman asks him. 'What dye take me for' Behan bellows back, 'a bloody chronometer?'"

Obviously all this did not come out at our first meeting and I am condensing the fruits of several subsequent conversations here, to provide an immediate flavour of the man. He was above all an anarchist, like every true poet! With no time at all for the cant and hypocrisy of 'respectable' conventional life. How he had ever survived in the Corporation was a testament to its implacable inertia.

He even got away with walking out of the office, "for a cup of coffee", several years previously and returning three months later...

"I gave them a good story" he explained. "And they accepted it."

In fact he had taken a boat to Jersey, "bored out of me mind", and lived "a bohemian existence" there for the interim.

"When I landed I was flat broke and went to the local Catholic priest to ask for help. He refused me. A few days later I collapsed in the street from hunger and exhaustion and ended up in a hospital bed. They thought I was done for and called a priest. ...So I open my eyes and there is the bad samaritan himself, praying over me and asking me to repent. Jaysus I didn't half send him to heaven with a few hard oaths. Mind you, that wasn't what put me off the Church. I never had much time for it. But it helped!"

Why did he return to the office and stay on thereafter?

"They leave me alone. I do my own thing, by and large. And, money."

He greatly lamented losing his "best friend. Now Finian was a character! Very warm. It was coming off his motor-bike that crippled me. I don't know what happened him. I think he's in England now."

Apparently Finian made a habit of obtaining free meals in restaurants by sitting down and "shouting" until he was served, gratis.

"It was a treat to see" quoth Gerry. "He'd just sit there bellowing, until the manager came, pleading with him to stop before he drove all the other customers out...offering him anything if he'd only shut up. It got so that we had only to go

260

in to a place in Stephen's Green run by a Greek, and he'd be straight up to us with the menu! We had many a fine repast there, on the house."

"They never called the Guards?" I asked.

"And lose their good name with their customers? Finian was selective. He had the places well-taped, where the reputation overrode everything."

Leading on to another picaresque reminiscence:

"One night in fact, we got an off-duty *Garda* so drunk that we all ended up using his helmet as a chamber. – By the way, did you know that Joyce got the title for his Chamber Music poems after idly kicking a piss-pot?"

All this I found highly amusing, but it hardly had great value! Except perhaps as an illustration of the very fine line, between poetry and crime. But then, many revered saints were once of the Devil's Party...When I met him, Gerry was shedding his horns and tail. "That accident took a lot out of me. No more exile now, only silence and cunning."

What about writing – was he doing a 'Ulysses' of his own?

"Maybe...A few years ago I sent half a novel off to Hutchinson and they wrote back raving about it, asking for the rest. But you know...it was enough for me to know they wanted it. I never bothered with it again..."

(That incidentally marked Hutchinson out as a name for me.)

* * *

After a second lunchtime session a day or so later, when we drank until closing time, he decided that we wouldn't just walk back to the office, "like peasants. We'll have a hansom." He called out to the barman: "Have ye got a runner?"

"A what, Sir?"

"A runner to go and get us a cab. Do you know what a cab is?"

All taken by the barman in the best of spirits. Indeed he was soon on the phone to order one of the few hansom cabs still in service. So we travelled back the few hundred yards to the office by hansom, alighting like two nineteenth century aristos to pay the jarvey and pat the horse, before ascending the steps to twentieth century work.

Our long absence and late arrival hadn't gone unnoticed by a certain senior salary man. I noticed him scowling as we came in, but he said nothing. He was biding his time. A few days later he was once more in ambush, this time remarking acidly to Gerry that he should "know better. Some of us here keep office hours." Gerry was polite as ever, even making apologetic noises, for the sake of peace and quiet.

It wasn't finished yet, for me. I was back in my own office, chatting up a pretty country girl on the establishment staff, joking with another temp, feeling slightly tipsy and pleasantly drowsy...when the Senior appeared on the scene, his face black with fury.

In front of everyone he really laid in to me, berating me as "a drunk" and " a disgrace". More than that I had "shamed a family man and led him astray" and "him trying to find his feet after a terrible accident".

By then I was dazed, speechless, humiliated. But there was no stopping it, or hiding from him...and I slowly realised that he was actually enjoying every minute of this.

As Gerry said later: "It was me he was attacking. He hates my guts. But he knows my hide is hard and that I have a bite as well as a bark. He went for the soft underbelly – you my friend - a defenceless gombeen of a temp."

'Defenceless' was a polite way of not saying what Gerry probably really thought: 'useless'. (He became noticably cooler towards me afterwards.) For of course I should not have taken that tongue-lashing as I did, without even a murmur of protest. Even if I allow for being a bit addled and guilty in the first place, my lack of spirit was abysmal. The man himself was everything that I detested: a pompous creep, a bully; yet I let him dismember me like a lamb. Shades again, of a certain earlier shaming incident, in the Phoenix Park.

By the time he blew out of the office I was well chastened.

In the ensuing 'awkward' silence no one dared look me in the eye, while the young lady was busily sorting papers, her face scarlet. With shock maybe...hardly sympathy, for a man suddenly stripped to the schoolboy.

For I only felt and no doubt looked, like a kid balled out by the Head. Gerry himself did get formally 'reprimanded' in turn, to the extent that we never had another 'late' lunch together. – Not least because they transferred him to O'Connell Street, a few days later. Game, set and match to the power-players-that-be, I fear.

And not the last bollocking I would get from a Boss – but none of them remotely in that category. Meanwhile I saw less and less of Gerry, until our paths finally parted after I left the Corporation in January 1960.

*   *   *

Vanity thus pricked, it was not seriously punctured, and I was otherwise pursuing the usual diversions, just a little wiser to the ways of the working world perhaps, or the ever-threatening unpleasantnesses of life. Knowing also, that there are always people like Gerry about, to make a final mockery of the brute reality brigade...in mayhem and merriment.

My parents were somewhere between the two camps, being on the one hand as 'straight' as the rest, with a saving tendency to spasmodic abandon. I actually got on very well with both of them now, often drinking with one or both of them. Drink predictably loosened tongues and I began to understand them both a lot better in consequence. Or to feel something as close to actual affection as a selfish youth like me could manage.

My biggest problem was their mutual antagonism, which was never far below the surface. There were perpetual arguments between them, often escalating into real shouting-matches, to the extent that near neighbours must have worried too. But no one ever complained, in a street where family feeling took everyone into account: a nice bunch...

I gave my mother four pounds a week from my Corporation pay, which delivered our improvident household from the worst of poverty. My own share was ample to keep me topped up during the week, while another bonus took care of the week-end.

A friend had built up a nice little income from a football pools 'round' he did Friday nights – about thirty shillings in commission for collecting the weekly subscriptions, door-to-door. This he passed over to me and I found that I could easily complete the round, on my bike, in a couple of hours. Manna.

However, late into January, unemployed again and now on the dole, the parental imprecations to "get a job" began anew. I wasn't even doing much writing then, nor had done since the Corporation. It became obvious to me that another trip to England was favourite and I made plans with the trainee radio officer to venture back in May.

He had a lead to Walls' ice-cream factory in Acton, where, he'd been told, we could earn big bucks during the long summer season. In the event we did fairly well – much better than I had in The Berkeley.

Meanwhile I was back to relying on my generous handsome pal, who consistently came up trumps. We now had a new refinement for the nightly pleasure jaunts: a car. The only driver among us, he could also start an engine by crossing the ignition wires. So, he took to 'borrowing' a Ford saloon that was often left parked (unlocked!) near his home, by a medical man who spent a lot of time away. Compared to braving wind and rain on a Lambretta, this was a lot more like it.

We took to driving to the 'bona fide' pubs, outside city limits, where normal closing hours did not apply and you could often drink into the early hours. Drunken driving was not a great crime in the Fifties and as long as you stayed roughly on the left-hand side of the road, you were fairly free from any 'interference'. My friend drove perfectly, as far as I could tell, drunk or sober. Certainly the car always got back to its spot without so much as a scratch.

Although we were both doing strong lines this time, we never took the girls out. Instead, some nights, we'd drive to a tennis club dance in Donnybrook or out to Laurel Park Ballroom in Bray, hoping to pick up "a bit of stray". The car was a help and sometimes we'd end up with a couple of high-heeled gigglers, game at least for "a good coort" – lotsa kissing and pawing. I always got the plainer one, given his nibs superior pulling power. But it was 'grate gas' (fun) all the same.

* * *

Before I knew it Spring was in the wet Dublin air and I was preparing for the second trip to London.

We sailed on a fine warm Sunday evening, this time driven to the Mail Boat in style, by a former classmate of my travelling companion.

The previous night had been one to remember, for a long time!

A group of us gathered in the local, sensing that this might be the last time we'd meet in force, for life-paths were starting to diverge generally. So it was quickly decided that we would make a real session of it and we began by bussing into the centre of town.

We worked our way through several pubs in the Grafton Street area – Dublin's longstanding Bohemian Quarter – until we hit Davy Byrnes. There we got talking to several sleek young men who we knew well to be "ravin pooves". But they were all admirably arty and could talk literature well.

Although we easily fell into the habit of making disparaging jokes about brownies, none of us had any real prejudice in the matter. They were 'different', they were exotic; that was about it.

Whatever they thought of us, likely lads on the town maybe, we were invited to "a party" come closing time. Although some now made their excuses and left, two or three of us were game to give it a try.

My good friend had come to town on the Lambretta and we jumped on that to find the South Side address on Pembroke Road – near the US Embassy. There we found ourselves being admitted, not to say welcomed, into the spacious drawing-room of big old Edwardian abode.

This was indisputably Men Only territory – not a sliver of the other sex in sight. Drinks shoved in our hands we watched, fascinated, as several male couples danced, entertwined, to the strains of Ravel's 'Bolero'.

Others stood around or sat in small groups, talking and drinking.

While a small earnest man attached himself to my pal and began to talk to him about music, I drifted off to explore. Plumped alone on a big sofa I picked up a paperback biography of James Dean, by William Bast. I slyly slipped that into my pocket. On the shelves behind me I noted an interesting and varied little library of books on Art.

Making, no doubt, a measured move, an extremely good-looking young man sat next to me, asked if I'd like another drink. I would and yes, wine was fine. All my curiosity well up by now, I was as eager to talk to him, find out about him, as he was obviously keen to 'know' me. Indeed I found him very likeable. He had a beautiful cultured voice and it didn't surprise me to learn that he worked behind the mike for Radio Eireann.

"They're very stuffy of course! I'd lose my job if they knew

I was...well, gay. Otherwise they can be delightful employers."

Sparked by my interest in poetry he began to recite Donne. "I do so adore him."

And so on, until he was suggesting that I might like to go back to his flat...Looking around I couldn't see my friend anywhere – it later transpired that he'd been propositioned by the small man and decamped in something of a panic. I wasn't ready to panic, yet.

That built up when we got back to the flat, two sumptious ground floor apartments a few streets away. A spot more wine, a few more poems, sat cosily together on a big settee...and he suddenly put an arm around my shoulders, drew me closer and kissed me full on the lips.

Now had he known my real type and paused, say to convince me that James Dean was bi-sexual, he might well have been in with a chance, who knows. As it was he must have thought that I knew what I was doing, going home with him in the first place...or...the unthinkable (to the prude in me) sensed that I was basically a closet queer.

Me, I was playing the Rimbaud for awhile...until that kiss suddenly jolted me back to reality and reminded me that Rimbaud's own 'search for experience' resulted in his being buggered by a platoon of French soldiers.

I decided that I wasn't quite ready to "systematically derange the senses", after Scamp Arthur's (highly questionable) advice, just yet.

So I crushed the Beau by saying (I think!) that I wasn't feeling too well! (I might as well have said that I wanted to wash my hair, as the moths did when they didn't want to go out with you.) I wanted to go home...(To Mummy, he must have hissed to himself – I've picked the wrong kind of moth-er's boy here.)

I was a bit worried that he might suddenly drop the quill for the knout, become aggressive and turn violent on me. No fear. He remained the perfect gentleman that my Mammy always hoped I'd be...and 'withdrew' graciously, even giving me the price of a taxi home. I left the flat unsullied, much relieved to be out in the air again, sobering up fast.

* * *

The following day, my case packed for the boat, I met the crowd for one last hair of the dog at lunchtime. My adventure of the previous night was already common currency – insofar as going to "a queers party" went. With no mind for consequences I told a couple of the lads about the semi-final in the flat. They only thought that smooch a real hoot.

Not quite so for...my mother...after the word spread somehow beyond the safe confines of the cognoscenti, when I had left for England and was too far away to console (or correct the item).

"Missis So-And-So" she told me much later, "came up to me in the street and said 'There's something you should know about Gay'. What's that? I asked her..."

"He's been involved in orgies" the Good Neighbour confided.

"With...women?..."

"Worse, Missis Duffy. Far far worse!"

Oh Geezus Mary and Joseph – was Gay gay?